The Wallflower's Pickle

Mayhem and Petticoats Book 3

Anya Wylde

For Marcus And Daniel

Copyright 2025 Anya Wylde

A note from the Author

I have reworked the Fairweather Sisters series to create a spicier version. You will find new scenes woven throughout, along with a deeper dive into the male perspective. I hope you enjoy this hotter take on the series.

Chapter One

"A new kind of light," Dorothy remarked, staring at the glittering glass orb. "No shadows, no flickering, a steady, bright, blazing light. A wee sun in your breakfast parlour."

"Only a few residential homes have managed to procure gas lighting, and we happen to be one of them," Penelope said proudly.

They were in Blackthorne mansion, an aristocratic abode and home to one of the most powerful dukedoms in history, which was astonishing considering Dorothy's parents were not aristocratic, wealthy, or anyone of note, and it was all due to Penelope, her eldest stepsister. The duke had done an unfashionable thing and gone and fallen in love with her, and then, to the horror of the *ton*, proceeded to marry her.

Apart from her two married sisters, her little nephews and nieces, ranging from one to three feet tall, dotted the room.

"Your upstairs maid, Della, thinks the lamp is witchcraft," Celine said, looking up from her needlework. "The butler scolded her earlier because she refused to enter this room, and when he tried to force her, the poor girl attached herself to the hat stand and wouldn't let go. The servants had to carry her to the kitchens. The last time I saw her, she was still wrapped around the stand, soaking bonnets and parasols with her tears."

Dorothy smiled, letting her fingers dance across the glass lamp. Everything was magical until a few grumpy old men explained it away. The sun, moon, and stars were magical. Pretty flowers, shimmering lakes and misty forests were magical ... Love, she sighed inwardly, was magical.

Her long, thick lashes flickered. Her sisters had married for love, surely, they would understand?

Penelope, the Duchess of Blackthorne and the eldest of the Fairweather sisters, had her bare feet tucked up on the green and gold chaise longue. Happiness dusted every inch of her sun-kissed skin. Her dark hair had long given up pretending to resemble a bun. It now tumbled down her back, unruly, free, and joyous. Her wild beauty had been enhanced by motherhood.

In contrast, Celine, the wife of the incorrigible Lord Elmer, sat with her back straight, her hair wrapped in a low coif with not a strand daring to escape. Her gold-rimmed spectacles sat at the edge of her nose while she concentrated on pulling the needle in and out of her embroidery. She was different from Penelope but just as beautiful in her way. Her features seemed to have been carved out of marble by the finest sculptor in the King's court.

When the two sisters entered a room together, they overshadowed even the freshest and prettiest debutants. They had a presence about them, and their titles had further enhanced their stature.

They were like grand blazing fireplaces, instantly warming every room they entered, while Dorothy was a flickering firefly, challenging to spot. Before them, her presence accounted for nothing at all.

She was certain they would be grande dames one day because of their love and loyalty to their husbands, excellent conduct in society, and charitable natures, which made them perfect examples of propriety.

She would have been envious had she not loved them so much.

"What is it, Dora?" Penelope asked, staring at Dorothy. "I can see your thoughts curling around your head like little puffs of steam."

"I—" Dorothy glanced uncertainly at Celine.

"I won't scold," Celine looked up briefly. "I promise. What did you do?"

"Nothing. I didn't do anything . . . Not this time. At least, I don't think. . . ." Dorothy took a deep breath and turned to face her sisters. "I have something to tell you."

Penelope nodded encouragingly.

"I-I have found a man," Dorothy said, and the tips of her ears turned a delightful pink.

"You were bound to," Celine said, dipping her head back to her embroidery. "Lots of men in this world. I reckon half the people in the world are men."

"In fact, we employ some," Penelope agreed. "Don't know why, but we do. Useless creatures, the lot of them."

"Now, women," Celine bobbed her head, "are far more capable."

Dorothy turned redder. "I don't mean a man. I mean the man."

"Not another one, Dorothy," Penelope said worriedly. "The last homeless young man you had asked us to employ absconded with the family silver. I had to get the Falcon to steal it all back. The duke was not pleased."

"And the old fellow you had asked me to give shelter to escaped with George's prized Arabian," Celine grumbled.

Dorothy ran a hand through her dark brown hair in frustration. Pearl-tipped pins slipped out and clattered beside a teapot on a silver tray. She looked like a wilting peony with her pouting, unhappy countenance, rounded shoulders, and long, fragile fingers viciously mauling the gold brocade cushion.

She had a charm about her that she was unaware of, the sort of charm that a soft, warm pudding exuded, so sweet that it made some people's teeth ache when they looked at her.

Provided they looked at her, most of the time, they didn't.

"Cherry wine!" the youngest of Penelope's children suddenly demanded from the corner of the family room.

Crash!

A spoon flung by little Johnny broke a vase.

"Leather shoes do not make a pleasant meal!" Penelope wrestled with a two-year-old.

Dorothy watched her sisters try to untangle the chaos, and her heart squeezed. Would her children also run away with the wool, bash each other on the head and fling peas at the window one day?

"Penny," Dorothy called out softly. "Celine?"

The din drowned her voice. She wondered if she needed to behave like one of the children to garner her sisters' attention. She briefly contemplated chewing on the tassels of the blue silk cushions.

She shook her head, dismissing the maddening thought, and took a deep breath, squished her shyness and hollered over the din, "I am in love! In love with a man! I have found the one I want to marry!"

Penelope stuffed the shoe back into little Richard's wailing mouth. Celine snipped a curl off poor little Johnny's head.

"Truly?" Penelope asked in delight.

"You are not bamming us, Dora?" Celine echoed.

Dorothy shook her head, her eyes sparkling like a pair of brilliant cairngorms—smoky brown with a translucent veil of shimmering gold. Her small, delicate face beamed shyly at her sisters. "It's true. After three whole seasons, I have found him."

They appeared stunned by the news and then burst into tears of joy, racing to Dorothy and wrapping their arms around her.

They sobbed all over her new morning gown, soaking her satin ribbons with happy tears.

"My sister," Penelope wailed.

"My little Dora," Celine howled.

Nurses and governesses materialised in the room and whisked the children away. Champagne was called for, poured into sparkling crystal glasses, and sipped at eleven in the morning.

"I cannot believe my little Dora has grown up," Penelope sniffed, and her eyes moved to the gas lamp. "You are like one of those. A soft, gentle light, a miracle amongst black-hearted rogues, but only someone with a discerning eye can see you amongst the celestial blobs. I am glad someone discovered your brilliance before it was too late."

Celine wiped a tear and asked, "Does he wear eyeglasses?"

Dorothy flung a cushion at Celine's head.

Gentle.

People often called her gentle and soft, and she despised that word. Being gentle was akin to being a helpless lamb in a ton filled with roaring tigresses. She was forced to cower in the corner, too fearful to offend and hurt someone's feelings. No wonder she was still unmarried after three seasons.

"Dora," Penny poked her arm. "Drink."

Dorothy obediently drank, glad of the distraction from her brooding thoughts.

"Who is the man who has dared to steal your heart?" Celine asked, taking a big gulp of champagne.

"Lord Lumley," Dorothy replied demurely.

A small silence fell in the room.

"Who?" Penelope finally asked, dabbing her eyes with the handkerchief.

"Theobald Grey," Dorothy replied with a blush.

"Who?" Celine frowned.

A voice near the entrance chirped, "Lord Theobald Grey, the Earl of Lumley."

The three sisters turned to find Miss Kitty Norwood, resplendent in a beautiful green muslin gown, framing the doorway like a dewy spring leaf. Her thick black hair, contrasting sharply with her pale skin, was plaited and coiled around her head like a crown, while her eyes, which changed colour depending on the light, were a bright, happy emerald green today.

Dorothy grinned in pleasure and patted the seat next to her. Kitty was her beloved childhood friend. They met at the Academy for Daughters of Gentlemen when they were twelve. Kitty had good-naturedly boxed a girl for making fun of Dorothy's twiggy legs. They had been best of friends since then.

Penelope rang the bell to ask for more tea. Her forehead scrunched up in concentration. "Lord Theobald Grey... Earl of Lumley... I think I know who you mean . . . What does he look like?"

"His clothes are always frayed," Kitty said helpfully. "And every time I look at his golden hair, I want to hold a bit between my fingertips and squeeze to watch the oil, drip, drip, drip."

"Impoverished?" Celine asked.

Kitty nodded. "Looks as if he could do with a bath or two... or ten. Lovely blue eyes," she added hastily. "Large . . . err . . . blinky."

"I have met him!" Penelope crowed. "I recall a few years ago, I had gone to Littlebury, the milliner's shop in Mayfair—"

"Bloody robbers, the lot of them," Celine remarked. "I know a milliner who is far better and can produce the same hats at half the cost."

Penelope ignored her sister and continued. "Lady March, the grande dame, was seated next to me. We were looking at some ostrich feather hats when a young man came hurtling in through the door. Lady March recognised the fellow and, quicker than lightning, lifted her massive, old-fashioned skirts and told him to hide."

"She did not!" Kitty gasped.

"She did. The shopkeeper swooned at the sight of her blue-stockinged hairy legs, but Lord Lumley was not fazed. He dove across the room in a trice and slipped under her petticoat. She had just adjusted her skirt to hide him from view when a group of debt collectors entered the shop. Naturally, everyone denied seeing Lord Lumley, and the men could hardly ask to peek under Lady March's skirts.

After they had left, Lord Lumley peered out, his head charmingly framed by the pink Chantilly lace petticoat. And even though his countenance was rather green, he fluttered around long enough to thank us most beautifully. I have always nodded and smiled at him since."

"He is titled," Celine said thoughtfully, "but his family is in dire straits. I recall George telling me that they are about to lose Knaptoft Hall, their family seat."

Dorothy nodded sadly. "My dowry can help him. Surely, it is enough to allay some of the debts? Imagine how wonderful he will look once he has some security and peace of mind—"

"And a bit of flesh on his bones," Kitty finished dreamily.

Penelope and Celine exchanged a glance.

Penelope cleared her throat and asked carefully, "You do know Lord Lumley is a man, Dorothy. Not a dog or a cat that you are adopting?"

Celine clasped Dorothy's cold hands and peered into her eyes. "Are you sure you love him as a woman loves a man? Is it a passion that draws you to him or his impoverished state? Do you want to kiss him or fatten him up?"

Dorothy frowned at her sisters. "I love him," she said firmly. "Surely, I am old enough to know my mind. I am no longer a child asking for a chimney sweep as a pet, Penny. I want to marry him."

"Are you certain?" Celine asked again.

"I am," Dorothy replied.

"Then we are with you, love," Penelope said. "I am sure the duke can help somehow."

Dorothy squealed and leapt on her sisters, knocking them back on the chaise longue.

"And George is a genius at speculating. He will ensure that your Lord Lumley is rich before the year is out," Celine said, extracting herself from Dorothy's enthusiastic hug.

"When are the two of you thinking of marrying?" Penelope asked.

Dorothy's smile froze. "Well... he-he has not asked me yet."

Penelope blinked. "Does he have cold feet?"

"No matter," Celine shrugged. "We can tie them up and hold

them over a blazing fire until he is entirely warmed up. George likes that sort of thing; leave it to him."

Dorothy drooped as the joy eked out of her. "We need to catch him first." She twisted the lavender ribbon attached to the cuff of her sleeve. "You see, I have only danced with him twice and seen him four times. He seemed keen… but he hasn't proclaimed his undying love."

"Oh, dear," Penelope pursed her lip.

"He wants her," Kitty spoke up. "I have seen the way he looks at her. Like a dried, leathery camel eyeing a wet lake."

"Now what?" Celine frowned.

"Now we shop," Penelope said, eyes on Dorothy's wilting expression. "She needs a whole new wardrobe, and this time, we have a goal in mind. We have much to plan, and the season is almost over."

A slow grin spread across Celine's face. "We have a man to catch for Dora and no time to lose."

"We will buy ribbons and bonnets and a lot of gooseberry shoes," Dorothy grinned back.

"Eh?" Kitty asked, perplexed.

"It rhymed," Dorothy shrugged, sending them all into peals of laughter. She beamed at the giggling women, her heart full of affection and hope.

Chapter Two

Celine rapped the carriage walls, and the landau jerked to a stop.

"Celine has become a tad strange since her marriage to Lord Elmer," Dorothy muttered to Kitty. She has a soft spot for thieves, and the mere mention of poets has her erupting in tiny boils."

"I wish I had sisters," Kitty whispered back enviously. "The Duchess, with her beloved pet goat, Celine and her pirate friends. Never a dull day with the Fairweather sisters. Never a dull day."

"Have you been to Gin Lane?" Penelope approached them.

"Gin Lane?" Kitty's eyes widened in delight. "No lady of quality ever goes there."

"Well, we are," Celine adjusted her eye patch. "It will be fun."

Dorothy slipped her arm through Penelope's. "I love you," she said affectionately. "No other duchess would put her sister's happiness before propriety."

"I am willing to take this risk since we are well disguised," Penelope said, avoiding her eyes. "But even a duchess has to bow down to the rules of society, Dora. We can't afford another scandal. I have to think of the future… of my children."

Dorothy understood what Penelope was trying to tell her. She had to be careful . . . She had to behave like a perfect young lady to water down the memory of their sister, Lily's indiscretion.

A young woman thrust a basket full of fruits into Dorothy's

face, pulling her out of her troubled thoughts. She had walked the length of an entire street without realising it and now wavered on the cusp of one of the wickedest streets in London.

Gin Lane snaked away from where she stood, brim-full of thieves, charlatans, pirates, animals, shops and carriages.

The street and its people seemed to be painted from a palette of browns and greys. They swelled and ebbed before her eyes like the muddy Thames, with an occasional flash of bright colour leaping out when the crowd shifted and moved.

She had expected Gin Lane to be restrained, like a shy wallflower creeping around the ballroom desperately trying to hide her existence. Instead, the street was the belle of the ball with no intention of trying to garb herself in a cloak of lawfulness. She roared out her presence as if daring the runners to curtail her blatant crookedness.

Vendors screamed, street musicians twanged, animals grumbled, carriages rattled, and if you happened to miss the noise … you certainly could not miss the smell.

The putrid smell of Gin Lane, resulting from various conflicting aromas, would have delighted a perfumer's nostrils. It was so potent that had it been possible to bottle up the scent, it would have rivalled the sale of smelling salts.

Celine expertly leapt over a puddle and gestured for the girls to follow. The girls quickly sprang after her, worried they would get lost in the tumult.

"Penny a lot," a young girl cried, swinging a basket of oysters.

Celine poked Penelope. "She said penny, heh heh."

Penelope rolled her eyes and poked her back.

"Buy me rabbits," hollered a young lad swinging a long pole, at the end of which were tied four gutted rabbits.

"Switch and cane for naughty boys," hissed an old woman through wrinkly lips.

Dorothy hurried forward, her eyes pinned on Celine's disappearing back. She slipped past a costermonger, avoided two more oyster sellers, ducked below a bunch of wildflowers and elbowed a gin-soaked creature aside before coming to a halt in front of a flower shop.

A wrinkled old woman sat among half-dead flowers. A young man snatched a pink rose from one of the baskets and disappeared into the crowd before the woman could get her ancient bones moving.

"Dora," Kitty whined nervously. "It stinks here."

The profusion of squished, dirty flowers couldn't disguise the awful stench.

Kitty inched closer to Dorothy. "And that man is leering at me... Dora, are you listening?" She shook Dorothy's arm. "We need to keep walking. Celine has gone ahead."

Dorothy ignored Kitty. Her eyes were riveted on a young boy with a dirt-streaked face slowly crossing the road. He stared at something in his hand, unaware of a flying wagon approaching him. He was so small that she doubted the coachman had seen him walking right into his path.

Dorothy lifted her skirts and began running.

The coachman saw her hurtling in front of him like a madwoman. He struggled with his horses while the little boy, hearing the sudden change in the tone of the roaring vendors around him, looked up and froze.

The coachman yanked the reins; the horses neighed and reared up....

Dorothy grabbed the boy by his waist and rolled away, missing the horses' hooves as they came crashing down.

She lay still for a moment, her arms wrapped around the boy and her heart beating so fast it ached.

Someone pulled the boy away, but she remained frozen, her nose grazing the ground, her arms lying limp and empty.

"Are you hurt?"

She tensed.

The voice so close to her ear was dark, rumbling, molten... a whisper more articulate than the rambunctious din around her.

Brisk fingers brushed over her leg, adjusting her skirt to hide every bit of bare skin from view. The fingers moved to her face and swiftly and expertly reattached the veil.

After a moment, she felt him move away, and a rougher, louder presence took his place. Sharp nails dug into her shoulders, trying to drag her into a sitting position.

She felt dizzy and sick to her stomach.

"Don't touch her." There it was again. That voice... like thick, viscous honey. When she next felt hands on her shoulder, she knew he had again taken charge of her.

"Don't take her coat off," Penelope's voice commanded somewhere close by.

"I have to carry her." His breath tickled her nape. "She landed in a pothole, and her pelisse is soaking with the contents of numerous chamber pots and butcher scraps. I would rather not smell it all the way to your coach."

"Take my cloak and wrap it around her," Penelope said.

The touch on her collar paused, and he spoke after a moment, "Ah, so you *do* like your stepsisters, your grace."

"Bah! They vex me to death," Penelope retorted, then, as if realising what he had said, emitted a shocked squeak. "Blast it! How did you recognise me?"

"You lost your moustache."

He wrapped Dorothy in the cloak while the duchess tried to find her voice. He moved her limbs easily and briskly as if she were a mere doll. Once done, he picked her up and threw her over his shoulder like a sack of coal.

Scoundrel! What manner of treating a lady was this?

Her stomach roiled as his hard shoulder pressed against it. She sucked her bottom lip and kept her eyes tightly shut. It would not do to cast up her accounts on her rescuer's coat.

"She is bleeding," Kitty said in a soft, breathy tone that she usually used when facing a handsome man.

Dorothy was intrigued and now eager to see the scoundrel's face.

In a trice, he flipped her over as if she weighed nothing at all and cradled her in his arms. He was staring at her. She could feel his eyes caressing her face like a physical touch.

She wanted to peek, but dared not, for fear of being soundly scolded for risking her life. Nay, it was better to pretend to have swooned and hurt herself badly enough for them to soften their admonishments when she 'woke' later.

Someone lifted a lock of hair away, and light fingers inspected the cut on her forehead.

"Will she be... Is she fine?" Kitty asked tremulously.

No one answered her.

"Be gentle with Dora," Penelope said through clenched teeth.

He is gentle, Dorothy wanted to assure her.

"Our coach is this way," Celine said politely.

He began walking while cradling her like a child. His breath was even, and his arms were broad and warm enough for her to be comfortable enough to start feeling sleepy.

"You are a canoozer of art," Penelope suddenly said.

"Eh?" The arms holding Dorothy tightened, forcing her face to squash against his chest and inhale his scent.

Dorothy groaned inwardly. In times of stress, Penny's Finnshire accent emerged like a shy mouse offering a gift.

"Connoisseur," Celine clarified.

His hold now slackened, and Dorothy hurriedly clutched his shirt in case he dropped her. No one noticed her discreet movement.

After a moment, her nose twitched as if it had missed something. She wanted him to squish her face back into his chest and drown the stench of this street. He had smelled wonderful, like exotic spices and dark florals with a hint of intoxicating cognac.

"You are threatening me, your grace?" His tone was cold, and his hold on her loosened even further.

Dorothy began panicking.

Penelope responded calmly. "I know your secret, and now you know ours. Forget about our little excursion today, and I will forget about your love for art."

They began walking again, and he gathered Dorothy more

securely in his arms. She calmed down, intensely curious about the strange conversation and the man's identity. His tone was cultured, and he recognised Penelope, Kitty thought he was handsome, while Celine had not scolded him once.

Someone of note, then.

Someone who could let slip that he had spotted them gallivanting on Gin Lane and cause a scandal.

They stopped, and he placed her inside the carriage, careful not to bump her. She felt a little cold when he moved away.

"I shall not mention this matter," he finally agreed to Penny's demands.

They bid each other goodbye, the tones stiff and polite.

Finally, Kitty and her sisters entered the carriage. Skirts rustled as they sat down, and the drapes were adjusted so that no speck of light could enter.

"Who are you?" a young voice asked. The boy she had saved, perhaps?

"Duchess of Blackthorne," Penelope absently muttered under her breath.

"And me mum's the queen," the boy replied. "Last week, she was a French seamstress. I couldn't understand a word she spoke. Not as bad as the time she thought she was a worm . . . Worms don't talk much."

"What's your name?" Celine asked.

"Blinker," came the proud reply. "My name is Blinker, my lady."

And that was the last thing that Dorothy heard before the darkness took over because, this time, she had truly swooned.

Chapter Three

Dorothy opened her eyes to find Penelope sitting across from her, surrounded by three of her youngest children. Her sister's expression reminded her of Madonna Terranuova . . . She had seen an excellent replica of the oil on wood in the duke's gallery. The only difference was the presence of Lady Bathsheba, Penelope's pet goat, lying peacefully at her feet.

"You are awake," Penelope said, quickly standing up and knocking the chair over. "Let me inform the duke. He has been worried."

Kitty popped her head in soon after Penelope left. Seeing Dorothy awake, she rushed to her side. "How are you?" she asked.

"Not smelling too good," Dorothy responded, wrinkling her nose.

"Her Grace refused to dump you in the bath," Kitty said apologetically. "You do smell like a dead rodent . . . Here, I brought you some orange blossom water."

Dorothy eagerly poured some over her wrist and neck. She sniffed experimentally. "Now I smell like a dead rodent in a coffin surrounded by blooming flowers."

"I don't care how you smell," Kitty grumbled. She stood up and began pacing the room. "You have been asleep for four hours. Another moment longer, and I would have gone mad."

Dorothy was touched by her friend's concern. Her heart warmed, and her eyes turned wet.

Oh, Dorothy," Kitty wailed. "I am so glad you had that accident—"

Dorothy gasped.

Kitty hurried to explain. "Nay, I mean, I am not glad you are hurt, but I am glad he saved you. I knew it was meant to be, and this is a sign. He appeared right when I needed him to save my bosom friend from peril. I am certain he couldn't see me in distress—"

"Ack?" Dorothy gasped in confusion. Her throat felt dry and gritty.

"Him . . . He saved you... My Endymion."

Kitty loved only one man, Lord William Huxley, and to call him Endymion... Dorothy rubbed her temples. He did not look like a hero of legends capable of enchanting a goddess; rather, he would suit the villain role with his cold, remote face and inky locks leaching every bit of colour from his skin. His thin lips never turned up in a smile, and his frighteningly tall, muscular figure was never seen dancing at a ball.

She could imagine him with a blood-stained blade more easily than picture him with fair Diana lying seductively across his lap.

"Huxley... Lord Huxley saved me?" Dorothy asked to confirm what to her seemed absurd.

"Yes, and her grace allowed him to help," Kitty replied.

"The duke will not be pleased," Dorothy said, trying to sit up.

"He was not," Penelope entered the room again. She adjusted the cushions behind Dorothy and gave her a vile-smelling tonic to drink.

"Your Grace, why do you dislike him so?" Kitty asked. "Doesn't his estate adjoin yours?"

"I don't dislike him," Penelope said slowly as if weighing her words. "The feud between Blackthorne and Huxley goes back well before the current duke was born."

"What happened?" Dorothy prodded.

"Ask the duke," Penelope said. It was clear she wouldn't speak of family matters in front of Kitty.

"If I marry him," Kitty asked, only half-jesting, "will I be welcome here? Can Dorothy still be my friend?"

"Drink up," Penelope told Dorothy, avoiding Kitty's gaze.

Kitty frowned in confusion while Dorothy squeezed her friend's hand and gave her a look that promised she would find out the source of the trouble soon enough. Surely, the feud was not so great? She knew the two families never acknowledged each other in public, but that didn't mean the next ten generations of the families would continue to harbour mutual loathing.

"Preserved pineapples will put you right," the duke strode in, holding a paper bag.

"Dorothy is no longer a child," Penelope reminded him. "Sweets won't pacify her."

"Yes, they will," Dorothy said, fluttering her fingers towards the bag.

"It's late. Father will be getting worried. I have to leave," Kitty said, standing up. She leaned over and, on the pretext of kissing Dorothy goodbye, whispered in her ear, "Don't forget tonight... wear the green satin. It goes well with your hair."

Once Kitty left, Dorothy dug into her bag of sweets. The moment she put a bit of pineapple in her mouth, the duke began to scold her.

"Penelope should not have taken you to Gin Lane, but you, Miss Dorothy May Fairweather, should have shown some sense and not dashed towards the carriage," he said sternly.

"The boy!" Dorothy interrupted, her eyes wide and troubled. "Where is he? Was he hurt? How could I forget about him?"

"Blinker is safe," Penelope said.

"But not for long?" Dorothy guessed from her sister's tone.

Penelope nodded, "When we arrived, his mother was sitting atop a wobbly cupboard pretending to be a fruit fly. He refused to leave, and since she seemed safe enough for the moment, we allowed him to remain. I will keep an eye on him, Dora."

"I want to see him," Dorothy said.

"He will visit you in a few days. He was awfully keen to

thank his saviour."

Dorothy knew her sister would not leave the boy unprotected. Even now, she was certain that a kindly neighbour would have been paid to keep an eye on him and ensure he was safe and fed.

The duke spoke again, "Now that you are satisfied with the boy's wellbeing, let me tell you that such behaviour is uncalled for in a lady—"

"Wait," Dorothy interrupted again. "Can you tell me about Lord Huxley? Why do you hate him so? And will Kitty never meet me once she marries him?"

"Why do you even pretend to scold her?" Penelope asked ruefully. "You can never do it."

"I will," the duke insisted. "This time, she deserves to be scolded. But first, I think I should tell her about Huxley. If Miss Norwood has set her cap for him, then it is only right that Dorothy knows the truth."

Dorothy leaned forward and cocked her ears.

"The feud between Lord Huxley and our family is complex," the duke said, sitting on the chair by her bed. "It began when Huxley's father, Lord Edward Ferrington Huxley the Third, began wooing my mother. A week before their impending wedding, he eloped with seventeen-year-old Mary Boone, leaving my mother and her family distraught."

"But your mother made a better match in the end. She married the Duke of Blackthorne," Dorothy pointed out.

"The dowager was heartbroken at the time," the duke said. "She married my father, not out of love, but necessity. Jilted so close to the wedding . . . she had no choice when he proposed, or she would have ended up on the shelf gathering dust, moths and flies. My father was ten years older than her and a tad bit eccentric. He adored slugs. He desperately waited for the rains so that he could watch the creatures crawl out of the muddy depths of the Blackthorne grounds—"

Penelope cleared her throat.

The duke shook himself out of his reverie. "Where was I?

Ah, yes, slugs. Slugs are not romantic. Add to that the fact that Huxley was her neighbour ... It made it difficult for my mother to reconcile to her new situation. She would often broodily eye the Ansley estate from the window in the west wing. But time worked its healing magic, and slowly, my mother learned to find my father and his slugs endearing, and she fell in love."

"How romantic," Dorothy cooed and then frowned. "If everyone lived happily ever after, then why this continued bitterness with the Huxley family?"

The duke stared at his fingernails. "My father loved slugs, but he had also secretly loved my mother from the day he had overheard her threatening the Count of Fox with her pointy parasol and hatpin. He never proposed thinking he was too old for her, and her attachment to Huxley was well known, but when he saw Huxley cruelly abandon her, he swooped in and saved the day."

"What about Huxley?" Dorothy asked. "Did he and his wife live happily ever after?"

"Huxley adored his wife," the duke replied darkly. "Some say a little too much. She was a delicate thing."

"Ill and indisposed," Penelope said, waggling her eyebrows suggestively. "Which meant Huxley began seeking his entertainment elsewhere."

"He began having affairs?" Dorothy asked, making the duke blush.

"He did," the duke muttered. "And then the blasted man tried to rekindle his romance with my mother. My mother scorned him publicly."

"Why didn't your father call him out?" Dorothy asked.

"My mother begged him not to. She knew Huxley was a better shot," the duke replied. "But the fact that Huxley had tried to canoodle with my mother was not forgiven or forgotten. It turned the bitterness between Huxley and my family into outright hatred."

"Then the land came into dispute," Penelope said. "A miserable, worthless piece of land in the middle of the Ansley and Blackthorne estates. Neither family would concede defeat and give up the land, nor compromise."

The duke leaned forward in his seat. "It became a matter of pride, and that dispute lingers till today even after both our fathers have given up the ghost."

"Is that the only reason you hate him?" Dorothy asked. "Because of the land dispute?"

The duke narrowed his eyes, "How can I acknowledge the son of a man who slighted my mother? Who eloped like a coward instead of admitting to his change of heart? Apart from our family dispute, Huxley was known to be cruel. A man obsessed with money, going to any length to grab what he wanted. The gold and jewels the current Huxley sits on today have been accrued by depraved means."

"Is his son the same?" Penelope asked.

The duke nodded. "I have heard he is just as ruthless. Not a kind bone in his body. He is not sociable and tends to keep to himself. He acts like a man who has something to hide. If he had wanted to, he could have amicably settled the matter with me when our fathers died. Instead, he has chosen to keep up the enmity."

"But, perhaps he is waiting for you to befriend him?" Dorothy offered. She could not understand why such a man would come to her aid. Something did not ring true.

"His father slighted my mother. The piece of land clearly belongs to my family. He should be the one apologising to me," the duke roared.

Penelope patted his hand soothingly. She turned to Dorothy and said, "I am not asking you to cut him in public, but keep a polite distance."

"And if circumstances force me to speak to him?" Dorothy asked.

"What circumstances?" Penelope asked.

"Events like today." The duke narrowed his eyes. "Events that force her to run in front of speeding carriages. Events that force even a man like Huxley to look the hero and come to her aid."

"What of the boy?" Dorothy argued.

"Someone else would have saved him," he snapped.

"And what if no one had? It would have been on my conscience forever. Besides, you would have done the same."

"Yes, but not at the risk of your life—"

"Do not scold her," Celine charged in, cutting the duke short. "She is in no state to hear your grumblings, Your Grace. She just had an accident. Here," she said, turning to Dorothy, her tone becoming soft and tender. "I brought preserved pineapple."

Dorothy had eaten the entire bag that the Duke had brought. She looked at the new bag thrust in her direction, feeling rather green.

"Eat," Celine threatened.

Dorothy quickly popped the smallest bit into her mouth.

"Did someone call the doctor?" Lord Elmer, Celine's debonair husband, asked from the doorway.

"Yes. Dr Johnson is on his way," the duke said.

Lord Elmer frowned. "Not that old man? He will leech the blood out of her. You need a man like Dr Chadwick, someone sensible who knows what he is doing."

"Dr Johnson is experienced. I am not letting some unlicked cub near Dorothy," the duke said firmly.

Dorothy popped another pineapple in her mouth and chewed. Her large, golden-brown eyes darted from Lord Elmer to the duke, watching them argue. She wondered if she should mention that she wasn't feeling the least bit ill anymore.

Penelope planted her hand on her hips. "If you two do not stop arguing and let my sister rest, then I will let no doctor near Dorothy but pull out my medicine chest and begin dosing her."

"We will discuss this outside," the duke said in a dignified tone.

"I agree, no need to trouble the ladies," Lord Elmer muttered hastily.

Once they left, Dorothy caught Celine's hand. She widened her eyes, batted her lashes, and said, "Tonight is Lady Derby's ball. The biggest ball of the season. Can I go?"

"No," Celine said.

"I promise I feel well enough. Besides, the two of you will be there to keep an eye on me. You can whip me away if I change colour in the duke's well-sprung carriage."

"Absolutely not." Penelope fluffed a few pillows and put them behind Dorothy's head.

Dorothy hung her head and whispered tremulously, "You are a Duchess. I am nothing but a country bumpkin. I would have spent my life in Finnshire, married a schoolmaster and lived a dreary life if it hadn't been for your and Celine's generosity." She wiped invisible tears from her eyes and sniffed loudly. "The two of you have sponsored three seasons for me, but I have not made a match. I am indebted to you, and if you say I have to miss the biggest ball of the season with eligible men prancing around or all balls henceforth—"

Penelope and Celine melted like ice in a crowded ballroom, and within an hour, they had turned into puddles of warm, agreeable mush.

It wasn't long before a maid strung emerald beads through Dorothy's hair while another fluffed her skirts to prepare for the biggest ball of the season.

Lord Lumley was bound to be there, Dorothy mused, eyeing herself in the mirror. She wondered if he would like her in green satin or think she looked like a well-fed toad.

Chapter Four

Dorothy sat with spinsters, chaperones and old dames in one corner of the ballroom. Her foot discreetly tapped in tune with the music while her fingers danced on the arm of the uncomfortable wooden chair. She should have been used to it by now, and yet every time she had to sit out a dance, it hurt.

She sighed and turned her attention towards the door, hoping for some entertainment to distract her from the ache in her heart.

People were most fascinating when entering an occupied room or approaching a large picnic party. Some habitually looked awkward and stiff as they stepped over the threshold. Some strode in, booming loudly to hide their vulnerability, while others slithered in, hoping no one had spotted them yet.

Dorothy watched Lady March enter with her daughter and Lord Huxley's younger sister, Sophia Huxley. Lady March was the booming sort. She stubbornly stuck to the idea that fashion had been best in her day, and in hopes of reviving it, she always insisted on wearing towering lavender wigs, brocade skirts and colours so garish that you had to squint when looking at her.

Tonight, Lady March's old-fashioned hairstyle was so tall that a servant trailed behind her, holding the delicate construction in place with a long stick. Dorothy spied an ivory elephant nestled between the powdered curls as well as a tiger, a parrot, and a family of sheep.

Miss Huxley followed the sweating servant, wearing a miniature solar system arranged around a blue silk turban. Her hairstyle was fashionably less elaborate than Lady March's. A few dark curls had artfully escaped the turban to frame her small face. Everything about Miss Huxley was small in stark contrast to her brother. Her teeth were small, and her hips, hands and feet were small. Even her ears were ridiculously small, making her look like one of Swift's Lilliputians.

Miss Huxley and Miss March were considered to be well-accomplished ladies. They were the sort of girls Penelope and Celine had hoped Dorothy would turn out to be.

Dorothy's father was not titled but impoverished landed gentry. The duke and Lord Elmer had come to her aid by adding to her dowry and increasing it to a fair sum. Penelope and Celine further armed her with fine clothes, social graces, education, and excellent connections, hoping that when Dorothy made her bow in the royal drawing room, she would be accepted by the ton.

And just as her sisters had wished, Dorothy had been accepted with barely a murmur.

Dorothy sighed, watching Lady March's hair tilt precariously near the beautiful chandelier glittering with candle flames.

She had been accepted by the ton, but her sisters' efforts could do only so much. Even they couldn't coax an eligible man to notice her.

In three seasons, she had only two offers for her hand, which the duke rejected since one had touched eighty and the other fifty.

Perhaps it was Lily's scandal that shadowed her, or it could have been the fact that while Penelope and Celine were celebrated beauties, Dorothy was not. Oh, she was passable enough, sometimes even pretty, but when her days were spent standing next to Kitty and her sisters, her little light was overshadowed by brighter ones.

"Dora, have you spotted him?" Kitty sank into the seat next to her and rapidly fanned her cheeks, flushed from dancing.

"Huxley? Not yet," Dorothy replied. "Have you spotted him?"

"No," Kitty slumped. "Not Lord Lumley nor Huxley."

"I am bored," Dorothy griped as she enviously watched a few elderly women leave the ball. "The Mechlin lace on my neck is attempting to strangle me; my bosom feels like it will escape its casing any moment, and the heat is making me sweat and itch in odd places."

"You look lovely," Kitty said. "Like a beautiful white rose about to unfurl its petals."

"My dress is green, not white," Dorothy replied. "And which of your admirers was spouting such unimaginative florid lines?"

"Mr Selwyn," Kitty replied apologetically.

"Aaron Selwyn? He is nice," Dorothy said. "But, don't you get tired of being compared to innocent lambs, goddesses and angels? If I were so admired, I would like the man wanting to court me to call me a mouldy flower. It would have stood out amongst the repetitive prattle."

"Don't be so unromantic," Kitty scolded. "Think of love… of being in love. How wonderful the feeling is. The anticipation of seeing our beloved, our eyes straying to the door again and again, our hearts beating in excitement—"

"Like two synchronised swans in a shimmering lake. If he goes one way," Dorothy swayed to the right, "then the other swan follows. If he goes the other way," She swayed to the left, "then again she follows. Left, right, left, right, right, left, right, left." She sighed, her eyes glazing over.

"You are mad, Dora," Kitty giggled.

"Madly romantic, dear heart," Dorothy replied, fluttering her lashes.

"Oh!" Kitty started violently. "Don't look, don't look towards the door. He just walked in."

"Where?" Dorothy arched her neck and scanned the crowd.

"Stop looking!" Kitty hissed. "He is staring right at us."

"Then smile," Dorothy laughed and swatted the air to show what a wonderful time she was having. "Men like women who laugh. It makes them believe they are getting a creature of pleasant countenance, dim-witted and charmingly biddable. Celine told me so. We must keep up appearances until we are well and truly wed."

Kitty obligingly bared her teeth while Dorothy snuck another glance towards the door.

Lord Huxley stood near the entrance, towering over Lady Grimly and Lord Remington, who were by no means short themselves. The ballroom was lit up by a hundred little lamps and five chandeliers, and yet, the space he had found was dark... shadowed.

Dorothy thought he looked remarkably like a ghostly giant oozing upwards from the carpeted floor. A handsome, Machiavellian giant, she conceded, noticing the lovely shape of his eyes, the hard mouth and the sharp angles of his face. His hands were so large that her entire waist could fit into his palm.

And it had.

Her ears turned red, and she blinked rapidly.

Lord Huxley suddenly turned his head as if sensing her regard and unerringly pinned his dark gaze on her. Lady Grimly shrank at his sudden movement while Lord Remington stepped back.

Dorothy wrenched her eyes away, wondering why people acted like they were stepping on hot coals around him. As if they were afraid, he would truly gobble them up like an ogre.

She frowned. Why did people fear him so?

Even Kitty admired him and proclaimed to be in love with him, but every time he came near her, she seemed to stutter and tremble in fright.

Her thoughts veered off course once again as she followed that trail of thought. Anger, sadness, and happiness were emotions just like love, and they all seemed to strike everyone equally, making them behave in an almost similar manner, but love struck everyone differently. Why?

"He appears even more handsome with the pain of his

tortured past lurking in his eyes," Kitty interrupted Dorothy's brooding thoughts.

"He has that sort of a face," Dorothy agreed after a moment of furtive ogling, "the sort you want to hold tenderly between your hands, attach to your bosom and murmur soothing words."

"You want to tickle his ribs, feed him dumplings and fatten him up," Kitty breathed.

"You want to kiss his brow and soothe his writhing soul," Dorothy sighed. "He cuts a profoundly pathetic figure."

"His expression is sombre and wretched," Kitty nodded feelingly. "His Napolean Tie superbly crinkly, his hairy brows going every which way and his shooooess," she cooed, "caked with dirt."

Dorothy frowned, "Lord Huxley's cravat is tied in a perfect Trone d'Amour style."

"Lord Huxley?" Kitty yipped in surprise. "How can you think he is unhappy or in pain? He is rumoured to be wealthier than the Regent. His stepmother adores him . . . Why, he has always lived a privileged life. I was speaking of poor, poor Lord Lumley."

Dorothy followed Kitty's line of sight and spotted poor, poor Lord Lumley battling his way through the crowd to reach them. He looked remarkably like a piece of paper that had been rolled into a ball, scrunched up and then opened again.

He finally reached them, sweating profusely and looking exhausted yet deliriously happy.

Dorothy smoothed her skirts and was about to get up to accompany him to the floor when he turned to Kitty and asked her to dance.

Kitty stared down at her dance card, which was visible to Lord Lumley. He could see she was unclaimed.

"I—" Kitty glanced at Dorothy uncomfortably.

"Perhaps you can learn more about him," Dorothy whispered to soothe her friend. "For me?"

Dorothy continued to smile until Kitty disappeared from

view. It wasn't Kitty's fault that Lord Lumley had asked her to dance and not her.

She tucked a stray curl behind her ear and stood up. Her maid had told her to let the curl kiss her cheek the entire evening. It looked pretty, she had said. But since no one seemed to be looking at her, she didn't think it mattered where the bloody curl lay. She moved towards the refreshment table, hoping a cup of tepid lemonade would calm the envy threatening to erupt inside her.

For the first time in her life, she was jealous of Kitty Norwood, the sole heir to her titled father's vast fortunes. She was beautiful, fashionable and accomplished. Why wouldn't Lord Lumley want her? Why would he even look at Dorothy when Kitty was in the room?

"I have a little terrier that growls just so," a voice said behind her.

Dorothy whirled around with a squeak, splashing lemonade everywhere.

"Lord Huxley!" She had to tilt her head right back to look at him. "I am sorry," she whipped out a handkerchief. "I spilt lemonade on your shoes. Let me—"

He caught her arm before she could dip towards his feet. His dark gaze raked her face, pausing at her forehead.

Her artfully arranged hair concealed the cut.

She gazed back at him, entranced. When had he become so breathtakingly handsome? His dark eyes seemed to pull her in, making the noise, the heat, and the people fade into nothing. All she could feel was his hand on her arm; all she could sense was the warmth radiating from his body, and as for her ears, they felt as if they were stuffed with big clumps of cotton wool.

A peacock feather attached to a young lady's bonnet caressed Dorothy's cheek, yanking her back to her senses.

Embarrassed, she wrenched her gaze away and found a blonde head staring at her.

Startled, she shrieked and leapt into the air, this time splattering lemonade all over Huxley's shirt.

"Oh, Mr Selwyn," she gasped, a hand on her heart. "I didn't notice you come up."

Mr Selwyn raised an eyebrow. He was one of the most handsome men in England, with blonde ringlets and blue eyes... He looked like a grown-up cherub. It was a rare thing for a female creature not to notice him.

Huxley laughed. It was a delightfully warm, rumbly sort of sound.

Dorothy watched him, fascinated. She didn't think a man like him ever laughed. He appeared to be the gloomy sort. The sort that one would rather believe had sprouted out of the ground fully grown than ever have been a vulnerable child.

She sucked on her bottom lip, moistened by sweet lemonade. She supposed that was an absurd thought, but some people tended to look more adult than others. Why sixty-year-old Miss Cross, back in Finnshire, still behaved like a petulant child—

"Miss Fairweather?" Mr Selwyn eyed her in concern.

Oh, dear. She had missed his question, and from his expression, it was evident she had missed it more than once. Her skin flushed, wondering how to ask him to repeat himself without sounding like a nitwit.

"She has promised me the waltz," Lord Huxley cut in smoothly. He plucked the offending lemonade glass from her fingers and handed it to a startled Mr Selwyn.

She opened her mouth to object when Huxley placed his gloved fingers on her arm.

"Come, the dance is about to begin," he said, silencing her.

She had no choice but to let him lead her. To argue would have been childish.

"You should have stayed at home," he said, holding his hand towards her.

She looked at his palm and then at his face, confused.

He rolled his eyes clearly, thinking she was a dramatic dimwit, what with all the shrieking, leaping about and dousing him with lemonade. He caught her hand with an impatient sound and placed it on his shoulder. Next, he put his hand on her back and pulled her closer.

She had been right in her estimation. His hand covered the entire width of her waist.

Her stomach clenched at his warm touch, and a soft sound escaped her lips.

He eyed her sharply, a slight frown appearing on his brow.

"Did I hurt you?" he asked.

"N-nay, I was just surprised. I didn't know we were going to waltz... You never asked," she said agitatedly.

His eyes glittered, making her think he was picking apart her answer.

He never danced.

Ever.

People were beginning to stare, and for someone used to being ignored, all those eyeballs made her feel jittery.

Had the duke noticed her dancing with him? If he had, would he never buy her pineapples again?

"Move, Miss Fairweather, the dance has begun," he murmured.

Her limbs, which usually melted when the music began, felt rigid and foreign. Her gloved hand, in his grip, began to sweat.

She forced her legs to obey. One, two, three... one, two, three, she counted, her heart stuttering.

His movements were surprisingly fluid. She had not expected such a giant of a man to move so gracefully. When she missed a step, he steadied her, his fingers briefly digging into her back.

Perhaps if they conversed, she would feel better. It would be good to learn a bit about him, for Kitty's sake.

"I heard," her voice came out all squeaky. She cleared her throat and began again, "I heard you procured the Aëdon. It is the talk of the town, My Lord."

He nodded his head but didn't speak.

Dorothy tried again. "Was it very dear? I heard the Regent was envious. Is it true that Raziel, who painted it, was the first artist you ever sponsored?"

Again, a short nod was her only reply.

She noted that he now held her further away than necessary, as if she smelled funny.

"I am sorry you have to suffer my company," Dorothy's mouth turned down. "You did not have to dance with me."

"You should not have come," he repeated his earlier words.

"Why?"

"Have you forgotten your little adventure this morning?" His eyes again tried to see past the hair swept over the cut on her forehead.

"I am not so delicate."

"I beg to differ."

"Perhaps to a man like you, I may seem delicate. But I assure you, I am a healthy country girl. I grew up in Finnshire, not London."

"Not delicate... then why the terror? I am hardly going to devour you in public."

"I am not frightened. And this is hardly my first season for me to act the simpering innocent."

"Your fingers are digging into my shoulder as if you want to separate the flesh from the bone," his lips tilted up in a half smile. "And you have danced the waltz before and never missed a step. You have stumbled twice now. If it is not fright, then what is disturbing you?"

"You have watched me dance?" The words slipped out in surprise.

He chose that moment to twirl and dip her.

When she was again upright, she took a breath, forced her body to relax and loosened her grip on his shoulder. "You asked me to dance because you were worried about my welfare? Because of the accident this morning?"

A muscle jumped in his jaw, and his lips pressed together mutinously.

He was concerned, she realised in shock. There could be no other explanation for his odd behaviour. She further noted that he was holding her as if she were made of glass, so carefully, as if he was afraid of snapping her in two.

It was not disgust, as she had first assumed, but concern that made him treat her so gingerly. Perhaps he was not as bad as the *ton* believed him to be.

She smiled at him.

The mask slipped, and she caught a hint of emotion.

"Are you in pain?" she asked.

"In pain? Did you step on my toes? I never felt it."

"Not that sort of pain," she said.

They danced a few more steps in silence before she spoke again. "Did you know when I was a child, I had asked the duke if I could have a pet?"

"I don't know how I missed such an important event," he said dryly.

"Hear me out," she coaxed. "I asked the duke for a pet, and he agreed I could have one. The pet turned out to be a six-year-old chimney sweep. I had seen the same pain in his eyes that lurks in yours."

Lord Huxley stilled, his pupils turned flat and dark.

"You often look hurt," she continued bravely. "Like you are suffering from a lack of something. Like the poor hunger for food, gin, shelter . . . You need . . . Oh! I don't know what someone like you might need, but you yearn for something important. I know it sounds absurd... You have everything, and yet... I see the same emptiness—"

He dropped his hand from her waist.

"The dance is not over," Dorothy said in confusion.

"It is, for me," he responded with his face scrunched up in a ghastly manner.

She stared at his departing back in horror. He was walking away... leaving her alone in the middle of the ballroom, abandoning her mid-dancing, and with all those eyeballs directed towards her, too.

Her entire body flushed, and she swayed as her vision slowly darkened. She was ruined, and her prospects were ruined.

No one would marry her now.

They would all think she stank like she had never washed since the day she was born.

Dashed his wrinkled, disgusted nose!

"Please, my lord," she called weakly, praying he would change his mind, twirl and say he was simply jesting.

Alas, he never turned back. Not once.

Chapter Five

If it hadn't been for Lady March's hairdo catching fire from a low dangling chandelier, Huxley's actions would have inevitably ruined her chances of marrying for good. While she had been busy feeling humiliated, the ton had been watching Lady March race around the ballroom with her lavender wig ablaze.

Dorothy leaned against the carriage walls, glad to be finally leaving. She had almost swooned when he had abandoned her, but her powerful will had forced her to return to her senses.

Swooning was no longer fashionable, and she had to overcome this awful habit.

"Did you catch sight of Lady March?" Kitty asked, massaging her tired feet.

"I saw people throwing wine, water and leftover food at her wig to extinguish the fire," Dorothy replied. "Some of them aimed badly, and naturally, the ones that were hit took offence. Soon, people were no longer concentrating on the wig but on each other. The servants joined in bringing up all they could find in the kitchens. It was the flying roast pig that frightened me into escaping."

Kitty laughed. "No one is going to forget this day. You will be glad to hear Lady March leapt into the fountain, effectively dousing the fire. The entire ton cheered at the sight, and the musicians promised to write an ode to her towering lavender hairdo."

Dorothy nodded sombrely.

"Dorothy?" Kitty placed a hand on her shoulder. "Is something the matter?"

"Oh, that awful, awful man!" Dorothy moaned.

"What happened?"

"Huxley asked me to dance and then promptly abandoned me before the song ended."

"Goodness, are you certain?"

"Nay. I simply enjoy making up absurd stories."

"Dora!"

"He did leave me mid-dance, Kitty. You know me well enough to ascertain if I am jesting or not. I have never felt so small in my life. Like a worthless, detestable, useless earwig. How could he be so cruel?"

Kitty turned away from Dorothy. "Surely, you said something to make him behave so cruelly."

Dorothy's mouth dropped open. "I did not... the only thing I said was that I thought he was hurt, in pain and wanted something. And then he walked away."

"I don't know how your silly prattle could have hurt him," Kitty said. "Perhaps it was something else? Did you hint at something indiscreet?"

Dorothy gripped her reticule, and her knuckles turned white. She understood now that her friend was torn. She was defending her beloved, who had become more important to her in the few months she had known him than her best friend, with whom she had spent her entire childhood.

When Dorothy didn't respond, Kitty caught her hand and said with affected cheerfulness, "It cannot be as bad as you think. Lord Huxley, perhaps he recalled something urgent."

"Still," Dorothy said, jutting her chin out. "He should not have been so unkind."

Kitty smiled forcefully. "I don't want to fight, Dora. Not because of a man. I refuse to be one of those women."

Dorothy's shoulders sagged. "I agree. I- I don't want to see you hurt. He is so... unpredictable. I am afraid he will hurt you."

"You and the whole ton think of him as a monster," Kitty

responded. "He helped you when you had the accident, when he could have walked away. He was concerned enough to do what he had never done before. He asked you to dance to ascertain your welfare, and in return, you tried to judge him like the rest of society and pick apart his character. It is bound to vex anyone."

"Let's not talk about him," Dorothy begged. "My head is aching."

Kitty softened at her pained expression. "I have something to tell you that will make your headache vanish instantly. My experience with Lord Lumley was far more pleasant. He is kind and attentive, and oh, he is so impoverished that it breaks my heart. Do you know he drank gin once? Gin! Can you believe it? And he does not have a valet! How can a man survive without a valet? No wonder he always looks crinkled. He brought me lemonade before I even asked him to! And when I was too warm, he steered me towards the balcony even though I had never voiced any discomfort. He is lovely, Dorothy. You will be very happy with him."

Dorothy was glad of the shadows around her. Her mind was too full of Lord Huxley's slight to take any joy in Kitty's words.

Dorothy danced her sixth dance in a row, thinking this was too good to be true. Her waltz with Huxley at Lady Derby's ball had not gone unnoticed. People had assumed that Huxley had stopped dancing because Lady March's hair had caught fire, and he had wanted to help the poor dear.

So, instead of her prospects being ruined, she was now in demand at dinners and balls. Men wondered what someone like Huxley had seen in her that they had missed.

Why, just tonight, Mr Selwyn had danced with her twice and even led her to the balcony, his eyes ardent and warm. Lord Lumley had danced with her once, while Lord Huxley had not bothered to grace them with his presence.

It was a novel experience, being visible for a change. It was . . . disconcerting. She felt like a fraud. She knew she didn't deserve this change in fortune.

She also knew that Huxley had seen nothing special in her but had only been doing his duty.

He wanted to ensure that the woman he had gone to such lengths to save did not overexert herself and expire on the dance floor, thus negating his noble act.

This last thought prevented her head from swelling from the sudden influx of compliments blown her way. She kept the image of Huxley walking away from her vivid in her mind.

It was during Lady Croft's dinner that Dorothy saw Huxley again.

When the men were busy passing the port, Kitty extracted Dorothy from Miss Branson's clutches and led her to the couch.

"I am going to ask Father to speak to Huxley," Kitty said the moment they sank into the soft cushions.

"About what?" Dorothy asked.

"About me, silly. About marrying me," Kitty replied.

"Shouldn't you wait for Huxley to ask?"

Kitty pouted. "I don't want to wait, and Father always gets me what I want. And I want him."

Dorothy frowned. Asking her father for a prized horse and getting it was different from demanding a husband. In the past, she had often found Kitty's absurd demands and the lengths her father went to fulfil them amusing. He had once got his ship to carry a camel from India to England simply because Kitty had wanted to see one up close.

But demanding a husband? Dorothy cocked her head and searched her friend's face for signs of jest.

Emerald green eyes filled with impatience and sincerity

gazed back at her.

Dorothy bit back a sharp retort and spoke in a measured tone, "I think you should learn about his feelings for you before asking your father to approach him."

"Help me then," Kitty responded. "He runs away every time he sees me. Perhaps you can corner him and speak to him about me?"

"If he runs upon seeing you, he will fly at the sight of my face," Dorothy exclaimed.

"Don't be silly. He has been watching you all night … I think he wants to say something to you. Please, please speak to him."

"After what happened at Lady Derby's ball?" Dorothy asked, shocked. "Besides, Penny would not be pleased. You know how the duke feels about him. I am supposed to keep away from him, not seek him out."

"I am certain Huxley feels bad about leaving you during the waltz. Why else would he look in your direction so often? I have caught him three times with his eyes pinned on your face. He wants to apologise and is waiting for an opportunity to do so. He wants to explain."

Dorothy put the lemon cake back on the tray. It tasted sourer than she had expected.

Kitty went on cheerfully, "I think I will accost Lord Lumley. It was heartening to see him eat a choice bit of meat instead of a cheap cut of beef at dinner tonight. Poor thing. He was swallowing it as if he had eaten nothing all day, which he probably had not. I will lure him into a corner, speak to him, and try to find out if he has any feelings for you. You do the same for me."

"But why rush things?" Dorothy asked agitatedly.

"I have never waited so long for anything I wanted, Dora. I don't know how anyone does it."

"I can't, Kitty. I cannot speak to that man, not after last time."

Kitty's eyes filled with tears. "I am trying to help you with Lord Lumley. I am willing to speak to him. Even your sisters are trying to help you, but I... I have no brothers or sisters, and not even an indulgent mother. Father can only help with coins and jewels. I don't want a treasure box; I want love. I want a family."

Dorothy's heart broke at her friend's plea. "What am I to say to him?"

Kitty brightened. "Just find him alone for a moment. On the balcony or library, perhaps? Nothing scandalous. Leave the door open and stand under a brightly lit lamp. No lurking in shadows. Talk about the weather or the last ball. Then suddenly—"

Dorothy jumped.

Kitty continued more calmly, "Mention my name and see how he reacts. Does he sigh? Does he ask you to speak more about me? If he asks questions about me, then it means he feels something for me."

Dorothy slowly bobbed her head from side to side. It did not seem so difficult. Wasn't it making polite conversation? Why, she had done it countless times. She had even begun speaking at eleven months old. Her first word had been a duck. Anyhow, she could do so again. Yes, she could do it.

It wasn't so bad. Was it?

Chapter Six

Dorothy skittered forward; her footsteps muffled on the lushly carpeted floor. She couldn't believe she was following Huxley of all the people.

Things one did for friendship... She shook her head wryly.

At first, following a giant of a man had seemed easy. His dark head had towered over others in the drawing room, making it simple enough to spot him. But the blasted man walked faster than anyone she had ever met. She had lost him the moment he had left the crowd and disappeared into the depths of Lady Croft's townhouse.

She wondered if he had gone left or right, peering at either side of the corridor. This was the first time she had attended Lady Croft's party. She didn't know the large townhouse at all.

Where would a man like him go?

Many grumpy old men went to the library after dinner, and Huxley, if not old, was definitely bad-tempered.

To the library, then, she decided with a firm nod. Now, all she had to do was find it.

Footsteps sounded behind her.

In a trice, she pulled open a door on her right and leapt inside. She muffled a scream when she realised that she had entered a closet filled with coats, hats and a naughty kissing couple.

They stared at her wide-eyed; the couple did, not the coats.

She stared back, horrified, at the couple, not the coats.

After a moment, footsteps receded, and Dorothy sprang

back out of the closet.

"I saw nothing," she muttered to the couple. "Please, go on," she said, closing the door behind herself.

She decided to go right first. She walked on for a bit and came upon a pillar—an ornate pillar with giant leafy pots surrounding it.

A small forest in the corridor.

Dorothy paused to gawk at the beauty and the oddity of having a miniature forest in a corridor, possibly the longest corridor she had ever been in.

This time, it was a giggle that had her diving behind the plants. She landed right on top of Lady Grey and Lord Huffington, who were attached to each other as if seeking warmth on an abandoned frozen land.

She apologetically scrambled off Lady Grey's backside while Lord Huffington tried to stifle his groans. Lady Grey had shoved an elbow into his belly when Dorothy had landed on top of her.

They all stayed low and still as a giggling couple scuttled by.

"Library?" Dorothy mouthed to Lady Grey.

"Third door on your left," Lady Grey mimed back.

Dorothy bobbed her head in thanks.

"I didn't see anything," she assured the couple as she crept back out. "Please, go on." She carefully rearranged the leaves so that the couple was again completely hidden.

She saw Lord Huffington's hand emerge from the bushes and wave a weak goodbye.

She curtsied to the hand and made her way towards the library.

She was no stranger to skulking around; she had done it often enough. She even considered herself an expert in such matters. But normally, she had skulked for amusement, whereas today, her destination was making her feel terror rather than excitement.

She paused outside a slightly ajar door. A faint yellow light filtering through indicated that someone was inside.

Crouching low, she peered inside and found a few beeswax candles illuminating a large desk, bookshelves and... Lord Huxley.

He was staring right at her.

She sprang up and gulped audibly.

He tilted his head and raised a brow.

She stepped into the library, her eyes watchful and wary. No one else was around.

"Do you normally crawl into a room?" he asked as a way of greeting.

"I needed to escape the crowd," she lied boldly. "My delicate nerves can't bear all the noise, rush, and heat. I felt ill and needed a quiet place, and Lady Grey suggested this was where I could retire. I was checking to see if the room was empty—"

"It is not."

"What?"

"It is not empty." He turned back to the bookshelf.

His shoulders were broad, not too wide, but wide enough.

Wide enough for what?

She frowned, shook her head and inched into the room. "What are you reading?"

"Do you see a book in my hand?"

"What do you want to read?" she amended.

"A book."

She moved closer to where he was standing. "Why are you here?"

"My nerves," he mocked, "are delicate."

He was truly very difficult to talk to, as if he were a cold, white, ice-encrusted flower embedded on top of a frozen mountain. Everyone wanted to look at him and pluck him, but it was impossible. Halfway through the hike, they would perish, if not from turning into an icicle, then from being struck by lightning for having impossible thoughts about a heartless heavenly creature.

She rocked backwards and forwards on her heel, wondering what to say to begin a conversation that would eventually meander on a path that led to Kitty.

How did one speak to a frozen chrysanthemum?

He was staring at her, his gaze intense and unfriendly. He wanted her to leave.

She took a small, nervous step back.

In the dim, flickering light, he appeared sinister. His shadow was even longer, snaking up the wall and all the way to the roof.

Not a flower. He could never be something as frivolous as a flower.

A mystical cauldron, perhaps, or a bendy bamboo stick?

Something glinted by his side.

"What are you holding in your hand?" she asked in a low voice, as if afraid of poking a devil.

He was silent for so long she didn't think he had heard her. Just when she was about to ask again, he bit out a word.

"Snuffbox." He tossed it towards her, and she deftly caught it.

"Pretty," she said, admiring it. "I like the embossed eagle. Lovely birds."

"They break the necks of helpless rodents and eat them," he replied.

"Kitty likes them." Dorothy thought it was time to introduce her friend into the conversation. It was a little hurried, but considering her beating heart, she would rather mention it quickly rather than on her deathbed.

"Rodents?" He asked.

"Eh? Oh, Eagles. She likes eagles."

Or at least Dorothy hoped she did.

He moved to another shelf.

"This is a very big library," she observed, following him. She felt a touch braver since he had done nothing yet except send scathing looks.

He moved deeper into the library, holding the candle as he walked.

She raced after him. "Though mice can be sweet. Dangerous

but sweet."

He eyed her irritably. "You could be describing yourself. Mousy, dangerous—"

"And sweet?" she finished and then flushed.

He turned away. "I thought you were ill."

"Ill?" She frowned. When was she ill? Oh, she had told him she was sick and looking for a quiet place to rest and then forgot. Blast it!

"Hmm?" A smile began tugging at the corner of his mouth.

"I am feeling better." She hurriedly peered over his shoulder to look at the books he was eyeing. Kitty would like to know his taste. "Kitty likes reading, too."

"Who is Kitty?" he asked, slamming a book in place and pulling another out.

"Miss Norwood," she frowned. "She is charming, is she not? I have known her forever."

"Stop bouncing," he spun around and glared at her.

"Bouncing?" she squeaked.

"It's vexing. Do you have to continuously rise and fall on your toes? Do you have to chatter on and on? Can you never stay still?" He walked over to another shelf.

She tried to walk at a more measured pace. Her nose bumped into his back, and both froze.

A man and woman unchaperoned, together in the evening, alone in the library . . . she gulped and turned scarlet.

"No bouncing," she promised his back in a small voice.

"And no talking. Better yet, leave. We don't have a chaperone."

Ah, he had read her mind. Did he have supernatural powers? He seemed eerie. Was he eerie? A ghost, vampire, or mayhap a cannibal? Bah, what nonsense!

"Kitty always has a chaperone—"

In a heartbeat, he had her arms in a rough grip. His fingers dug into her flesh. "I said leave. One more word and—"

She stilled at the look in his eyes. What did he mean? One more word, and what?

"Will you kill me if I speak?" she asked in a hushed voice. It was entirely possible. "Where will you hide my dead body? This entire place is riddled with couples, and dragging a dead creature through the corridor unseen will be a task. You could fling me out of the window, I suppose ... Penny would be sad if I were dead, but the d—"

"Not. Another. Word," he snapped, jerking her close until she was flush against him.

She felt every ridge, every hard plane of his body against her soft curves. She took a shallow breath, gulping in a heady scent of whiskey and dark amber.

He gazed down at her, watching every emotion flicker across her face. His eyes lingered on the blush staining her cheeks.

Something shifted in his expression, and the air became charged with anticipation.

How did the atmosphere, which had been unfriendly, cold, and biting a moment ago, change to something so warm and intimate?

This-this was not seemly. Nay, a man and woman should not be so close. Her heart thundered as his warmth began seeping through her dress and spreading over her skin like an upturned bucket of water over her head. Sensations coursed through her, touching every part of her body and soul.

She had thought he was icy, but he was so warm. Perhaps it was the burn of frost lashing her skin.

Her lashes dropped, feeling heavy, while her entire body blushed. She should have stamped on his foot and moved away, but that thought never entered her head, for her head was swimming.

Swimming as if she had drunk a glass of wine too fast.

Her lashes flickered, unknowingly beckoning him as if every long, gleaming strand held an ancient enchantment.

"Look up." He placed a finger on her chin and gently raised it.

Her neck elongated, revealing the vulnerable, sensitive expanse of skin from her red-tipped ears down to her collarbone as she gazed at him. The gentle swell of her breasts and small waist, wrapped in the excellently tailored dress, further enhanced her femininity, making her appear warm, sweet, and delicious.

Her expression was open, dazed and confused, while her skin was a faint pink and glowing in the candlelight. So unbearably trusting, defenceless and good that it made one's heart ache.

He inhaled sharply and took a step closer.

The sound of trees swaying and rustling in the evening breeze was suddenly magnified, along with the scent of imminent rain and desire.

Her breath seemed caught by something invisible when his eyes dropped to her lips, and then she stopped breathing altogether.

With deliberate slowness, he placed his lips on her as if he wanted to enhance every excruciatingly sweet moment.

He lifted his head after only a light brush of lips to find her eyes glazed and guileless. Her every emotion was etched on her face for him to read and comprehend.

A flash of guilt flickered in his eyes, but then the tip of her tongue snuck out to lick her bottom lip.

His eyes darkened, and he captured her lips again, this time allowing a bit of his darkness to reign. He lightly nipped her mouth, tugged her chin until she opened her mouth and delved in, tasting every bit of her.

Her mind went blank, and only the feeling of being caught and teased mercilessly remained.

His fingers had encircled her wrist at some point, testing her rapid pulse and moving slowly and deliberately up her arm.

His light, fleeting caress was too much and not enough at the same time.

It made her head spin. He made her head spin. She could not think, only feel these incredible, strange sensations coursing through her, heating her until a faint layer of sweat formed on her back.

This maddening attraction addled her. It was as if his

scent, heat, and touch held a magical spell that bound her, eliminating her rational senses and capturing her most intimate thoughts and desires.

How did he know how lightly, deeply, and sweetly to touch? How did he know where she ached, what part of her was most sensitive and how to make her quiver?

How could a man understand a woman's body so well as to make her melt into a thoughtless mess in a few heartbeats?

It was frightening and yet exhilarating.

She wanted him to stop, but go on, and these contradictions were making her insane and uncertain to the point where she surrendered and allowed him to have his way.

His exploring continued to sweep over her collarbones and breasts and finally settled on her waist. With a swift tug, he pulled her closer still, so close that every inch of her could feel his hard, muscular body.

Her head reached his chest, and she unknowingly nuzzled him from instinct and accidentally brushed against a hard nipple.

Instantly, he sucked in a breath, and pinched her breasts in playful retaliation.

Lightning shot through her at his touch, and she gasped in surprise and tried to move away.

Her hands were instantly captured and pulled above her head, and he made a low, angry sound in warning.

He was taller, stronger and far more powerful than her. A trickle of fear, like a cleansing stream, suddenly flooded her muddied head.

How could she allow herself to become intimate with a strange man? What was wrong with her body to betray her so easily? Shame and horror at her behaviour made her eyes red and teary.

She had fallen into his arms like a pup, eager for his caress.

No more.

Now that her sanity had returned, she squirmed to get away, panting slightly.

"Please, I—do not . . . I—"

At the sound of her trembling voice, his fingers tightened their grip on her fists, and the sharp metallic edge of the snuff box lying in her palm sliced through her skin, making her hiss in pain against his mouth.

In a heartbeat, she was free, cold … bereft. She hugged herself, feeling as if something wonderful had been cruelly snatched away.

She looked up to find his face mirroring her shock.

"I..." She touched her sensitive lips, unsure how to continue. Her lashes dropped again, still not brave enough to meet his, while her mind continued to flicker like a dying oil lamp.

He didn't hear her. His attention was on the smear of blood on her palm. His entire body was rigid, his face pale, and his breathing shallow.

The sound of his rapid, laboured breathing in the silent library made her look at him again and observe his condition.

He had turned so white that he was glowing in the candlelight. Every bit of blood had drained away from his face, leaving his lips almost blue.

Uncertain of what to do or say, she held out the snuff box. When he didn't move, she took a step toward him, worried he would swoon.

With a strangled curse, he snatched the box and spun away from her. A moment later, he stormed out of the library with the candle, plunging her into darkness.

She rocked on her heels, watching his back disappear, wondering what to make of it all.

Was kissing her so terrible that it made him want to swoon?

Her mouth turned down, and she discreetly checked her breath.

It smelled like sweet wine.

A tear sparkled at the corner of her eye. Her first kiss had been stolen, and the one who stole it had been sickened by the experience.

It couldn't get worse.

And then it did, as another thought struck her. Her mind, which had finally started up again, began whistling out information like a steaming kettle.

The man was her bosom friend's beloved, and she had been tasked with bringing them together, not tearing them apart.

Her head spun, and she felt the familiar fainting spell coming on.

Chapter Seven

What in the world was she supposed to tell Kitty now?

Dorothy headed towards the front of the library, using the faint light of the moon filtering through the window to guide her. A polished silver candelabra on the desk with lit candles threw a pool of light, alleviating the darkness.

A mirror hung over the desk, and Dorothy scrutinised herself. Apart from her flushed skin, which could be blamed on the warm weather, it did not appear as though she had been kissed.

With a final glance at the mirror, she turned away. She would have to find Kitty and tell her the truth. Tell her how he had grabbed her, kissed her and tried to seduce her ... except, the way he had looked afterwards—shocked and shaken—she doubted that had been his intention.

Her face felt hot, and her ears burned as if singed by embers.

Had the snuff box not scratched her palm ... what would have happened next? She increased her pace down the corridor, hoping to outrun her thoughts.

She paused outside the drawing room, half afraid of running into Huxley. She didn't know how she would ever face him again. She lurked near the doorway, and only after ascertaining that Huxley was no longer towering over the other guests in the room did she make her way towards Kitty.

Men were fluttering around Kitty like bees circling a sweet, sweet flower. Lord Lumley, standing closest to Kitty, whispered something in her ear while she giggled into a hand encased in soft white lace.

Dorothy tried to reach Kitty through the barrier of admiring men, but no one listened to her requests to be let through.

The music was loud, the chatter even louder, and Kitty's hypnotic laugh the loudest.

A young man thoughtlessly stepped on Dorothy's toes as he eagerly joined the crowd surrounding her friend.

Dorothy wilted and turned away. It seemed the magical days were over. She looked down at her pink dress, wondering if it was an unflattering colour to have her rendered invisible so swiftly.

Lud! The confession could wait. She headed to a corner reserved for women on the shelf and grabbed a glass of wine. A giggling couple near the food table stood with their pinkies touching, a little secret that they thought only they were aware of.

Dorothy swallowed the wine while glaring at the blushing pinkies. She, too, had recently touched someone... someone's lips.

Lips that belonged to Kitty and not her.

Confound it, she was a thief.

She could tell Kitty that she and Huxley had pressed lips, but Kitty had nothing to be concerned about because the act had sickened him so much that the giant had almost fallen to his knees in horror.

Would this make Kitty happy or disturbed?

She swallowed more wine.

"Dorothy?" Kitty placed a hand on her shoulder. "I am sorry. I escaped as soon as I could."

"Hic."

Kitty grabbed the wine off her and set it aside. "You look different ... Did you do something to your hair?"

"Someone stepped on my toes," Dorothy replied, turning red. Could people tell she had been kissed?

Lord Lumley popped up next to Kitty. "Your champagne," he

offered her with a bow. "And this," he said, producing a second fluted glass with a flourish, "is for you, Miss Fairweather."

Dorothy took it with a grateful smile. He had remembered her! Her heart warmed towards him. Such a kind, generous man .... It was a pity he suffered while men like Huxley rolled in wealth.

She eyed him fondly, overcome with the same sort of maternal feelings she got when she spotted skinny cats and unhappy dogs. Oh, she would love to take him home and feed him a big hearty meal until his pale cheeks flushed with colour and his concave stomach became convex.

Now, if only her true love would scamper off ... She needed to speak to Kitty alone.

Alas, it was not to be. Not only did Lord Lumley remain stubbornly stuck to them, but Mr Selwyn joined them as well.

"Maria plays well," Mr Selwyn said, nodding towards Mrs Aston's eldest daughter at the piano. "Would you like to dance?"

Oddly, his eyes were fixed on Dorothy's face rather than Kitty's.

"You must!" Kitty whispered in her ear urgently. "He seems to be half in love with you."

Dorothy blushed and allowed herself to be led. She danced with him, enjoying the fact that, for this young man, she wasn't invisible.

The chat with Kitty could wait until they were in a more private setting. Kissing and such could not be discussed so blatantly with many eager ears surrounding them.

∞∞∞

The next day, two maids rushed into the room, one holding walking boots, the other a parasol.

"Boots don't match the gloves," Penelope said critically. "Dora, eat some more. You will swoon in the heat—"

"I don't care if they look odd." Dorothy pushed her feet into the boots and slammed an old, frayed bonnet on her head. She didn't have time to look for another one since she was already late. She had to meet Kitty and confess it all. "Goodbye," she kissed Penelope on the cheek and raced out.

"She is worse than the children," the duke commented as he watched Dorothy slide down the bannister in hopes of saving time.

Once Dorothy settled in the carriage and was on her way to Hyde Park, she relaxed. It wouldn't be long now before she would unburden her heart and get rid of the guilt gnawing her. She had to tell Kitty about the kiss, and the sooner it was done, the better.

Her fingers strayed to her lips ... they still felt more sensitive than usual. Yanking the glove off her right hand, she stared at the faint red dot on her palm where the snuff-box had dug in.

Proof that she had not imagined the kiss.

She squeezed her eyes shut, feeling little darts of sweetness run through her at the thought of his lips on hers.

It wasn't right to feel this way ... not about him.

She found Kitty soon enough. Today, Kitty's chaperone was her aunt, an old spinster who disliked gossiping. She gave the girls a disapproving glare as she followed them down the well-worn path of Ladies' Mile.

It wasn't long before the girls' quick steps left the aunt far behind.

Dorothy would have linked her arm through Kitty's at this point, but the guilt gnawing at her held her back. "Did you speak to Lord Lumley about me?" she asked.

"No," Kitty replied. "We were rarely left alone. Even the balcony was crowded since it was such a warm night."

Dorothy cleared her throat. "Kitty, if I stole your favourite dress, how would you feel? One you have never worn before and recently procured from Paris?"

"Eh? I wouldn't care. Father will simply buy me a new one."

"What if I steal a precious necklace from you?"

"What is going on in your silly head? Did you want something of mine?"

"Nay! But, if I did, what would you do?"

"You wear it, I wear it, makes no difference. You can take anything of mine."

"Anything?"

Kitty suddenly stopped as if a thought struck her. "Dora, d-did you see something last evening?"

"Hmm?"

Kitty searched her face. "I... well, it was unexpected."

"What?" Dorothy stared at her in confusion. Why was Kitty looking guilty when she should be the one feeling rotten?

"Nothing." Kitty began strolling again. "I wanted to ask you something."

"Yes?"

"Don't be offended, but it is positively eating me up. What happened with Lily?"

Dorothy paused and readjusted her thoughts. She had been so fixated on Huxley that this completely different topic threw her for a moment. "I suppose I can tell you. Lily had her season four years ago. She dislikes Penelope, what with her being our half-sister, so she stayed with Celine in London. I am not sure about the details since it was hushed up, but Penelope discovered that Lily was with child in the middle of the season. Lily refused to name the man responsible, and she was sent back to the Finnshire. She was quickly married off to an old admirer of hers living in the village. He may have guessed the truth, but loved Lily too much to let her go."

"Is Lily happy?" Kitty asked.

"She is content. I always thought of her as someone who would have loved the London life, but it seems I was wrong. She enjoys her married status, being the prettiest girl in the village and ruling over unmarried women. She thinks of herself as a grande dame of Finnshire. She would have never had so much control in London."

"A happy ending for her then," Kitty mused, linking her arm

through Dorothy's. "To share something so personal with me, to trust me so wholeheartedly ... I am not sure I deserve it."

"It's me you shouldn't trust," Dorothy choked out. "You are kind, wonderful ... a true friend and, yet, I—"

"Hush," Kitty placed a finger on Dorothy's lips. "I think I heard someone say, Fairweather," she whispered.

Dorothy had heard nothing, but Kitty's ears were remarkably sharp. She had learned to respect them over the years, so she obligingly pressed her lips together and crept forward.

They found Lady Huxley and Miss Huxley sitting on a bench.

Kitty and Dorothy sprang behind a tree and strained their ears.

Lady Huxley, Lord Huxley's stepmother, had a plump, youthful face. She was speaking now with a gleam in her eye that indicated a good gossip session was underway. "I don't know how she does it. Mrs Fairweather must be an awfully clever woman."

Miss Huxley smiled, showing a row of tiny, even teeth. "She should move to London and set up a school to teach young, unmarried adventurers how to ensnare rich men. She would make a fortune. After all, she managed to get both her daughters hitched to wealthy, titled men."

"The third one left mid-season, I recall," Lady Huxley mused. "I sniff a scandal there, but it was hushed up well."

"The Duchess can join her mamma then," Miss Huxley giggled. "While the mother teaches the women how to trap hapless, rich men, her daughter can hold lessons on how to hush up scandals."

"Although they seem to have lost their touch. Three seasons and the latest spawn has not married," Lady Huxley observed.

"Mushrooms, the lot of them," Lady Huxley shook her head in disgust. "Their luck had to run out sometime."

"Ooh, the vulgar circulators!" Dorothy hissed under her breath.

At this point, Penelope would have cried, Celine would have ignored the scandal-mongers, but Dorothy ... Dorothy refused to let the insults go unchallenged. Her Fairweather blood was all fired up. Her family name was being tarnished. It was up to her to scrub the rust, to right the wrong, to teach these half-witted yahoos that no one could insult her mother and sisters and go unpunished.

She straightened her bonnet, squared her shoulders and curled her fingers around her pointy parasol, ready to pounce —"

"What do you think you are doing?" a dark voice spoke in her ear.

Dorothy whirled around to find Huxley peering down at them.

He was dressed in his walking gear. A large blue–grey overcoat hung over his broad shoulders, and a light waistcoat had the good fortune to hug his sculpted chest. Wisps of hair had escaped the gold-brimmed hat to give him a wonderfully tousled look.

Her shoulders drooped, and her anger fizzled out. She stared up at him, overcome by a sudden feeling of smallness.

Dark, furious eyes glared down at her. "You were eavesdropping on my mother and sister," he said sharply. "Why?"

"Your refined mother and sister were gossiping about my family and me. Why don't you ask them to tell you what they said?" Dorothy replied, indignation rising once again in her heaving bosom.

"We were only talking," Miss Huxley said. She and her mother had heard the raised voices and had come to investigate. She widened her eyes and blinked at her brother. "It was harmless gossip."

Huxley's eyes softened. "Take Mother back to the carriage. I will join you in a moment."

"They called us mushrooms! Mushrooms, I tell you!" Dorothy made a squawk of protest. Were they not to be held accountable? She lunged at them, but Kitty grabbed her waist and held fast.

"You believe that vicious little minx?" Dorothy turned on Lord Huxley. "What they were doing was not harmless gossip. It was malicious, evil—"

"It is none of your concern," he cut in.

"They were talking about my family," she spluttered.

"They were," Kitty bravely spoke up. "She is not lying."

"I think she is," he replied in cold, clipped tones. "You both are."

"We will apologise for eavesdropping if your mother and sister agree to apologise to Dorothy about the things they said about her family," Kitty said in a soothing voice.

"This is planned, is it not?" he suddenly asked.

"What do you mean?" Kitty asked in confusion.

"You are Miss Kitty Norwood, are you not?"

Kitty nodded.

"The same woman whose father has been spying on me … I had thought he was interested in my latest shipment, but that's not the case, is it, Miss Norwood?"

Kitty paled while Dorothy caught her hand and held it tight.

"What are you trying to say?" Dorothy challenged him.

He shook his head in disgust. "This empty-headed butterfly," He jabbed a finger in Kitty's direction, "has set her sights on me. This is one of her ploys to increase the intimacy between herself and my stepmother and sister … First, she sent you after me in the library, and now this …. How is it that you knew where to find me? Do your father's spies inform you about my whereabouts, Miss Norwood?"

"How dare you?" Dorothy stepped towards him and jabbed a finger in his chest. "Is this how you speak to a lady? Kitty has not set any spies on you. What a ridiculous notion!"

"Is it ridiculous?" he asked, his eyes on Kitty's face. He didn't wait for them to respond but continued, "I don't want to see either of you again. Don't test my patience or…" He let the threat hang in the air for a moment before turning on his heels and leaving them alone.

"Kitty, don't you dare cry," Dorothy said the moment his back disappeared from view.

"I am not crying," Kitty replied through gritted teeth. Come, let's find my aunt. We should head home."

Chapter Eight

Dorothy watched Kitty twirl around the ballroom like a sparkling silver top. Her shoulders drooped unhappily. She was not envious of Kitty's dancing partner, a renowned foot stomper who had left numerous women with bruised toes.

No, she was unhappy because Kitty had stopped speaking to her since their stroll in Hyde Park a week ago, and she didn't know why.

Dorothy had sent letters to Kitty's home and got no response. She had called Kitty's house and found her unavailable every time. At every ball and dinner, Kitty created a wall of admirers around herself, making it impossible for Dorothy to approach her.

Dorothy was not one to let friendships go without a fight. She narrowed her eyes and tracked Kitty's movement across the drawing room. The moment the song ended, Dorothy knew Kitty would head to the retiring room. Lord Bray had clumsily spilt some wine on Kitty's skirt, and Dorothy would take full advantage of the fact.

Just as she had hoped, she found Kitty dabbing at her skirt in the retiring room. A maid stood next to her, wringing her hands in agitation.

"Can I help?" Dorothy asked.

Kitty squeaked in surprise. "I didn't know you were here. When did you arrive?"

Dorothy let that slide. She knew Kitty had spotted her a long time ago. "Is the stain bad?"

"It's barely noticeable."

A short silence followed, and neither of the girls said anything.

"I need to talk to you," Dorothy finally said. "You have been avoiding me."

Kitty laughed, a high-pitched artificial laugh. "Don't be silly. I am doing nothing of the sort."

"Are you certain?"

"Yes."

"Have you given up on Huxley?"

"Nay," Kitty mumbled uncertainly.

"But he threatened us." Dorothy grabbed her friend's shoulders. "He said we better leave him alone or—"

"Or what?" Kitty responded coldly. "What can he do? If he is wealthy, then so is my father. If he is titled, then so is my father. If he is—"

Dorothy stared at her. She had never used that cold, arrogant tone before when mentioning Huxley.

"Kitty," she cut her short and glanced at the door. "Not here. Too many ears. Come over to Blackthorne, and we will talk about it."

Kitty nodded reluctantly.

"Promise me you will come," Dorothy said forcefully.

"I will," Kitty replied. "I promise."

Dorothy decided to believe her.

The next day, Dorothy lounged on the window seat in the morning room of the Blackthorne mansion. The summer sun had warmed her up nicely and lulled her into a half-asleep, half-awake state. One of her gloves was draped over the precious gas lamp, while a baby goat was sitting on the carpet, chewing on her blue slipper.

"Have they arrived?" Penelope's voice floated in from the hallway.

"Not yet," the butler responded.

Dorothy yawned. Who were they expecting?

She shot upright, knocking off a cushion.

By Jove! The morning callers! The Duchess was expecting ladies of the ton.

She smoothed her hair, leapt towards the goat and attempted to get her slipper back. It was chewed up beyond repair.

She groaned and rang the bell.

Two maids strode in quickly enough for her to suspect they had been lurking outside, expecting her to call them any moment.

"My slippers," Dorothy yelped. "Gloves? My hair is tangled … perhaps a cap—"

The butler poked his head in—

Dorothy froze. This was it. The end of her season. The ladies of the ton were going to see her with a chewed-up slipper, untidy hair, wrinkled skirts, grit in the eyes—

"Miss Kitty Norwood," the butler announced with a twinkle in his eyes.

Dorothy wilted in relief.

"Oh, I am so glad it is you," Dorothy said the moment Kitty floated in. "I thought the ladies had arrived to meet the duchess, and as you can see—"

"You are not ready," Kitty replied without any amusement. She perched on the very edge of the chair longue and continued, "You cannot behave like this once you are married. How will you keep your husband's home if you can't even keep yourself?"

Dorothy slowly sat back on the window seat. "Is it Huxley? Is he the reason you are so anxious?"

A maid entered just then, bearing tea and cake.

Dorothy noted Kitty's flushed skin and realised that perhaps her friend was embarrassed. Kitty had never known rejection before, and Huxley had been scathing in his putdown.

And the only witness to Kitty's humiliation had been her.

"Kitty," Dorothy got to the point as soon as the maid departed. "Why are you avoiding me?"

Kitty stirred sugar in her tea and continued to stir even after it was obvious that not a single granule could have remained undissolved after all this time. Finally, she said, "I am in love … It is making me irrational … not myself."

Dorothy tilted her head to one side and eyed her friend. "I know you are in love, but I did not know love increases in ardour every day … you are looking almost feverish. Kitty, stop stirring the tea and look at me."

Kitty set the spoon down but continued avoiding her eyes. "I am so happy, Dora … so, so happy. I cannot think of anyone but him."

"I didn't think Huxley could make anyone happy, but if he is truly the reason for your chirpiness, then I am glad for you and willing to forgive him for being horribly rude."

"Will you forgive me, too?" Kitty cried suddenly. "I have been a terrible friend."

"So have I," Dorothy said, thinking of the brief kiss she had shared with Huxley. "I wanted to talk to you about it."

"I don't want to talk about it," Kitty hedged. "Not today. Today has to be perfect."

"But—"

"Please."

"It is important and eating me up."

"If the subject is unpleasant, I do not want to hear it." Her eyes appeared almost manic in desperation as if a wrong word would turn her brain into soup.

Dorothy was puzzled, but she reluctantly agreed when she sensed her fragility. "Perhaps another time. Right now, I have some good news. I have been thinking that the duke said I won't be able to meet you once you marry Huxley. But I have thought of a way out. We can send letters, meet socially, and once I am Lady Lumley, the duke won't care if I am friendly with Huxley's wife—"

The cup trembled in Kitty's hand, and she slammed it on the table. The tea sloshed over the rim, pooling in the saucer.

Dorothy leaned forward in concern. "Did you burn your hand?"

"No."

"Kitty, are you feeling unwell? You are trembling."

"It's nothing. I simply need to rest. The season has been busy, has it not?" she laughed, tucking her quivering fingers under her pale pink skirt.

"Has Huxley said something? Frightened you … or hurt you?" Dorothy asked gently. "I have never seen you so agitated. Let me help—"

Kitty sprang up. "Nothing is the matter," she said through clenched teeth. "I am simply overtired. Why do you have to make more of things than they are?"

"I was concerned—"

"Emotions don't have to have layers, Dorothy. Sometimes, the answer is simple enough."

Dorothy watched her friend storm out of the room. The sun slipped behind the clouds, and the room felt suddenly chilled.

What was going on? What was Huxley up to? Was he trying to seduce Kitty with no intention of marrying her, just like his father had left the dowager at the altar?

Had he already seduced her and rejected her? She shivered at the ominous thought.

He was the only one in the ton who could afford to play with Kitty's feelings with no care for her fortune. He had far more of his own.

∞∞∞

"Kitty is missing," Penelope burst into Dorothy's room the next evening.

Dorothy paused in the middle of unwrapping her paper

curls. "What do you mean she is missing?"

"Her father is here," Penelope said urgently. "She has been missing since yesterday. He says you were the last person to see her, and her carriage returned empty from Blackthorne."

"She came to see me just before noon," Dorothy replied in a panic. "I thought she was acting a bit odd. Oh, why didn't I keep her longer and ask her more questions? She left in a hurry—"

"Calm down, Dorothy, and think. What was she talking about?"

"About Huxley. How much she loved him. He had been rude to her before … but perhaps they made up? Oh, I don't know. She barely spoke to me the entire week—"

"Dorothy," Penelope squeezed her hand. "You need to breathe. Lord Norwood thinks you know something, but I can tell that's not true. But perhaps she let something slip? She shares everything with you. You have to know where she went. Think!"

"Did Lord Norwood pay a visit to Huxley?" Dorothy asked.

Penelope nodded. "Huxley said he hasn't seen her since Lady Darwin's picnic, which was four days ago."

Chapter Nine

Dorothy sat at the dressing table, absently twirling a diamond-tipped comb. It flashed like a tiny white flame in her hand whenever the sun hit it.

Kitty had been gone for two days and an entire night. Lord Norwood was convinced she had been abducted and was awaiting a ransom note. Penelope was worried that she had met with an accident, while the duke believed Kitty was hiding from her father on some childish whim.

An abduction was a possibility, but what of her odd behaviour that morning? As for an accident, Lord Norwood had said that Kitty had arrived at Blackthorne and sent the carriage back home.

Blackthorne was too vast and isolated for anyone to leave without a carriage or a horse—unless one counted Ansley Hall, Huxley's residence, which was a brisk hour's walk from Blackthorne.

Huxley had told Lord Norwood that he hadn't seen Kitty, but what if Huxley had lied? He had warned them to stay away, but Kitty did not take the threat seriously. What if she went to Ansley Hall to convince Huxley to take her as his bride? He had lost his temper, ordered his servants to tie her up and left her to starve in some cold, dark place.

She frowned. It sounded excessive, and perhaps the truth was far tamer … but she was certain that Huxley was behind Kitty's disappearance.

Whatever the truth, the answer lay in Ansley Hall.

She stood up and began pacing the room. After a short, silent debate with herself, she concluded that she would have to go to Ansley Hall. She couldn't sit in her room and do nothing.

Perhaps she would find Kitty sprawled on the way with a broken leg?

The poor thing could be writhing in pain, hungry, thirsty … dying—oh, she had to leave now!

Dinner was still three hours away, and three hours would be enough time for her to ride over the border, sneak in, look around, listen a bit and then return triumphantly with the news that she had found Kitty.

She couldn't let anyone know—not her maid, stable hand, or anyone—since she didn't want Penelope to be alerted too soon. Otherwise, she would send the duke out after her, and the entire plan would be foiled.

Once decided, she spurred into action.

First, she told her maid not to disturb her until after dinner. Next, she slipped into her riding dress and boots. Once ready, she slithered down the ivy outside her window with practised ease and made her way towards the stables.

This was not the first time she had ridden to the border where the Blackthorne estate ended, and the Ansley estate began.

After Penelope had become the Duchess, Dorothy had visited Blackthorne every summer. The duke had allowed her to do everything except step onto Huxley's lands. That little bit of curtailment had chaffed at her.

She had often escaped on horseback in part defiance, galloping across the field to come to a standstill on the edge of the Blackthorne border. She would sit with her back against a gnarled oak tree, staring at the mysterious paths disappearing into Ansley woods. She would admire the pillars of a Venus temple here, the tip of an ornate bridge there, and when the light was just right, the shimmering waters of an artificial lake winking into sight.

But what fascinated her most was Ansley Hall, which rose beyond the lush, vibrant gardens. It was a refurbished monastery, aloof and distant amidst its excessive surroundings. It was a stone-grey mass that seemed to sink into the ground. A few florid Roman editions added to its bleak beauty and prevented it from being altogether too stern.

To her young eyes, Ansley Hall had appeared enchanted. She was convinced it was a gateway into a forbidden world filled with fantastical creatures. She had imagined an ogre living in the house, and the duke's warnings further convinced her of the fact. Fear had kept her from crossing the border then; now, it was the rules of propriety.

And just like she had countless times as a young girl, she, once again, stood on the border staring at the mansion glittering like polished silver in the summer sun.

She had not found Kitty on the way, so she could only continue to search Huxley's home.

For a moment, she baulked, unsure if what she was about to do was wise, but the thought of Kitty lying frightened somewhere gave her the courage to leap over the wooden fence.

She tied the horse to an apple tree and made her way towards the house. She felt like an ant navigating through a lush Persian carpet. The gardens were bursting with plums, berries, currants, wild strawberries, roses, sweetwilliams, peonies, and many other flowers she had never seen before.

The air was heavily scented with fruits and flowers, which seemed to beg her senses to stay a moment and breathe deeply. She refused to let herself fall prey to the heady spell and quickened her steps.

Using the bushes as a cover, she snuck closer to the house and peered into the window closest to her. She spotted Lady Huxley, Miss Huxley, Lady March, and a few other women of the *ton* gathered in what appeared to be a beautifully furnished morning room.

A maid standing in a corner in a grey livery holding a tray

laden with cakes and biscuits appeared to be looking right at her.

Eek!

Dorothy ducked, her heart in her throat. She wasn't certain that the maid had spotted her, but it was too late to turn back.

She had come this far and would not go back without exploring further.

Gritting her teeth, she scuttled forward and avoided the next few windows. At the fourth window, she once again gathered her courage and peeked. The room was filled with dark red roses and soft white lilies. Perhaps Huxley was preparing for a ball or a dinner party, and the flowers were being stored here for the moment?

To her delight, she found no one in the room, and the window was ajar. She sprang over the ledge in a trice and landed on a pile of pink and yellow freesias.

"What are you doing here?"

Lord Huxley sat behind a large rosewood desk at the far end of the room, which was not visible from the window. His eyes and nose were red, and he appeared to be holding back a sneeze.

Dorothy squeaked. "I-I lost a goat. I mean the Duchess ... She has some goats as pets, and one of them escaped, and I was trying to find it—"

He held up a finger to halt her babbling and sneezed into a large white handkerchief. He said irritably, "You are a horrible liar."

Dorothy bristled at his tone and decided to be direct. "I am here to find Kitty. What have you done with her?"

"I don't know where your precious friend is. And hasn't that Duchess of yours taught you better than to barge into a gentleman's study unchaperoned?"

"This is a study?" Dorothy asked in surprise. "It looks like a flower shop."

"My sister needed to store the flowers," he replied moodily. "I don't know why they always choose my study. Three hundred rooms in this deuced place, and yet—I think you should leave."

Dorothy blinked at the abrupt change in topic. "I shall not. Not until I find Kitty."

He strolled over to where she lay sprawled on the ground and held her gaze, his lips twitching in amusement.

She self-consciously patted her hair and averted her eyes.

A pale, beautiful hand devoid of unsightly veins appeared before her nose. The long, masculine fingers waggled impatiently. "Do you want to sit on the bed of freesias all night?"

She flushed and leapt up without taking his help.

He spoke coldly, "Your Kitty is not here, and that is the truth."

"You mean she is somewhere else?" Dorothy asked, stepping closer to him. "Oh! You mean she is in heaven. Y-you killed her!"

"What sort of a monster do you think I am?"

"The worst sort," she replied tremulously.

"And yet you have taken two more steps closer to me. Your lips say one thing and your actions another," he observed softly.

Her eyes widened in confusion. She hastily stepped back, and her ankle knocked into a stool covered with lilies. Her back arched, her hands flailed—

With a curse, Huxley grabbed her waist, but instead of saving her, his foot slipped over the petals strewn on the floor, and he crashed onto the floor.

She landed right on top of him.

He let out a soft moan, and his breath tickled the top of her head.

"You are going to squeeze me to death," Dorothy squirmed in agitation.

His arms immediately loosened their hold around her, but a powerful palm remained at her waist.

She spat out a cloth-covered button and lifted her head from his chest.

He was staring at her.

She narrowed her eyes and stared right back.

He had a fleck of gold in each eye, and his lashes were dense, dark and long.

She continued gazing at him, refusing to be the first to look away. Slowly, her expression changed. She became aware of the muscle beneath her palm, the rhythmic rise and fall of his chest, and his intoxicating masculine scent.

Her limbs turned liquid, and her body curved and softened to fit his. She shivered and, after a few ragged breaths, conceded defeat and dropped her lashes.

Then she noticed something strange. A blob nudged against her thigh, growing bigger and harder.

What on earth was that? A mouse?

He suddenly pinched the tips of her pink ears, making her squeak in shock.

"Aren't you going to ask me if I am in pain again?" he asked huskily.

She shook her head. "I remember what happened the last time I asked."

A lock of hair escaped from her bun and grazed his lip. He brushed it away. "If you had asked, now I would have replied that yes … right now I am in pain. A lot of pain. Now, will you get off me?"

"Hmm?" she asked dazedly. His lips were so close.

He gripped her waist and flung her aside. "I said I am in pain, woman! A thorn from one of these cursed roses has embedded into my back."

"I am sorry." She leapt to her feet, glad that the fog that had clouded her senses had evaporated so swiftly. "I am sure your valet will know what to do."

"He has gone away for the day."

She half turned away when guilt made her turn back around. This situation he was in was her fault, after all, he had been trying to save her. "Can you call for someone else to help?"

"Yes."

"Then I will leave."

"Wonderful." He gripped his waist and winced in pain, clearly eager to dismiss her from his sight.

She stepped towards him, the guilt now gnawing at her like a dog with a bone. "Who will pull out the thorn?"

"I will do it myself."

"Eh? It is embedded in your back… can you even reach it? What about the butler or the servants?"

"Nay."

Her brows rose in surprise. Was he, mayhap, bashful? "I suppose I have to help you now. This is all my fault, and it wouldn't be right to leave you like this—"

"It is perfectly acceptable to leave me. It would be the ideal thing to do—"

"I have pulled out many thorns from hooves and paws and children. I must say I am something of an expert. I know just how to get the thorn out clean without breaking it—"

"I can manage. The doctor—"

"For such a silly thing, you want to call a doctor? Let me try. I promise, in a heartbeat, I will have it out."

"Fine, but I have a feeling you won't be able to do it."

"We shall see."

He smirked. "The thorn is embedded in my lower back."

"So you said. Turn around … I can't see it."

"It might have gone through the coat."

"Well, then, take it off!"

"If you insist."

"Hmm, I still can't see it. Perhaps you will have to take off your shirt."

He whirled around. "Do you have no maidenly modesty? I thought the moment you realised I would have to undress, you would give up this fatuity."

She raised her nose and addressed him in a tone she had heard the village doctor use with particularly nervous patients. "In Finnshire, I assisted the doctor. Old men, children … sometimes, they had to take their shirts off. Oh, don't look so horrified. I always had a chaperone with me, and the doctor wouldn't let me help if things got too delicate ... Oh, I see what the trouble is. Are you shy? Or do you have a particularly hairy back? I understand you are sensitive—"

"I am not shy," he bit out. "And my back is not hairy." To prove his point, he pulled off his shirt and flung it on the chair.

Her mouth turned dry.

His back was broad, sculpted and pale gold. Heat radiated from it like a blazing fireplace. Muscles rippled when he shifted his shoulder in impatience.

She wrapped her hand around her skirt to still her quivering fingers. Seeing skinny little village boys without shirts differed greatly from the breathing, manly specimen before her. Perhaps she should let the doctor take care of this. She didn't think her heart would last like this. It was galloping so fast as if a hungry lion inside her chest was chasing a thousand deer—

"Did you find it?" He growled.

"Hmm?"

"The thorn!"

"Oh ... yes, oh, no, that was a mole," she stammered. "A moment."

She could do this.

Her fingers traced his warm skin, lingering longer than necessary. She traced his shoulder blades, dipped lower and lower until it reached the edge of his breeches.

She finally spotted the thorn poking out of his skin; the surrounding area had turned red. But, as if possessed, her fingers dragged across his skin, circling the place.

It was like caressing the finest silk, and she was reluctant to stop.

He tensed and turned to look at her.

She looked at him at the same time and froze.

"Seen enough?" He raised his brow.

"Place a chair in front of you and brace yourself," she said, her voice sounding foreign to her ears.

His mouth pressed into a hard line, and he turned back. "I

am ready," he said, gripping the chair.

She dragged in a big, shaky breath and gently ran a finger over the brown thorn sticking out of his lower back.

"I might have to … err … the breeches … your breeches are in the way. I have to pinch the skin around the thorn, and I can't."

"I will not take off my breeches!" he snapped.

"No, just wriggle it down a bit. No, too much … just a tiny bit."

He pushed them slightly lower.

"Now, this may hurt, but don't worry, it will be over soon."

He gasped. "Bloody hell—

"Now, now, it is almost done. You will feel wonderful after this."

He cleared his throat.

"I should suck it out… but don't worry … I think my nails are long enough to grab the little thing."

"Miss Fairweather—" He moved to get away.

She gripped his waist and held him still. Her hands appeared ridiculously small against the vast expanse of his skin, but her gentle touch seemed to have the power to freeze him. "Shush, no talking. Let me concentrate."

"But—"

"Hush! If you move too much, it might break," she scolded and returned to prying the thorn out. "A moment longer, and you will compliment me on my excellent skill."

Something thudded on the floor, and a gasp rent the air.

She slowly pulled the thorn out and whooped in triumph. "I did it! It was a long one. Do you feel any better?"

Someone screamed.

Dorothy froze. That did not sound like Huxley.

"Did you just scream, My Lord?" she asked fearfully.

"No," he forced the words out.

She slowly peeked around his thigh and looked towards the door.

Lady Huxley, along with Lady March and other ladies of the ton, were staring at them while three maids, the butler, Miss

March and Miss Huxley, were lying on the floor in a dead faint.

"I am so sorry," Lady Huxley was the first to break the silence. "But it seems my future daughter-in-law and my son wanted to spend some time together. We will, of course, get them married far sooner than we had planned—"

"What were they doing?" someone whispered loudly. "She was … and he was … and then she whooped … and he groaned … very odd position for—"

"Who is the young lady?" Lady March asked loudly.

"Miss Fairweather," Lady Huxley replied sourly.

"When is the wedding?" someone else asked.

"Registered wedding … as soon as the Duke of Blackthorne can procure a license," Lady Huxley said, ushering everyone out of the room. "She is his sister-in-law, a well-connected family."

"Ah, your neighbours," someone said, "and childhood friends. How thoroughly romantic."

Huxley spun around the moment they had left, his eyes blazing with anger.

"Have a nice day," Dorothy squeaked and dove out of the window.

Chapter Ten

"It wasn't his fault," Dorothy cried. "I snuck into his study and was only trying to get the thorn out. Surely, I don't have to marry him over something so trivial?"

Penelope eyed her gravely. "I am afraid this time your thoughtless action has consequences, Dorothy. You will have to marry him. Knowing you were at fault, the duke cannot call him out with a clean conscience. And what's more, I won't allow it."

"But Kitty loves him," Dorothy wailed. "Oh, why can't I move away from London? Hide from the world. Surely it is better to live a frugal spinster's life than ruin Huxley's and Kitty's happiness."

The duke lifted his head wearily. "Kitty married Lord Lumley early this morning in Gretna Green. We got the missive just before you arrived."

Dorothy looked as if she had been slapped. "Must be some mistake," she whispered.

"None at all," the duke responded, unable to hide the pity in his eyes.

Penelope rose to her feet, looking every inch the regal duchess. "Dorothy, the duke will procure a special license, and your marriage will be registered by the end of the week. I had already begged you to refrain from causing a scandal … you are not a child anymore to have made such a foolish mistake and to think you will marry Huxley of all the people—" Her voice shook, she bit her lip and quickly left the room.

After a moment, the duke said gently, "If he hurts you, come straight to me. The marriage will silence all tongues, but do not allow him to treat you cruelly. I am angry and disappointed in your actions, but you will always be welcome here if you need help or a home."

Dorothy watched him leave through a veil of tears. How could she have made such a horrible mistake?

Her foolish act had alienated those who meant the most to her.

Her heart felt utterly broken, shattered into a million pieces. How could Kitty betray her so? Now, even her family abandoned her to a stranger.

∞∞∞

Dorothy sank into the soft leather carriage seat and carefully adjusted her satin skirt in Evening Primrose.

Penelope and Celine popped in after her and sat in the opposite seats. Both looked how Dorothy felt, funeral.

Penelope stared out of the window, refusing to look at Dorothy, while Celine appeared to be preparing herself for a favourite relative's guillotine.

The carriage lurched forward, and Dorothy's stomach lurched along with it.

"I will write to Mother and tell her about this," Celine waved a hand at Dorothy. "She will be pleased enough."

Penelope gave a short nod.

"I am sorry," Dorothy said for what felt like the umpteenth time.

"If only it had been anyone but him ... this has hurt the duke, who has been nothing but kind to you," Celine replied tiredly. "I don't want to talk about this again, Dorothy. You know how I feel ... how we all feel."

"Will you never speak to me again, Penny?" Dorothy's voice shook.

Penelope pressed her lips together, the only indication that she had heard her.

Dorothy refused to give in to tears. She hugged the pink and white long-stemmed roses lying in the crook of her arm and inhaled their fresh, sweet scent. The roses were from the grounds of Blackthorne mansion ... from Penelope's patch. This gave her hope. Penelope and Celine may be angry now, but they wouldn't be for long, she silently vowed. She would make sure her sisters forgave her.

"We are here," Penelope finally looked straight at Dorothy. "You will be married within an hour."

And Dorothy *was* married within an hour.

She now had a new home, husband, family, and title, and even her name was foreign to her tongue.

Lady Dorothy May Huxley.

The registry had been short, swift and dispassionate. So quick, in fact, that the momentous occasion felt anticlimactic ... unreal. To have her world turned on its head so simply and without any hullabaloo left her reeling in confusion. In one moment, everything that had been familiar to her was snatched away.

"Dorothy," the duke gripped her arm to halt her.

Dorothy blinked in the harsh sunlight.

"You are going the wrong way. Huxley's carriage is behind ours."

She blinked again and focused on the gold Blackthorne emblem emblazoned on the carriage before her. She dipped her head to hide the fear that suddenly engulfed her and retraced her steps towards her new life.

Huxley sat before her, drenched in sunlight. His skin gleamed like pale gold while his eyes stayed glued to the passing scenery. The carriage was well furnished, well sprung and roomy, but it felt like a miniature, with his tall and broad physique taking up half of it.

His icy aura and the sense of alienation in his eyes annihilated any warmth that the blazing sun brought to this late morning of her newlywedded life.

She wrung her hands, wondering how to speak to him and thaw the tension.

He sat with his broad back resting against the seat, dressed in a dark blue velvet coat that appeared almost black in the dim light. His long fingers encased in fawn kid gloves lay loosely on his lap, relaxed and still, while his legs were tucked close to himself, careful not to crowd her.

A sense of calm permeated from him as if he were a monk, not of this world. This matter of hastily being married did not seem to concern him.

The carriage lurched and dipped as it bounced over a large pothole. The horses neighed and carried on, unaware of the escalating emotions of the passengers they carried.

"My lord, I am sorry," she finally said in a voice as low as a mosquito's buzz.

His face remained frozen like a true aristocrat, promising not to move even if the stars fell to earth and set everything ablaze.

She swallowed and continued, "I- this is my fault. I should not have been so irrational, presumptuous and bold. I promise to do my duty henceforth as your wife. After a year, once everything is settled, I can move to the countryside and leave you in peace."

He remained impassive, not even bothering to acknowledge that he had heard her. A moment later, he yawned, making her blink.

They had just been married, a calamity had occurred, and he had the audacity to yawn. What was wrong with his blooming head?

She stuffed her irritation deep into the bosom. She had no right to be vexed; he could dance a jig or set sail for Africa, and she would have to endure it.

Endure everything this man flung at her from now on.

At least he was easy on the eyes. So handsome... but what did that matter if they lived on different continents?

Nay, he could not detest her so much as to move away from his homeland.

She smacked her head, forget him, what in the world was wrong with her? Why was she suddenly envisioning romancing him in an exotic jungle?

The carriage moved on, and the galloping horses entered the lush avenue that led to the Ansley estate.

"I will not trouble you," she said desperately, hoping to melt the man before they reached his home. "I am truly sorry and feel terrible."

His lashes flickered so briefly that she would have missed them had her gaze not been pinned on his face.

She leaned forward and clutched her knees, eager for just one comforting word or glance from him.

He did not acknowledge or dismiss her, treating her like a nonverbal decorative cushion lying dead on the velvet seat.

As if she were of no consequence at all.

A soft, gentle breeze caressed her face and then moved on to play with his hair.

How could anything be so light and frivolous when the entire world was crashing down around her aggrieved ears?

The silence stretched on, finally broken by the footman, who knocked on the door to announce their arrival.

Dorothy watched him descend without a backwards glance while she moved more slowly.

She glanced at the broad shoulders of the man in front of her. Her husband ... who had complete control over her life now.

She felt like a fisherman caught in a storm. A roaring gale was pushing her along an uncharted path while all she could see around herself was the endless grey sea.

She clutched her stomach, feeling sick and breathless. Her

attempts at improving the tumultuous atmosphere had failed spectacularly, and her path to redemption now appeared more gnarled and twisted than she had thought.

That brooding, silent man would take much work to break and soften, but she had always been hardworking and persistent. Why, once she had found a kitten with a burnt ear and vicious personality, nursed the hissing demon back to health, coaxed it until it fell in love with her, and slept on her bed until it died of old age.

Surely, it would be easier to win over a man who grew up healthy and wealthy than a traumatised kitten?

He pushed open Ansley Hall's giant, exquisitely carved rosewood doors and strode in.

Even his back appeared cold like a snow-capped Himalaya, unreachable and foreign.

No matter. One little failure did not indicate a bleak future. She gritted her teeth and hurried to join him.

Argh!

Someone screamed the moment she crossed the threshold.

"Why did he have to marry her?" A young woman's wail rent the air.

"Hush, she will be here soon." A voice replied.

Dorothy froze. She recognised the voices floating down the grand staircase. Miss Huxley and her mother were once again discussing her.

"He was to marry Miss March," Miss Huxley sobbed hysterically. "Why, he kissed her last night. I saw him do it!"

"Sophia!" Lady Huxley scolded. "You have yet to marry the prince. He will have nothing to do with a family riddled with scandals, no matter how generous your dowry is. We must behave appropriately. I will allow nothing to tarnish the Huxley name nor ruin your excellent prospects."

"Mother," Lord Huxley called out belatedly. "She has arrived."

Dorothy pasted a smile on her face and took another step inside. "Oh!" The exclamation slipped past her lips, and for a brief moment, she forgot herself as she stood transfixed by the sight that met her.

Sunlight streamed in through luxurious glass windows, illuminating intricate tapestries. Her eyes moved upwards to admire the high ceiling, exquisitely painted to portray various mythological scenes.

There was also a pond in the hallway, with blooming white lilies and fish. A soft blue Persian carpet sat at the bottom of the grand staircase, and lush green plants in ornate vases dotted the marble-pillared room.

She took a deep, steadying breath. She could do this, she told herself. It was a big change, but what seemed foreign and intimidating to her now would soon be familiar and comforting in the near future … or so she hoped.

She looked around the stunning hallway again and could barely believe she was the mistress of it all.

Huxley's foot began to tap impatiently, his eyes pinned on the staircase, while the staff that had lined up to greet the new lady of the house tried not to fidget.

Lady Huxley and Sophia had still not come down to greet them.

When Sophia let out another indignant shriek, Huxley muttered in annoyance and bounded up the stairs.

Dorothy rocked on her heels, feeling awfully awkward. She didn't know where to go or what to say.

Forty eyeballs of the most essential indoor servants watched her expectantly.

She took a deep breath and stepped forward. It seemed she would have to acquaint herself.

The staff eyed her pityingly as she greeted them one by one. She kept her shoulders straight and her chin up.

Her smile never wavered.

She quickly assessed the staff, trying to memorise the names and faces of the most important servants.

The housekeeper looked like a goose feather quill. She was a woman of few words and cold. The butler was a tall, dignified fellow who always appeared to sneer. The cook was a whimsical young woman with a flowery cap, mismatched shoes and delicate gestures.

It wasn't long before the names and faces began to blur together, and Dorothy's head began to throb.

She glanced up at the stairs for the fifth time. It had been a good while, but no family member appeared.

Finally, she requested two upstairs maids to lead her to her chamber, where she flung open the windows, crawled into bed, cried, and then slept.

Chapter Eleven

Late in the evening, long after the sun had gone down, she woke to find a wide-eyed maid staring at her.

"What is it?" Dorothy yawned.

"Would you like dinner?" the maid squeaked.

"I will join the others," Dorothy replied.

"They have already eaten," the maid replied apologetically.

Dorothy forced herself to appear cheerful. "Well, I am hungry. I would love something to eat."

Dinner was a lonely affair. She barely tasted the lamb, too busy brooding over the fact that what should have been the happiest day of her life had turned into a tragedy.

She pushed aside the little sugar basket filled with candied roses, violets and jasmine. No more brooding, she scolded herself and leapt out of bed.

Her fingers lay on the door handle for a few moments before weakly dropping to her side. It was better to explore her chamber first. After all, she was already here.

It was lovely. Far lovelier than she had expected.

Three enormous fireplaces lit the room and the adjoining parlour, and ornate silver candlesticks with beeswax candles cast a sparkling golden light over everything.

The toilet table was strewn with new silver combs, brushes, and pots of creams and oils. The teak wardrobe occupied an entire wall, while at the other end sat two ornate chairs covered in gold brocade. The four-poster bed was draped with yards and yards of gossamer cloth, and the linen was made of the softest fabric edged with satin and lace.

She discovered a beautiful bathroom with blue and silver drapery, silver fittings, and a small private parlour to entertain her guests.

Back in her bedchamber, she found yet another door next to the wardrobe. It was wide and made of rosewood. She intuitively knew it led to Huxley's room.

Naturally, she didn't dare open that door and hurriedly scuttled away.

A delicate, cool breeze rustled the white lace curtains framing the window, drawing her eyes towards the lush rose garden lit with twinkling lamps. A fat moon hung over the garden, further illuminating the Albas, Cuisse de Nymphs, Banksias and the arching, nodding old cabbage roses.

It was clear that whoever decorated the room had spared no expense.

She slipped down to her chemise, not bothering to wait for her maid and got ready for bed. At least Huxley was not a miser.

That was something to feel hopeful about.

She might, henceforth, live a lonesome existence, but a luxurious one at that. She decided to drown her sorrows while drinking the most expensive champagne and dressing in pearls and emeralds henceforth.

If he did not love her, she could indulge in delicious treats and grow fat without a care.

Her mood improved as she spent her husband's money in a wonderful daydream. She snuggled deeper into the soft bed, imagining her desolate future of luxuries stretching before her.

She could see herself roaming the corridors of Ansley Hall wearing a diaphanous white gown, dripping diamonds from her neck and wrists, while her heart ached for a drop of love.

She could imagine crying bitter tears as her family and friends shunned her. She would be so frightfully unhappy that even after her death, people would hear her pathetic wails as she floated from room to room, searching for companionship.

Her tale would be told over and over again as a warning to all men who decide to take wives. It would be a lesson for cruel, heartless, wealthy husbands who abandoned their—

"Are you asleep?" Huxley's deep voice echoed in the room.

She yelped and dragged the covers to her chin.

"I am coming in," he warned.

Nay, she wanted to cry. How dare a despicable creature of the opposite sex enter her room in broad evening light?

He appeared at the foot of the bed while she was still trying to form appropriate words to ask him not to behave like a scoundrel.

He was dressed in a deep blue house robe with a thin silver border that gaped at the neck, revealing gleaming skin. His hair was slightly wet and appeared even darker and shinier. Droplets of water escaped the tips and trickled down the side of his left ear until they disappeared beneath his robe.

She gazed at him in horror.

He quickly placed his finger on his lips and pointed to the door. The robe fell back when he lifted his hand and exposed his wrists. His skin was clear and spotless everywhere she could see. Not a freckle or a scar marred him.

His eyes narrowed, and she quickly yanked her wandering gaze back to his face. Eh? What was he trying to say?

She followed his finger and spotted a flitting shadow beneath the gap between the door and the floor.

Someone was listening.

He moved closer to the bed and leaned towards her.

Her heart began to thud as his face came near enough to brush hers. Warm breath splayed on her lips and cheeks, sending tingling sensations down her spine.

He inched even closer until his mouth almost touched her scandalised left ear. "Do not scream. Get off the bed and sit on the chair."

A drop of cold water fell on her forehead as he moved away, and she buried herself under the quilt.

Nay, she would never let this quilt go until her dying day. He would never see her face again, and she would die on this bed, starving, thirsty and mouldy.

She was only wearing a chemise! How could he expect her to expose herself like a hussy to his male gaze? Ah, the heartless dimwit.

He waited for a moment, and when she did not twitch, he picked her up, quilt and all, and deposited her on the high-backed chair near the window, which was the farthest point in the room from the door.

Then, he patiently and gently proceeded to dig her head out of the blanket.

Her red face finally appeared in his view, and he, once again, placed his finger on his lips and whispered, "My stepmother's maids are listening at the door to ascertain that we consummate our marriage."

She wanted to stuff her head under the quilt again at his words, but she had somehow become wrapped so tightly that she couldn't get her hands free without an exaggerated struggle. She did not want to appear foolish before her husband, so she stared at the carpet with a flushed face.

He watched her quivering lashes for a moment before asking, "Did your mother tell you what to expect on your wedding night?"

She nodded, her motions jerky and unnatural.

"What did she say?" he asked.

"It is a long story," she whispered in embarrassment and then tried to divert his attention by changing the topic. "You should sit. Kneeling for so long must be painful. Should I call for some tea?"

"Long story?" He rose to his feet, pulled open the window to let in the sharp, cold breeze and then moved the second chair in the room close to where she sat. "Speak."

"Your hair is still wet, and you opened the window. Are you not afraid to catch your death?" He picked up the chair and placed it on the other side of her, closer to the fireplace and away from the breeze.

So obedient? She stared at him suspiciously.

"Now, tell me."

"Would you like a sugar plum?"

"I want to hear what your mother told you about the wedding night." His tone was patient, like a quiet, frozen lake, as if nothing could cause ripples in his demeanour. The man who had growled at her so often was suddenly steady and unruffled.

Why didn't he rage at her like everyone else? After all, in this entire debacle, he had been wronged the most.

She dropped her lashes and once again admired the carpet. "She told me a story about a warrior mouse."

His expression contorted, but he waved at her, indicating she should continue.

So, she continued, "The mouse had a home, but a wall blocked it, so the mouse took a spear and rushed at it. He was homesick, very homesick, so homesick that he was desperate. He rushed at the wall again and again until he was battered, bleeding and bruised."

His eyes became cloudy with confusion. "Continue."

"Then the warrior mouse died."

"Oh."

"Then the next day, he came alive again."

"An immortal mouse?" his brows rose with incredulity.

"Hmm. So, he fought again with all his might, slamming into the wall again and again. Then he coughed up blood and died."

"And came alive?"

"Yes. But on the third day, he managed to pierce through and enter the hole in the wall that was his home."

"It is always the third time, is it not?" He scratched his chin and stared into the fire until his eyes turned watery.

"Hmm."

"Is that all?"

"Yes."

"Did your sisters tell you anything?"

"Penelope told me that an elongated mushroom falls down the well on wedding nights."

"Ah, and the other married sister?"

"Celine. She said that on the fateful night, the sword was sheathed."

He rubbed his temples. "Do you... need someone else to explain?"

Her eyes widened, and she almost leapt off the chair. How could one hear such things from the lips of a man? Had his father taught him nothing? "Nay! I grew up in Finnshire... on a f-farm. I know enough."

He swiftly stood up, and she squeaked in fright. That brooding, dark expression on his face was back.

Was he going to ravish her?

Nay, she would rather tear apart the chair and become the stuffing inside.

He raised his hand and wiggled his fingers.

He was waving at the window. Was it a ghost?

She turned to look and found a man clambering into the room. Because of his beautiful appearance, which included delicate features and pretty green eyes, she recognised him as Huxley's valet.

This time, it was her eyes that clouded in confusion.

Huxley bent from the waist and placed his lips close to her ears again, his entire being hovering over her, giving the illusion that they were embracing. "What will happen next shall not surprise you since you grew up on a farm. All I ask is that you stay quiet and let us work."

Then the valet sat on the floor with his back leaning against the bed while Huxley pulled out a deep red cloth bag from his robe and placed it on the table.

She stared in befuddlement as her husband took twenty quills from the bag. His long fingers pinched one, held it up, and inspected it from all sides; then he started sharpening it.

Why did he need so many quills? Who would need to write

so much? But that was not the confounding thing.

What on earth was going on?

Was she a pervert who had misunderstood the meaning of a wedding night? Here, it seemed it was a heartwarming time of bonding in the most innocent way by sharpening quills.

Ahhh!

The valet suddenly made the ghastliest sound. It sounded like a ghoul in pain.

Puch, puch, pucheee.

Next, the valet puckered his lips and made kissing sounds.

She stared at the valet and the unperturbed Huxley, then back again.

The valet giggled, sounding remarkably like a woman.

Her eyes widened. The valet was meant to be her! He was pretending to be ravished, or rather behaving as he thought she would sound while being ravished.

Naturally, she could not sit and do nothing about this. This was unacceptable, unseemly and embarrassing. So, she freed her hands, yanked the quilt up and hid again.

This was all too much! The scandal, the quick wedding and now this strange, strange night. She could not bear it. Her skin could not turn redder, or she would go up in flames.

That might not be so bad.

Oh! If only she could spontaneously combust!

The valet spoke softly, amused by her behaviour. "Pardon, I play the part of an actress during stage plays since I am small-boned, and that's why my lord asked me to help. Rest assured, I will remain discreet."

"Shh," Huxley warned, picked up a new quill and began scraping again. "They may hear us."

After some time of listening to the valet mewl, it became stifling under the quilt, what with being so close to the fireplace, so she revealed her nose and then replaced it with her eyes.

Huxley had moved at some point without her realising and was now standing near the bed with his arm out. A dagger glinted in his other hand.

She watched in horror as he raised the dagger as if he was about to offer a sacrifice to pagan gods and slashed his arm.

Both the valet and she cried out.

Two feminine screams had rung out.

Huxley, the valet, and she froze. How did they explain this anomaly to the eavesdroppers?

Add to that, blood poured out of Huxley's arm onto the bedsheet, becoming a little red pool.

There was so much blood that it appeared as if a small animal had been killed rather than a virgin losing her most precious treasure.

Goodness, what would the household think?

The valet paled and swayed before bowing to Dorothy in apology.

"I told you to be quiet," Huxley muttered, pulled down his sleeve and clutched his arm to stop the bleeding. The blood now dripped from the bed to the floor as he walked towards their connecting door.

The valet hurried to Huxley, pulled his collar aside to reveal his sharp shoulder blades, mussed up his hair and then raced towards the window. His leg had just been thrown over the windowsill when the connecting door was opened by a timid kitchen maid and Dorothy's lady's maid carrying a tub of hot water and muslin cloths.

They spotted the dishevelled duke, the valet, and the blood splattered all over the floor and bed while Dorothy stood trembling like a branch on a windy day, tightly wrapped in a quilt.

Time seemed to freeze, and no one knew what to say. The maids began swaying, the valet began slithering, and Huxley frowned.

"Change the sheets," he ordered.

The valet disappeared down the ladder; Dorothy pretended to swoon and landed back on the chair while the maids inwardly swore never to marry.

They peeked at Dorothy worriedly as they quickly worked while Huxley kept his arm hidden in his house robe, his finger pressing hard on the wound to stop the blood flow.

Soon, the maids left, and Dorothy sat up. "Wait," she called when he was about to head back to his chamber.

She shuffled to the wardrobe, dragging the quilt across the floor, pulled out her medicine chest, rummaged amongst the contents and then shuffled back towards him. "Here, this balm is good for your wound. And this b-bandage."

He pocketed them.

"Your quills," she reminded him softly.

He picked that up as well.

They stared at one another, both realising that this maddening night would be the first secret between them as husband and wife, and there would be many more to come.

"I am locking the door from my end. I don't want you taking undue advantage of me." He pulled the fabric of his robe closer together.

"I am not going to sneak into your room to … take advantage of you!" she spluttered in shock. "If anything, I should be concerned about you doing the same to me."

He hmphed disbelievingly. "That is highly unlikely, considering I am far more tempting a specimen than you can ever hope to be. Besides, if I had any such intention, I wouldn't have needed to create an entire play. Goodnight."

Dorothy spent the rest of the night fuming. How absolutely, frustratingly, vexingly arrogant! Tempting … he thought he was tempting! He was as tempting as a poisonous viper!

At least the anger kept her from feeling sorry for herself and sobbing the night away. She would be able to present herself fresh-faced and dewy-eyed at breakfast the next day… all ready for battle.

Then she recalled all the blood and the escaping valet.

Ahhhh! What would the servants think?

How would she face her mother-in-law?

This was all too embarrassing.

So, embarrassing that she was going to die.

Chapter Twelve

The next morning, Dorothy was woken by loud, thumping music. She opened her eyes to find two large, round eyes peering at her. It was the same maid who had attended to her the night before.

"Are you alive, my lady?"

Dorothy blinked rapidly, plucked out a few crusts from the corner of her eyelids and made a confused sound.

The woman stared at her with a soft, tender expression as if facing a wounded pup.

Ah, the blood; Dorothy suddenly recalled where she was and what had occurred. No wonder she was being treated like a dying creature.

Dorothy wondered if she should explain, but what on earth could she say? This matter was too convoluted, and no explanation seemed suitable.

"What's your name?" Dorothy asked.

"Milly."

"Who is pounding away at the piano with such enthusiasm, Milly?" Dorothy yawned.

"In the music room … they are practising—"

"Who?"

"Who, Miss?"

"I mean, who is practising?"

"Musicians."

"What musicians?"

"They play instruments, Miss," Milly responded with a look

that indicated that she thought her new mistress was a bit dim.

"I would like some tea." She rubbed her temples. The blasted din was torturous after a night of fitful sleep.

"And breakfast?"

"I will eat with the others."

"Pardon me, but you are now married—"

"I will not eat in bed."

Milly bowed and retreated, looking even less impressed.

Another maid entered with a tea tray, saw Dorothy's pale face and bit back a sob. "Tea, my lady."

Dorothy smiled weakly and accepted it. After drinking every drop, she slipped out of bed and walked to the basin.

She splashed her face with cold water and eyed herself in the mirror.

The lace-edged pillowcase she had admired last night had left an imprint on her cheek. Things didn't get any better thereafter.

Instead of looking like a glowing, blushing bride, she seemed to be emanating the physical traits of a vigorous gin drinker.

Her lady's maid arrived to help her dress, distracting her from the ghastly sight.

"Rosie! I hope you are settling in well." Dorothy wanted to cry in relief, seeing a familiar face. Rosie was the only servant she had brought as part of her dowry.

"The cook is very kind."

"That's good."

"Last night... miss... I mean, my lady," Rosie paused as she adjusted to the new title. "You, the blood?"

"Don't worry about it. I am unhurt." She quickly washed and dried her face.

Rosie burst into tears. "But—WHY WAS THERE SO MUCH BLOOD!"

Dorothy patted her maid's back and then continued getting dressed, unsure of how to respond. The pounding in her head increased.

"Wah!" Rosie howled. "You were doing this and that... how did it turn into a killing?"

"I am alive."

"So much BLOOD!"

A sad twang of a harp reverberated through the room, echoing the wistful mood.

"Oh, that blasted music! Do they have to play so loudly in the morning," Dorothy grumbled, poking her head through the neck of a soft green muslin dress. "I have to see what it's about."

"Your hair!" Rosie wailed. "Blood loss! You may swoon, my lady, stop!"

"To hell with it!" Dorothy yelled back and strode away to investigate the music room.

It wasn't difficult to locate. It was right below her bedchamber.

She pushed open the door and paused in surprise. This was not what she had expected. Instead of finding Miss Huxley twanging away at the harp to vex her, she found a group of men draped over various musical instruments. One man played the piano while another shouted instructions over the noise. In the corner, someone was tinkering with a citole. A fellow was lounging on the window seat, playing the flute while another was tuning a violin.

At the sight of her, they paused and stared at her boldly. A room full of men exuding hostility made her flinch in sudden realisation. This was not her home or her sister's residence; how could she recklessly rush in like this?

Lack of sleep had addled her brain and turned it into soup.

She took a small step back. The unfriendly and mocking gazes made her feel a little frightened.

A young, bacon-faced man who looked no more than sixteen boldly caught her hand and pulled her in.

"The bride is here," he smiled. "Sorry if we woke you."

"Ack," she responded in bewilderment.

The fellow at the piano twirled a hat on the tip of his finger.

"We were getting ready to play a song for you. We didn't realise you were an early riser ... but ready or not, here it is."

The young fellow who had pulled her in now came back to stand before her as if readying himself for a dance. The first music notes floated out, and she was surprised that the tune was bittersweet and wonderful.

And yet, contrasting with the lovely music, she was surrounded by strange men wearing smiling masks.

The sudden grins and affected lightness did not deceive her. After all, she had spent countless social outings skirting the rooms and observing people. She was unwanted, and they were simply putting on a show.

Testing her.

She frowned in confusion. What was the need?

The young man tugged at her hand, encouraging her to follow his steps. He seemed young, but his body resembled that of a mature man. This proximity, along with his probing looks, made her feel uncomfortable.

They were barely attempting to conceal their contempt.

She needed to get away.

She twisted out of his grip and began retreating towards the door. "Mayhap, later."

Her back hit a wall, and she turned to find Huxley standing behind her. Who knew when he had entered the room?

He placed his hands on her shoulders and faced the room. His eyes were like flints, sparking in warning.

The room chilled, and the lounging men immediately straightened. Some appeared confused at the hostility on Huxley's face.

"I hope you will extend the same respect and courtesy towards her as you do towards me." Huxley's words were polite, but the underlying threat was clear to all.

Dorothy's heart leapt at his words; she had not expected him to protect her thus, not after all that had happened between them.

A man laughed, and she recognised him. He was the valet!

The swarm of men in the room had hidden his delicate figure, and she had failed to spot him.

"You changed after one night of passion?" The valet boldly winked.

What passion? Why... oh, he was helping her. She hung her head and obediently pretended to be a shy bride on the morning after almost being killed.

"Dance," someone else cried.

After the subtle admonishment from the master of the house, the men turned meek and hurriedly began playing music to change the heavy mood.

A brave man approached her and bowed.

"Why, you are the cook's assistant!" she accused the fellow.

He grinned. "I am that. And the one at the piano is the butler, the fat fellow is the head gardener, that sour-looking creature takes care of the stables and hounds, the one playing the flute is the silver polisher—"

"Everyone works in the household?"

"Most of us do. Though we do have a guest or two amongst us," he replied.

"You are a talented lot."

"Why, thank you, miss," the cook's assistant bowed again. "Would you like to dance?"

A blast of frigid air suddenly seemed to engulf the room.

The cook's assistant raised his head, spotted Huxley's gaze behind Dorothy's head, and paled. He hurriedly changed tune. "Would you like to dance with my lord? We can play a waltz."

Would he be willing? Dorothy spun on her heel and found herself in Huxley's arms.

She stared up at him, and her heart began hammering loudly in the sudden pulsing silence. She was not very tall, her bones were narrow and fragile, and her pale skin had paled even further due to the difficult few weeks.

In contrast, he was extraordinarily tall, perhaps the tallest and broadest in the *ton*. His skin glowed with health, and his eyes were clear and bright as if he had slept well.

The contrast in their physiques made her tremble and realise just how weak and vulnerable she was.

Was he angry at the liberties his staff had taken? Would he become violent?

One twist, and he could easily break her wrist. She paled even further, and her eyes turned red in the corners.

The servants were watching them, watching every flicker of expression.

Aware of the curious, gossiping eyes, her hands fluttered over his arms, tapping lightly, uncertainly.

After a brief hesitation, Huxley curled his fingers around her waist and dragged her close.

He was going to dance with her.

She looked up at him in surprise. He wanted to oblige his staff instead of scolding them.

How odd.

The soft strains of the waltz oozed out and wrapped themselves around the couple.

The first few steps reflected the tension in Huxley's face. He meant this dance to be different from the one they had shared before.

He did not set her at ease or allow her limbs to relax into the familiar rhythm this time. Instead, he took charge and kept his body firm, his movements brisk, confident and sharp.

She felt as if he was no longer leading her but dictating when and how much she should move.

Every dip, turn, and step was guided by his determined touch, which left no room for her to think. It was as if she were a mere doll being tossed and turned as he wished... as if she were his from now on.

He pulled her flush against his body when her lashes briefly dipped. She looked up, startled, and was caught by his feverish gaze.

A complex emotion arose between them, rising higher and higher like steam trapped in a bubbling pot.

Was he trying to frighten her?

She tipped her head back in defiance, keeping her gaze locked on his. She refused to give him the satisfaction of knowing he was upsetting her.

His eyes were like deep pools of a placid lake gleaming in moonlight. They fell on her face, lingered on her brows, her hair, and finally slipped to her mouth.

He was not angry with her but with the men. This dramatic display was for their benefit and had nothing to do with her.

Her body went limp at this realisation, allowing him to take charge. She let him turn, spin, and dip her however and whenever he liked.

She softened in his arms like sun-warmed butter as all her grievance melted away.

He frowned at her surrender, and the resolve in his eyes suddenly blazed into something more torrid and acute.

He pulled her closer still, far closer than propriety allowed.

The dance changed, becoming sensual, slow, and rhythmic … a faint blush rose on her cheeks.

The men were forgotten, and now his attention was only on her.

The song ended, and neither of them noticed as they continued to sway.

"Kiss her," someone shouted.

So, he did.

He dipped his head and placed his lips on her cheek.

Her skin burned where he had touched as if he had left a mark whose heat would refuse to fade for a long time.

Someone whistled, and he stepped back. He looked at her shaken face in amusement, and there was laughter in his voice when he announced that breakfast was ready.

On cue, the musicians trickled out, leaving them alone.

Chapter Thirteen

"Why pretend?" she asked, gripping her skirt to hide her trembling fingers.

The music room was silent, with only their breaths and beating hearts ringing in their ears.

Amusement gone, his face was once again a mask when he replied, "In private, you may mean nothing to me, but in public, including amongst the household, you are my wife. Until my sister is married, we have to pretend."

"You don't trust your servants?"

"They are artists first. The moment they find their feet, they move away. They change so frequently that—" He clicked his tongue impatiently. "Your behaviour will reflect on my family name; thus, I will treat you with courtesy and respect that belongs to your status. In turn, I hope you will be loyal and discreet."

She nodded so hard that her head almost appeared to blur. "I am sorry. I have caused you trouble."

He was quiet for some time before suddenly reaching out and smoothing the rebellious curl waving atop her head. "This is not your fault. If anything, both of us were frivolous in our behaviour. This is our comeuppance."

"Eh?" Her head shot up, and she eyed him quizzically.

His lips ticked up, and he continued, "Lady Lu—Miss Norwood had been pestering me for a long time. Her father even started interfering in my business, and I lost patience. You happened to be the innocent victim of our battle. I was rude and deliberately created an unpleasant impression of myself in your eyes, hoping you would dissuade your friend from chasing after such an unreliable creature who kissed women with abandon and used harsh language to bully the weak."

Her eyes widened. Goodness! She was an even bigger fool than she had thought.

He took a step away from her. "In private, nothing will change. I will not interfere with your life, and as long as it is proper, you can do what you like."

"I see."

"Another thing, the artists here are fugitives and hiding. Some have created works that have offended powerful people, while others have a scandal attached. Their presence is a secret, so please keep this to yourself."

"You can trust me," she said sincerely.

He lifted his hand as if he wanted to pet her again before allowing it to fall back to his sides. "If you let it out, then not only my reputation but also yours will be affected. If I am imprisoned, so will you. After all, you are my wife."

She flushed and looked away. So many secrets. No wonder he stayed aloof and refused to mingle in society.

"I understand," she said. "Your secrets are safe with me for the sake of your head and mine."

"Even from your family?"

"You can trust me," she repeated.

He nodded. "One last thing, I do not expect you to warm my bed, but I will have to visit your room at night to keep up pretences."

"Until your sister marries?"

"You are not as foolish as I had thought. I had feared I had married a nitwit."

"You nitwit." It was out before she could help it

His eyes twinkled. "I will come to your room at ten and leave at eleven. Prepare something to occupy yourself at the time."

She nodded once again, surprised by his polite, respectful

tone, a far cry from his harsh manner these past few weeks.

She gazed at him, feeling suddenly strange, as if she no longer knew how to behave around him. She could no longer bristle and snap at him or be on the defence. All this while, anger and enmity had bound them together with an invisible thread and now that had been suddenly snipped.

An abyss opened between them, with nothing connecting them any longer except a superficial name. He was like a cold, aloof stranger whom she knew nothing about.

Oddly, it left her feeling bereft.

Once, she had chanced upon Lord Elmer and Celine canoodling. Lord Elmer had grabbed Celine, thinking no one was watching, and twirled her around until she burst into delighted laughter. The sun had streamed in on the happy couple, full of dancing golden dust, while the polished wooden beams and floor had shone in the light around them.

Alas, such a warm, intimate relationship was not meant for her.

Her heart suddenly ached.

Ah, well, she could always go to Mayfair and buy something whenever she needed a hug.

"Breakfast is ready." He interrupted her reverie and glanced meaningfully at the mass of thick, silky hair tumbling down her back in waves.

She obediently hurried back to her room to let Rosie finish doing her hair; her mind was stuffed with fragmented thoughts. A part of her felt relieved because, unlike everyone else, he had not laid complete blame on her feet. Instead, he made her realise that this entire situation was not her fault. She did not need to apologise; she had been tricked.

Tricked by her bosom friend, and yet, her heart still ached.

Yes, she had been tricked and had hurt many people because she had been a fool. If only she had not trusted so easily or been prejudiced against Huxley. He may be magnanimous about it, but the fact was, she was an idiot who had ruined his life.

∞∞∞

Some people were already seated at the long, gleaming breakfast table. On her husband's right sat his stepmother, Lady Huxley, and on his left was his sister, Miss Sophia Huxley. Four strangers and one of the musicians she had met earlier took up the next few seats.

She would have to sit at the end of the table, which, by right, did not conform to her status. Still, it was understandable, considering that everyone thought she had used unscrupulous means to marry into this aristocratic household.

She nodded politely and sat down.

Lady Huxley gave her a comforting look as she introduced the people at the table. The four strangers were visiting poets and painters. Her eyes were full of worry as she spoke, as if she had softened overnight to her plight.

Oh yes, the blood. How could she forget?

A bowl of porridge was placed in front of her by a maid, who also eyed her tenderly.

Dorothy obediently dipped her head and allowed her fingers to tremulously rise and touch her slim, long neck, acting like the damsel who had almost been slaughtered on her wedding night.

She glanced at Lord Huxley and found him watching her as well. He seemed to have been struck speechless by her tortured maiden act.

She smiled at him weakly.

His lips tightened in a straight line, promising retribution.

She gulped and quickly looked away.

Blackthorne Mansion had many rules; she wondered if Ansley Hall was also strict about mealtimes. Could she begin eating without ceremony?

The platter of toast was arranged in the shape of a fan. The edge of each slice was burnt artistically. It looked pretty but was cold to the touch. The boiled eggs were arranged like a fish, and the bacon was turned into flowers. Much thought had been given to the presentation, but none to taste.

She did not pick up her spoon until she saw Sophia picking up a grape and delicately nibbling it like a rabbit.

The meal was eaten in silence.

"He does not like excessive noise," a red-haired poetess sitting beside Dorothy whispered to her companion on the other side. "Or rather, likes the noise to be contained to an appropriate time and place. Music should be played in music rooms, and poems read in the library. This morning, he looks particularly pungent, so beware. He couldn't have slept much last night." She finished with a smirk and a nod in Dorothy's direction.

Dorothy's face flamed, and she concentrated on swallowing her tea.

Midway through the meal, Huxley put a slice of toast on Sophia's plate, indicating that she should eat more. Lady Huxley watched the interaction calmly, her eyes serene and full of affection.

Apart from this small exchange, the rest of the breakfast was finished in awkward silence, with Dorothy feeling like an unwanted pelican amongst bears.

Chapter Fourteen

"I want to look wonderful," Dorothy said, splashing cold water on her face. "If I look good, I can handle anything."

Rosie's eyes brightened, and she set to task.

First, she popped Dorothy into a steaming bath of scented water. After Dorothy had stewed for a good while, Rosie applied lotions and potions to Dorothy's skin until she glistened like a nymph.

Next, her cheeks were vigorously rubbed with Liquid Bloom of Roses, her lashes cleverly darkened with soot and her lips dabbed with crushed red berries.

Dorothy patiently endured every moment. She needed every bit of help she could get.

She wanted to look alive and full of fighting rigour.

No one seemed pleased with her arrival, not the family nor the servants.

Oh, the male servants were too polite to say anything, but the coldness emanating from them was felt silently and effectively. The smiles, the songs and dances were a sham.

She understood why now. They were suspicious and afraid that she would reveal their secret or, as the new mistress of the estate, throw them all out on a whim.

Meanwhile, the maids eyed her with sympathy and concern as if she were preparing to give up the ghost.

Why, even the housekeeper spoke to her in whispers, as if she were an ailing creature, and brought her a bowl of nourishing soup at noon and a bitter tonic in the evening, which promised to rejuvenate her blood.

She closed her eyes while Rosie brushed her hair and went over everything that had occurred the day before.

After breakfast, she had prowled around the house, followed by the housekeeper, and felt more like an unwanted thief than the new mistress. If she touched a precious vase or a bowl, the servants trailing behind her tensed, waiting for her clumsy fingers to break something.

It seemed that, even though she was the Duchess' sister, everyone still remembered that she had been brought up in the country, and although her father was respectable enough, he was no aristocrat.

She had tried her best to ignore the servants and instead attempted to learn as much as she could about her husband.

Huxley, she learned, not only employed some artists and helped them financially but also kept his house open to friday–faced visionaries who might need a home for a short while. The only condition was that they had to be exceptional at what they did.

On further perusal, she found sweaty sculptors in the garden chipping away at marble and granite, painters dangling dangerously near the reception room ceiling while eagerly varnishing Servius Tullius and Fortuna's love story, poets dozing open-mouthed on balconies and some eccentric singers living in tree houses on the Ansley estate.

The artists avoided the morning room, reception area, and anywhere Lady Huxley's guests might spot them.

"How would you like your hair done?" Rosie asked her, pulling her out of her thoughts.

"I will do it," Dorothy replied.

Rosie was a terrible hairdresser and only marginally acceptable as a lady's maid, but Dorothy couldn't bear to hurt the girl and ask her to leave. Now, she was glad she had kept her on. A new maid in this strange place would have unsettled her even more.

Once she was ready, she decided to explore the east wing, something she had missed on her tour yesterday. The housekeeper had been reluctant to take her, and that had piqued her curiosity.

The first thing she spotted when she entered the east wing was a giant painting hanging in what appeared to be a family room.

There was no doubt in her mind that this was the famous painting, The Aëdon, painted by Raziel.

The painting was like a gust of cold, grey breeze. The harsh, frosty hues leached the warmth from the room. It was a morose painting of a beautiful, frightened creature—a young woman draped in a mist of ice and snow, her mouth stained red and agape in terror. Her muscles appeared to be straining, trying to escape the painting, the silent scream echoing in every brush stroke. It seemed as if her eyes were silently begging Dorothy for help. They were so lifelike it was unnerving. A pomegranate lay broken and bleeding on the stark white ground, and a nightingale sat picking at the blood-red seeds.

Dorothy shivered and turned away from the painting. The artist was trying to tell a story, a story she would never know the end of. It left her feeling restless and angry. It wasn't that she didn't appreciate the artist's skill, but … it disturbed her. It was too depressing to be in a room that should have been filled with warmth and love.

The next room appeared to be another smaller, more private library. The green leather-covered desk was recently used. She touched the ink smeared on a piece of paper lying on the table and found it still wet.

Was this Huxley's writing?

Her hand flew to her cheek to the spot where he had kissed her, and the thought of running into him while they were alone suddenly made her feel unbearably shy.

He had not visited her on the second night. Perhaps he wanted to give the impression that he was being considerate and allowing her to recover.

Would he come tonight? Should she prepare some needlework to keep herself occupied?

Would the valet accompany them again? Should she procure a cat to make those odd mewling sounds, since having a strange man in her chamber to do so made her want to bury herself in the rose bush?

She was about to turn away and leave the room when she noticed something curious.

Next to the bookcase was a partial opening in the wall. It was so low that she had to bend down to ascertain that it truly was an opening and not a trick of the light. It seemed like someone had carved a door on the wall for a large doll or something fey.

Intrigued, she inched closer and curled a finger around the door, intending to open it wider, when something behind the wall caught her finger and held it fast.

"HELP, SOMEONE HAS CAPTURED ME! HELP!" Dorothy screeched in panic.

Huxley strode in through the door. "What's the meaning of this?"

"My finger," Dorothy begged.

"Let her go," Huxley ordered the mysterious creature hiding behind the door.

"Oh, I am sorry, Lady Diana," a man's voice said, sounding not at all apologetic. "I didn't know I was holding your finger. I couldn't hurt Lord Huxley's apple blossom—"

"She is not Lady Diana," Huxley cut in. "Let her go."

"Not Lady Diana," the fellow mused, "then who, I wonder—"

"He is nibbling my finger!" Dorothy squealed.

"Stop nibbling," Huxley snapped.

"Miss May?" the fellow asked calmly. "I shouldn't have mentioned Lady Diana. Why, I think Lord Huxley has not canoodled with her for a long time. But you ... he waxes lyrical about—"

"He is still nibbling," Dorothy said, trying to pull her hand away.

"That finger," Huxley roared. "Belongs to me. No one has the right to nibble it, Woodbead."

"I beg your pardon, Mrs Green. I thought it was that silly Miss May. But the passion with which he roars tells me it has to be you—"

"I am not Miss May, Miss Green or anyone you have ever met!" Dorothy growled.

"She is my wife," Huxley snapped.

The finger was immediately freed.

"Oh dear." Woodbead poked his head through the doorway. "I didn't know you got married."

A small, thin, bald man wriggled out and bowed to Dorothy. "My name is Philbert Woodbead."

Dorothy gasped. She knew all about him. He had been in love with her sister, Celine.

Woodbead took the gasp to mean she was flattered to meet such a famous poet.

"I know you are wondering why I was where I was," he said, gesturing to the wall. "Well, this is my hidey hole. Huxley keeps it for artists who are not too keen on facing the law."

"Why is the law after you?"

"It was all because of a poem. Would you like to hear it?"

She cautiously nodded.

He immediately produced a piece of paper from his pocket and handed it to her.

"What's this?" she asked.

"The poem."

"It's not a poem. It's two blobs."

"It's a poem that has been painted. Look at the circles. Two perfect circles. It's poetry in symmetry."

"Huh. What does it mean?"

"This is Peter," he pointed to one blob. "And this is loo."

"Err…"

"Here, this should explain it."

She was relieved to find the second paper he thrust towards her had words written on it.

Peter Loo, Peter Loo
You have turned the Thames a dodgy blue.
Have a heart and do your part,
And turn it back to greeny–blue
Oh, Peter, Peter looooo!

"That's the poem," he finished. "The government perceives my harmless ditty as radical and wants to book me for sedition. You must have heard of the new law—"

Dorothy nodded. "After the Peterloo Massacre. It's beastly, isn't it? To think they can curtail the press, the artists and everyone who dares to speak up. For years, we have sacrificed for the wars, and now that it is all over, we are rewarded thus."

Huxley's eyebrows shot up in surprise at her tirade.

Dorothy scowled. What did he think? Women only knew of the latest fashions and the colours of ribbons.

Philbert sighed loudly. "The poem is brilliant, isn't it? It is a pity I cannot publish it. It is hard being a poet."

"My maiden name is Fairweather," Dorothy said, turning her back on Huxley.

His eyes widened in recognition. "Little Dora? Is that you? Oh, I remember you." He sank into a seat close to her and shook his head in amazement. "Ah, the memories. How I loved your sister, and she was kind enough to refuse me. A hurting heart makes one a better poet."

"Why can't you be a happy poet?" she asked.

"No such thing. People like being miserable. And poets need to be the most miserable. First, you need a few people to die in your life to understand sorrow properly."

"How morbid."

"Precisely. The more gruesome your childhood, the better. A cannibal ate my father."

"Nay! Truly?"

"No. He is still alive. But I believe a cannibal ate him, and that is what matters. It truly depresses me. The thought that he was eaten by a cannibal when I was just six years old and my beautiful mother was married off to the cannibal's great–

grandfather as his twelfth wife . . ."

Dorothy didn't dare interrupt.

"The fact," he continued, "is that you have to be sufficiently morose to be a poet. Your life should be tragic, filled with a series of pathetic events and not a happy day to dwell on. You should have no hope, no money, no belief in humanity. You should be draped in dark clothes with not a drop of colour and wear a constantly haunted expression. You should look starved, your eyes unfocused just so. And when in large public gatherings, adopt a faraway look."

He stared thoughtfully at the ceiling, formed his lips into a pout and frowned slightly. "It is not easy to perfect this look. You have to brood convincingly to be taken seriously as an artist. You have to sulk, be moody, go away on lonely trips, and wear an odd assortment of mismatched clothes. You must pretend that material things do not matter to you. It is an art to look so lost and forlorn, to impart an aura of creativity. Yes, Miss Fairweather, it is hard work and a thankless job, but one day, when I am dead, the world will laud my genius."

"Lady Huxley," Dorothy corrected him and then asked, "Wouldn't you rather they laud you now?"

"Ah, but if they did, then I would be famous and rich and … happy. I would lose my creativity. It is not a compromise I can make. A hungry stomach is the best way to hone an artistic talent."

"Artists have a hard life," Dorothy obligingly nodded. "Are there many artists on this estate hiding from the latest law?"

"A fair few," he replied. "We keep away from the other artists and lurk in the east wing. That door," he gestured to the opening in the wall, "leads to an artist's sanctuary."

Dorothy eyed Huxley from beneath her lashes. No wonder he was so secretive and aloof in public. If a hint of this reached the ton … he would be in a pickle.

"Now that I am his wife," Her voice caught on the words. She hurried on, "Let me know if I can make your stay any more comfortable."

Woodbead smiled in delight. "I thought you would be packing us all off to the colonies since we are crowding your family wing."

"I … admire his efforts," Dorothy said softly, hoping Huxley wouldn't catch her words.

Woodbead whistled loudly. "Admire him! Yes, we all must admire him. If it weren't for Huxley, art would be dead in England. He is a great man… a great and wonderful man. Admiration is not enough. But," he eyed the flush on her cheek speculatively, "it is a start."

Chapter Fifteen

He arrived in her room on the third night, but this time, the valet did not accompany him. When he opened the door and entered her bedchamber, the church bell had just struck ten.

She was sitting primly in the chair, still wearing her dinner gown, a soft pink, spotted muslin. Her pale hands lay on her lap while her lashes quivered, giving away some of her anxiety.

"Good evening," he greeted her politely as if they had not been eating dinner together a short while ago.

She leapt up, her hands flapping like an agitated sparrow. "Please, sit. Would you like some tea?"

He shook his head and showed her the pile of letters in his hand. "I will work on these. You need not entertain me."

"The valet?"

"No one will listen at the door. They do not need to; thus, his presence is futile."

"Ah." She nodded and sat down, trying to shrink into the cushion as much as possible to minimise her existence.

He looked around briefly. The heat of the crackling fire and numerous candles made the chamber inviting. A tea tray sat ready in front of her, along with an assortment of sugarplums, after-dinner mints, bonbons, and sandwiches.

He ignored the food and drink and instead began working on the correspondence.

Dorothy picked up the knitting but could not concentrate. Her eyes kept flitting to the man sitting beside her.

He sat composed and relaxed; his long fingers gripped the quill as he dipped it into the ink and wrote earnestly and quickly. His thick, dark lashes were lowered, and his lips were slightly parted, making him appear sensual.

She looked away and resumed knitting. The sock started to look like a rabbit, but she didn't care. Her entire body was tensed as if poised to flee from danger.

At some point, it began hailing; the hard ice hit the window, creating a sudden racket. She paused and glanced at him again.

He seemed unbothered by the noise as if he were too engrossed to notice the change in the weather.

She spoke softly, as if talking to a half-asleep child, "How is your wound?"

He looked up to find her staring at his arm. He frowned, then his brows cleared. "It is healing."

"Mayhap, in the future, you can refrain from putting yourself at risk?"

His mouth twisted in amusement. "I did not have a choice."

"You could have used chicken blood. Or pig blood?" she suggested tentatively. "Maybe pigeon? Fish, if you are squeamish... do fish bleed? They must, after all, they are alive, or are they like plants full of sap?"

"The matter sprang upon me suddenly. I did not have time to plan. As for fish, we can visit the kitchens and investigate."

"No need," she quickly assured him. "Go on then, with your work. I will not disturb you again."

He obligingly dipped his head.

She glanced at the blazing fire and then back towards him again, her expression a little guilty. Surely, it was fine for her to have a good look at her husband. It wasn't as if she was stealing his money.

His features were noble, with a high-bridged nose and eyes that seemed calm on the surface but hid a volcano deep within. This time, he wore a black robe with a thin, almost invisible border of red silk embroidery that made him appear paler and his mouth redder than usual, as if he had just been bitten.

Every time he moved, a bit of the cloth moved aside to show part of his collarbone and a hint of his shoulder.

She felt odd and a little naughty. She had never sat with a strange man in her room before and felt this was wrong. As if at any moment, her mother's curly head would appear at the window and soundly scold her for doing something so scandalous.

And no wonder. He was so polite and distant that she didn't feel married at all.

He suddenly looked up and caught her watching him. Her face flushed, and she looked up at the ceiling and then at the wardrobe as if admiring the chamber.

His eyes blazed momentarily before his lashes dropped to hide his expression. "We cannot remain as we are."

She cleared her throat and carefully put down the knitting. "What do you mean, my lord?"

"We are married now. Perhaps we can start anew and forget the past?"

"I would like that."

"I had to get married to someone at some point. I suppose it is done now, and we must resign ourselves to fate. Are you upset with the outcome? Do I fall short of your expectations?"

She shook her head rapidly. "It is I who is not worthy. I fear you have been wronged."

He frowned. "Explain."

"You are wealthy, titled, and could have married the diamond of the first water, yet, due to my foolishness, you had to settle for a pastoral nuisance like me."

"I told you not to blame yourself. We both caused this pickle."

"Yes, but you suffered more."

"Are you saying that you are satisfied with me as your husband?"

Her face turned pink, uncertain as to how to answer. Her heart began beating fast in panic as she rooted through her brain for an intellectual spark to provide her with an answer.

He didn't wait for her response but continued to probe, "I thought you were in love with Crumbly."

"Lord Lumley," she corrected hastily and then scrunched her nose. Goodness, she hadn't thought of him in days. Besides, how did he know? She didn't recall mentioning him in all their interactions.

"Hmm?" He prompted.

"I do not love him anymore."

"Is he a roasted goose that you would like him one day, but are not in the mood for it again the following evening?"

"I am fickle," she snapped finally. "Fickle in my affections. Do you regret marrying me, my lord?"

"I am satisfied."

She stared at him. How could it be? Was he telling the truth?

"On the wedding night," he went on. "I was caught by surprise when I spotted my stepmother's maids crouching outside your door. I had to act quickly, hence the indiscreet play. But, rest assured, my valet shall not enter your chamber again without permission."

"I understand." Her heart settled at his words, and the small worry gnawing at her eased.

"It is late. You should call for your maid, but before that, muss up your bed and roll around in it."

She understood his meaning, quickly leapt to her feet, and wished him goodnight in a high and unnatural voice.

They stared at one another awkwardly before he gave a stiff bow and left her alone.

Rosie entered the room with a basin of hot water. She looked under the covers and sighed in relief. "This is better, my lady."

"He is gentle," she replied and bit her lip. "Very gentle. That day was not his fault."

Rosie stared at her disbelievingly, but Dorothy did not budge from her stance. She could no longer bear to let him take the blame for something he had not done.

∞∞∞

The next few weeks passed similarly, except she was now more relaxed when he visited late at night. The servants and artists also became accustomed to seeing Dorothy, and her sweet, gentle disposition began thawing some hearts.

She was courteous, polite and not overly friendly. Her presence was akin to a delicate flowering plant hidden amongst a group of wildflowers at the base of a tree. Only a waft of fragrance now and then would remind everyone of her existence before fading away—A light, sweet, inoffensive scent that tickled one's heart and made one want to seek her out, protect and cherish her.

Dorothy chanced upon Huxley after dinner one evening during a stroll. He was watching a sculptor at work in the garden.

"This is terrible," Huxley waved his hand at the clay in disgust. "I thought you were carving a flower."

"This is a bud."

"It is a characterless lump."

"Ah." The man fell silent. He had long hair and an impressive beard long enough to reach his chest.

"You will have to leave in the morning. I do not do charity." Huxley's tone was firm, even a little rude.

"I can work as your butler."

"No."

"A carriage driver."

"No."

"An ornamental hermit. It is all the rage in England." He stared up at the darkening sky, trying to look mysterious and druid-like.

"Leave."

The old man sighed and threw down the tools. "Fine."

"As soon as dawn breaks."

"Understood."

"Or your legs will break."

The old man became speechless.

Huxley gave him a final stern look before leaving.

"Disrespectful hobbledehoy," the man muttered at his back. "At least respect my age."

Dorothy felt a little sorry for the old man, and she hurried over to him. "I can offer you some coins to help you find a place for a few days."

The man waved her concerns away. "I deserve it. I tried to trick that brat."

Dorothy felt uncomfortable. Huxley's tone had been harsh and rude, and she was reminded of the coldness he had emanated before their marriage.

The man smiled, showing a few missing teeth. "He chooses to help only the best, and in return, they must leave everything they have created in his home before moving away. Some of the artworks are priceless, yet others will become priceless. Every time he is short of money, he needs only to sell a piece or two to fill his coffers again. A clever investment."

"I see."

"He is not charitable but shrewd," his tone was laced with bitterness.

"I am sorry," she said again, feeling powerless.

He shook his head and waved her away. "Maybe I can still turn this into a rose," he muttered under his breath. "Or eat one last dinner before departing?"

Dorothy left him alone and returned to her chamber. Undressing for bed would have to wait since it was the night Huxley would visit.

He came as usual at ten, his eyes showing no hint of lingering anger from earlier.

He watched Dorothy as she sat poking holes in a cloth, pretending to embroider. She was like an exotic treat—a glass of excellent champagne, an exquisite piece of art, or a precious pearl—that only those with a discerning eye and taste could perceive her beauty and rarity.

She looked up and caught his heated look. Her fingers fumbled, and her manner promptly became flustered.

He retracted his gaze and said, "We have to attend a few social events since many would want to host us as newlyweds. You should get some new clothes."

"Mmm."

"I will give you a generous allowance," he continued. "And once my sister is married, you can take over the household matters."

"Only then?"

He was unwrapping ink cakes that had just arrived from the east on a ship and inspecting them. He had told her they were more expensive than gold. The artists would be pleased.

His fingers continued unknotting the blue silk as he asked, "Were you unsatisfied with something?"

"Nay, it is nothing."

He checked the ink block by scraping away the smallest wafer with a sharp knife. Satisfied with the colour and quality, he turned to her and commanded, "Speak."

She quickly admitted it. "We need another cook."

"We have a cook."

"We have an artist, not a cook."

"The food is edible."

"You can have a decent cook and keep the artist," she said firmly.

"Tell Sophia."

"Nay, she will think I am trying to usurp her position."

He frowned. "What do you suggest?"

She explained. "Let her present the food. I spoke to her ... She doesn't enjoy cooking, and I think she would be more creative if she weren't forced to spend hours slaving over mediocre meals."

He shrugged. "Do what you think is best."

"Will you speak to your sister and explain? I mean, no ill."

"Leave it to me."

She beamed at him, unaware of how lovely her smile was, as she leaned towards him as if unconsciously asking for an embrace. Her eyes were wide and grateful, full of happiness, and bathed in the firelight, she appeared warm and soft.

He looked away from the domestic sight, and his Adam's apple bobbed as he swallowed.

He left her chamber earlier than usual that evening, explaining his behaviour away with a small white lie.

The simple acquiescence from her husband, which allowed her to add a new cook to the kitchen, changed several things. The servants became aware of the shift in power. It trickled away from Lady Huxley and Sophia and landed firmly in Dorothy's lap.

When Dorothy poached a new cook from the envious entourage of a distinguished personage, no one could deny it any longer—Dorothy had married the master of the house, and that made her the mistress with excellent manipulative skills.

She may not look like the brightest star in the sky, but her soft, gentle, dim visage was not to be taken lightly. A sharp mind was hidden behind her delicate, sweet demeanour.

She could now command changes in the menu, throw out all the cushions in the house, refuse to pay the tin money, let a servant go if she so fancied … The advantages were innumerable.

She, on the other hand, was unaware of why the servants suddenly began treating her with the utmost respect, as if she were a sabre and not a harmless, fluffy feather. But her joy was short-lived.

Blinker arrived with a note from Penelope.

She stared at the grimy boy muddying the soft pink carpet of the morning room.

"Lor'! You remember me, your 'ighness? I am the boy you

saved," he asked, moving from one foot to another.

"I do remember you ... How can I forget? I am delighted to see you well, and I am not the queen. No need to call me Highness. Lady Huxley will do," she replied distractedly.

"Lor'! For me, you are better than the kween. You saved me life," he smiled, revealing a chipped tooth.

A charmer. She rubbed her head and gestured for the boy to sit.

He sat, smearing mud and soot all over the cream and gold chair.

Dorothy smoothed out Penelope's letter and read it again ...
Dorothy,
Our dear neighbour, Mrs Mill, is once again convinced she is going to die. She has begun arrangements for her funeral for the fifth time this year. Do not be alarmed if you get a missive informing you of her demise. She has decided to send the letters out early to ensure enough people are in attendance for her funeral. She hopes the fateful event will occur in September when the weather is pleasant.

Now to essential matters. Blinker's mother took a turn for the worse and has been sent to live with her brother. Her brother refused to have Blinker, so I have sent him to you. You are now married and can take care of your responsibilities. I suggest writing to an orphanage or a school and sending him there.
Yours not so affectionately,
Penelope

Ordinarily, Dorothy would have been delighted to see Blinker and to keep him for as long as needed. But this was not the Blackthorne mansion. This was the Ansley estate.

While the duke suffered her unfortunate friends, Huxley was unlikely to do so. He might allow suffering artists a home and, in return, be a part of history and be responsible for nurturing the greatest minds of the future, but Blinker ... He was a boy with no talent to speak of. Huxley would never allow her to keep him.

Blinker let out a sneeze and wiped his nose on his shirt. He found her watching him and offered her another infectious, toothy smile.

She pinched the bridge of her nose in distress. What was she going to do?

Chapter Sixteen

"I didn't draw them," Blinker said, tilting his head towards the papers in Dorothy's hand.

"But you must say that you did," Dorothy said.

"You want me to tell a clanker?" he eyed her speculatively. "I thought genteel folk didn't lie."

"It's not a lie. We are simply twisting the truth for the greater good."

"Twisting the truth means lying. It's a whisker, a bouncer, a great big swinging lie—"

"I will give you a chicken leg to gnaw on if you do as I say," Dorothy cut in shrewdly.

"I will twist the truth."

"Now, hide under that desk," she said, pointing to a corner of one of the smaller family rooms she had found at the back of the house. "I will be back in a moment. Don't move. And remember to do exactly as I taught you."

"Chicken leg?" Blinker reminded her.

"You will get it after the performance."

Blinker was just a little sprig, Dorothy mused as she hurried down the hallway. Surely, he could pass unnoticed in a house this big and teeming with all sorts of people. It would be simple enough to hide him from Huxley, but the servants... They were bound to notice a child—

She slammed into a broad, warm chest.

The owner of the said chest gathered her close for a moment.

"Why do you feel the need to run rather than walk? What's the urgency?" Huxley queried.

She forced herself to step back and rubbed her arms. She felt guilty and could not hide it. Her eyes skittered all over the walls, moulding and skirting.

He caught her chin and lifted it, refusing to let her drop her lashes. His finger on her skin was so light and gentle that it surprised her. For such a large man to have so much control over his touch … the thought made her blush.

"You are a married woman now. I hope you will remember that in the future and not run around like a hapless child," he murmured.

She nodded, her eyes large and unblinking.

He searched her face; a tiny frown appeared and disappeared between his brows so swiftly that she failed to catch it.

"Is all well?" he asked.

"Yes," she lied and began gazing at the ceiling again.

He waited a moment, but when she refused to confess, he pressed his lips together and headed towards his study.

She watched him until he disappeared from her view and then once again broke into a run.

She had asked the head gardener, butler, housekeeper, chef and Rosie to meet her in the room where she had hidden Blinker.

She pushed open the door and was relieved to see that they were all present, and Blinker, hiding under the desk, had not been discovered.

She asked them all to take a seat, and when they refused, she chose to stand as well.

"I have asked you here today because I have something important to tell you," she paused, scanning their faces. They looked a little nervous. "Your jobs are safe," she assured them. "I am here to ask you for help."

The shoulders around her tensed up some more.

"I understand what every earned penny means to you. I am only too aware of the injustices in this world," she said, throwing out her arms. "The division between upstairs and downstairs, the elite and the poor … It is a shame this vast gaping difference between classes. Why should the rich have so much and the honest, hardworking souls nothing at all?"

Her maid and the cook nodded enthusiastically. The butler and housekeeper looked suspicious.

"I want to change this world. I want to do something for the poor," she declared. "I want to help the helpless, be a guardian of some forgotten soul, to give an unhappy, innocent creature a reason to live… and I would like your help to accomplish this."

"How?" the butler queried sceptically.

Dorothy dipped her head unhappily. "Let me tell you about a young, charming boy. A boy full of life and creativity. All he wanted to do was draw and paint. He used what he could to create his dreams. His mother often found him drawing people in the mud with a stick. He would make mountains and streams with the food on his plate or carve flowers into the bark of trees. A talented boy who could have been the greatest artist of the century … except—"

"Except," the cook asked, her eyes moist.

"Except, he had no money, barely any food to eat. He sold skinned rabbits on Gin Lane when he could find them … or ran errands for the rich folk. His father was dead, and his mother became mad…"

"Oh dear." Rosie sniffed into her handkerchief.

Dorothy wiped her eyes. "Oh, the poor, talented darling. He had nowhere to go."

"Where is the boy now?" the butler asked, his lips trembling.

"That's where I need your help," Dorothy replied. "I have a secret, and I would like you to help me keep it."

The servants straightened up, their eyes bright.

"I will compensate you for helping me keep this harmless secret."

The eyes brightened even more.

She pushed the drawings she had made earlier towards them. "Does he not show talent?"

They peered at the drawings of fruits and vegetables, looking suitably impressed. The apple looked like an apple, the pear was a pear, and even the grapes were recognisable.

Indeed, this was talent.

"But where is he?" the butler asked again.

Dorothy paused dramatically, letting the question hang in the air for a moment before whirling around and pointing at the desk.

"There!" she announced, and on cue, Blinker emerged, his hands folded in front of him, his eyes on his muddy shoes.

"This is the talented, pitiful creature," Dorothy said, allowing her voice to tremble. She held Blinker's shoulder and wiped an invisible tear from her cheek. "All I ask for is your silence and your cooperation. I have written to some schools, and the moment I hear from them, I will send him away. But until then, can we not keep him here? This estate has so many rooms. He will pick a dark little hole and sleep in it."

"Lord Huxley might approve of him. He shows talent," the butler suggested, his loyalty warring with his heart.

"Ah, but my wonderful, kind husband does not like noise. How is he to know this sad little child has no joy in him and that he would rather sit quietly with his thoughts than run around like any other boy his age," Dorothy replied. "He will tell me to send him back to Gin Lane. Gin Lane is the abyss of depravity. His innocence will be snatched before he knows it, and his talent squished to nothing. Would you like to have that on your conscience?"

"And if the master finds out," the cook asked.

"I will take the blame. You can say you knew nothing of him," Dorothy replied.

"What if he won't believe us?" the cook pressed.

Dorothy placed a hand on her heart in mock horror. "How can he doubt the loyalty of his wonderful housekeeper and musical butler who has served him for years?"

Blinker let out a large, dramatic sniff and looked up at them sadly.

They thawed.

"This poor boy," Dorothy pushed him forward, "so thin … barely any flesh on his bones … It's not fair that just because he was born in the wrong place, he cannot develop his artistic skills."

Blinker took his cue like a professional. "Please, sir," he said in a soft voice and then paused. He had forgotten his line.

Dorothy quickly faced him and mouthed, "Can I not stay?"

Blinker nodded in comprehension and turned towards the butler and asked beseechingly, "Please, sir, a bottle of gin for two pence fifty."

Dorothy slapped her forehead in disgust, but before she could think of something to save the situation, an odd sound filled the room.

A wheezing, whooping, dying sound.

She looked around in alarm to find the housekeeper and butler in each other's arms, sobbing as if their hearts were breaking.

"The poor boy," Rosie said, hugging Blinker.

"We will do what we can," the butler choked on his words.

The housekeeper nodded, and the cook swore to have the boy fattened up in no time.

The head gardener vowed the boy could run around the orchard to his heart's content and steal all the fruits he liked.

Blinker slipped his hand into Dorothy's and squeezed.

Dorothy, in turn, kept her promise and slipped him the chicken leg.

Chapter Seventeen

Dorothy sank into a chair, ready for dinner. Her stomach rumbled approvingly at the scent of mock turtle soup and Ox tongue. She caught Huxley biting back a smile. He had heard her belly gurgle.

She ducked her head in mortification. She had yet to master the art of feigning indifference to food. It was a Fairweather failing. None of her sisters had managed to subsist on clear broth or resist a pudding.

She watched Sophia delicately taste the brown onion soup and admired her phlegmatic expression. How utterly fashionable is it to appear as if you lived on air and nothing else? Even Lady Huxley managed to grimace at the sight of the luxurious white currant jelly.

"Did you want something?" Lady Huxley asked Dorothy sweetly. She had caught her staring.

"Thank you. I have everything I need," Dorothy replied.

"You could do with some clothes that befit your status," Sophia said, slicing into a pheasant.

Dorothy looked down at her soft blue dinner gown. It was lovely ... or so she had thought.

"She means, now that you are married, you should wear bolder colours," Lady Huxley explained.

Sophia snorted into her wine, "And pray that it helps your complexion."

Clink!

Huxley's spoon hit a porcelain bowl, silencing the chatter.

Dorothy's appetite dwindled, and her mouth turned down.

A servant appeared behind Dorothy and poured a generous amount of wine into her glass. The maid dipped low and whispered in her ear, "The butler has left some preserved pineapples in your room, and Blinker has been fed."

Dorothy felt a touch better, and she finally noticed the dishes dotting the table. The choicest dishes had been placed around her when Lady Huxley and Sophia had earlier been given that honour. She knew the reason for the servants' change of heart—the bloody disaster on the wedding night, shortly followed by the arrival of Blinker.

In short, she was a defenceless little kitten in the servants' eyes, and their maternal instincts had been prodded awake.

She quickly finished the meal and leaned back contentedly. Being a kitten was also good; at least she was coddled and fed.

Her stomach no longer growled, her head was nicely swimmy with wine, and Huxley looked more handsome than ever.

So what if she was not the diamond of the first water? She was still pleasant to look at, kind, and well-behaved, even if a little dim.

It simply added to her charm and made her adorable.

Yes, she was adorable, and once upon a time, her entire family had thought so. Surely, her sisters would soon recall her adorableness and forgive her, while Huxley would treat her like a wife and not an impoverished artist with no talent.

She frowned at the last stray thought. She wanted him to treat her like his wife?

Her eyes flew to him, and her heart began beating as if panicked.

Nay! The wine had gone to her head and addled her brain.

After dinner, she did not retire to the drawing room along with the rest of the family but hurried to her room and rang for her maid.

She became lost in thought while she waited. Blinker's arrival had elevated her loneliness a little, and now that most of the servants had begun to melt, the Ansley Estate began to feel more like home.

"Rosie," Dorothy cried the moment she entered her chamber. "Where on earth will Blinker sleep?"

"In a guest room?"

"With so many artists roaming the halls at all hours, he will be discovered."

"He cannot sleep here. Even if we ask him to sleep under the bed, he might overhear you doing this and that. It will burn his ears off."

"I am not doing this and that," Dorothy denied quickly and in a high-pitched, embarrassed tone. "But yes, he cannot stay here."

"Then?"

"I know," Dorothy said. "Your room."

"I share a room with two others. Not all servants are trustworthy. Remember you told us to keep it between ourselves?"

"Ah. Then?"

Rosie began helping Dorothy undress. She tossed the pins aside, unlaced her mistress, and helped her brush her hair. "Maybe your parlour?"

Dorothy pursed her lip thoughtfully. "I suppose that could work. My lord never enters the parlour, and the door is thick enough to muffle most sounds."

"I shall make a bed for him and then fetch him from the cook's room where he is eating supper."

"Will you sleep with Blinker? I am afraid to have such a small child sleep alone. What if he has a bad dream and cries?"

"He grew up on Gin Lane! What can possibly frighten him here?"

"Please."

Rosie sighed. "Fine. I suppose it will be nice to sleep in a room with a big fire and no one snoring in my ear."

"Thank you, you are wonderful."

∞∞∞

The first few days went by without incident, but on the third day, Lady Huxley's maid spotted Blinker.

"Rosie, what are we to do?"

Rosie yanked the pins out of her hair. "Wait for death."

"Stop being morose. Think!"

"You always make me think. Give your head a little nudge for a change."

"Rosie!"

"She only caught a glimpse of Blinker. A fleeing shadow."

"But, it is a matter of time before he is entirely discovered. Her suspicions have been raised, and she will be vigilant from now on," Dorothy cried.

Rosie stroked her employer's distressed head. "There, there, don't worry."

Dorothy scowled. "Think of something. Don't just pet me like I am a pup."

"I have thought of something."

"I knew it!"

"Tell everyone there is a ghost in your chamber. If they spot him again, we can say it was the spirit of a dead chimney sweep."

Dorothy eyed her maid with respect. "You are awfully good at deceiving."

"Why, thank you, miss. It is a talent."

Thus, the tale of a newly arrived ghost was spread throughout the mansion. It triggered the artists' imaginations, and for a while, many ghoulish sculptures, paintings, songs, and poems appeared within the walls of Ansley Estate.

The following days went by peacefully. The servants kept their word, Blinker behaved himself, and Dorothy took Sophia's rudely given advice and bought dozens of scandalous dresses. Since Huxley was one of the wealthiest men in

England, she didn't even look at the prices but shopped to her heart's content.

She bought silk taffeta, gold and silver muslin, delicious crepe dresses and plenty of satin ribbons, shoes and hats. She also bought a handful of evening gowns in Coquelicot, Jonquil, Evening Primrose and the popular Vienna green. Some dresses were cut shockingly low, but the modiste assured her it was all the rage.

She had tasked the butler with finding clothes for Blinker, knowing she couldn't go looking for little boys' clothes, or the news would be all over London. The butler did a wonderful job and procured a sack of clothes in near-perfect condition from a rag shop.

Thereafter, Dorothy fell into a repetitive pattern of supervising the servants, caring for Blinker, creating menus, practising the piano, attending parties, and, most importantly, shopping.

But the days that had flown by so leisurely were bound to end. It was the morning Blinker refused to wake up that she had an inkling that things would get volatile.

She stood over the sofa in her parlour, adjacent to her bedchamber, and irritably peered down at his sleeping face.

She smoothed her new morning gown in buttercream and once again attempted to rouse him.

"Dimber mort," he muttered in his sleep. "Leave me alone."

She narrowed her eyes, yanked the blanket off him in one swift motion and then dumped a large jug of water on his head.

He spluttered awake.

"You called me Dimber Mort," she told him once he had settled down for breakfast.

He looked up from his bowl of eggs and shrugged. "Was asleep."

"I am a lady," she reminded him coldly.

"Lawks! I meant no harm. Only called you a pretty wench," he replied defensively.

"No one is a wench in this household. I heard you call Rosie goosecap the other evening. You will mind your language from now on and learn to speak like a gentleman."

"Bloody 'ell!" He wilted under her flinty look.

"And no more bloody hell, damnation or any other rude exclamations."

"Lor'! A man can't eat in peace," he grumbled, his legs swinging with suppressed energy.

A smile tugged at her mouth. He looked particularly charming, all scrubbed up, with his curly hair brushed back and gleaming and his dark eyes narrowed in impatience.

"A walk in the gardens," Dorothy ordered. It was better to let him run around and tire himself out than wait for him to think up something naughty.

The moment they stepped outside, Blinker took off towards a towering, ancient Elm. Like a monkey, he leapt on the lowest branch and scrambled upwards.

Dorothy raced after him.

"Come down right now," she scolded.

Blinker ignored her and climbed higher still.

"Blinker!"

He swung forward, holding on to a fragile-looking branch, and stuck his tongue out at her.

"I am sorry I dumped the jug of water on you!" she called desperately. "I promise I won't do it again. Now, be good and come down. I don't want you to fall!"

"Lor'! Fall down a tree?" he scoffed. "Not likely."

Dorothy watched in dismay as the last of Blinker disappeared up the tree. She couldn't even see his feet amongst the thick, dark leaves.

What if he fell and broke his neck?

Horrified at the thought, she gripped the lowest branch and hauled herself up. If the little rascal wouldn't come down, then she would follow him and drag him back down if she had to.

But climbing a tree in her morning gown was not easy.

She had only managed to reach the second bough when her

foot got entangled in her petticoat, and her hands lost their grip. She hurtled towards the ground, eyes squeezed shut, praying for a swift death with no visible blood so that she would look as beautiful as the asp-bitten Cleopatra—

Strong hands caught her and held her close.

Her chest rose and fell rapidly as she tried to calm herself. The arms encircling felt warm, strong and … human.

She was not dead.

Wonderful! Some kind soul had saved her.

After a moment, she opened her eyes and found herself staring into Huxley's delicious peepers.

"Why were you trying to climb a tree?" he asked, raising an incredulous brow.

Dorothy peeked at the tree and was relieved that Blinker was well hidden from view.

"Why?" he repeated.

"You are looking very handsome, My Lord," she blurted out, hoping to distract him. Her cheeks turned pink, but she had no choice but to continue this uncharacteristic flirting.

He stared down at her, a little dazed as he gazed into her pure, bright eyes, soft mouth, and red-tinged cheeks. She looked soft and exquisite, like a quilt made of goose feathers, a joy to cuddle.

Her little scheme worked.

He promptly released her, and she landed on her behind.

She squeaked in indignation.

He smiled, his face lighting up and looking softer. "If you don't want to answer a question, then don't. Refrain from flirting, my dear, or you won't like the consequences."

"I wasn't flirting," she said. "You *do* look handsome today. It is the truth." And he did in his soft white shirt and brown breeches. He hadn't bothered with a coat since it was too warm, and the pleasant wind had ruffled his hair, making him look less stiff … more approachable … inviting … Perfect.

She sighed.

He searched her face and realised she was telling the truth, and then he did something she would have never imagined him doing.

He blushed.

His dark lashes fell over his flushed cheeks, and his lips pursed uncertainly, making him look even more handsome.

Seeing him like this, she felt a sudden urge to grab him and kiss him.

"Well," he said at a loss for words.

She stood up and dusted off her skirt. "I won't climb any more trees … unless you are around to catch me." She fluttered her lashes, feeling bolder than she had ever been.

He turned redder still.

"Well," he said again and cleared his throat a few times before giving up and striding away.

Dorothy chuckled. She had finally found a way to fluster the great and mighty Huxley.

She was still giggling when she found Blinker climbing back down the tree.

He offered her a cheeky grin before leaping off a high branch and plummeting towards the ground.

Chapter Eighteen

"Oh, keep still," Dorothy grumbled, dabbing Blinker's wound with a vile-smelling green paste. "Does it hurt?"

"Nay," he said bravely, though his mouth was pinched in pain.

"Good children don't lie."

"You did."

"I am not a child. I can do what I like," she snapped.

Blinker reached out to touch her cheek. "I am sorry."

"Promise me you won't lie again."

"I won't ... lie."

Dorothy forced herself to smile. "At least you did not break anything. Only a few scrapes ... but the fright you gave me!" She grabbed the boy and hugged him.

He wriggled uncomfortably.

"Now, go to sleep. I will come and see you before dinner."

She kissed him on his forehead and smoothed his hair. She looked down at him for a moment, her heart constricting when he rolled over and tucked his hand under his cheek.

She reluctantly left him and headed towards the morning room.

She hadn't had a chance to catch up with her correspondence since Blinker had taken up her entire morning. He was a handful, she sighed worriedly.

"Why doesn't she get the hint?" Sophia whined from the other side of the door.

Dorothy paused outside the morning room, her head tilted to one side. She had a brief internal debate about whether she should eavesdrop or not.

Well ... to be entirely honest, it wasn't really a debate; rather, it was a few mental token protests made to hush her moral, upright side, which had long become used to giving way easily and quietly.

"This is her chamber now," Lady Huxley replied.

"Pah! I have spent all my life laying down the domestic law in this household," Sophia said. "William has allowed me to decorate as I please, order what meals I like, entertain whom I want, and this deuced mushroom has dared to take over all that has been my right—"

Lady Huxley made a noise of agreement. "It was unfortunate William had to marry a commoner. It pains me to allow her to have her way in Ansley Hall ... where the King himself stayed for an entire week during the war—"

"Why did you consent to this awful union?" Sophia wailed.

"It was ingenious how Dorothy trapped poor William. She did it in a way that I had no choice but to give consent—"

"You didn't have to," Sophia said.

"There were too many witnesses, and I had no choice. I can't afford to ruin your chances of making a good match. The prince—"

"Oh, enough about that toad. I can't understand a word he speaks."

"That may be so, but you will continue to be pleasant and obedient around him. He is a foolish man. A wealthy, royal, foolish man, and that's the best sort of man to catch."

"What I don't understand," Sophia said thoughtfully, "is why you are so nice to Dorothy?"

"She has managed to win over the servants and taken over the household. Even the artists seem fond of her. She can make life very difficult for us if we are not careful. Besides, William is duty-bound to protect his wife. He is an absolute muttonhead. He should have thrown her out the moment he saw her climbing in through that window—"

"Don't speak ill of William, Mother," Sophia snapped. "You know I don't like it when you do."

Lady Huxley's childish voice turned shrill, "I don't know why you are so fond of him. Fine, I shall refrain from saying anything bad about your precious William. If only you had been a son, I would have gotten rid of your brother long ago. A push in the lake when he was young or some choice herbs sprinkled in his meals—"

"Mother!" Sophia gasped.

"Calm yourself. He is safe. The estate is entailed."

Dorothy felt sick and turned away from the door. She couldn't bear to hear any more or to sit in the same room as Lady Huxley. She had known Lady Huxley was a little prejudiced against those of common blood and that she put too much value on rank and wealth ... but she had never thought of her as a rotten, murderous creature.

All those soothing glances that Lady Huxley had thrown in her direction, the times she had stood up for her against her daughter ... It had all been a pretence.

Dorothy's heart ached for Huxley. To lose his parents at a young age and then be responsible for a stepmother who loathed him.

Pah! The thought made her grind her teeth in anger.

She spent the rest of the walk to the family room shoving Lady Huxley off various cliffs in her imagination.

The butler handed her a letter the moment she entered.

"Tea?" the butler asked from the doorway.

"Please," she responded gratefully.

"And something to eat," he muttered, not waiting for her to respond.

She sighed again. It seemed that, along with Blinker, the servants had adopted her as well.

She turned her attention back to the letters on her desk. Most of them were invitations from the ton for her and Huxley. She would have to ask him about those. A few charitable institutions wanted a donation or her involvement. She responded eagerly to those.

Marrying Huxley had one advantage: he was generous with her allowance, and she had ample resources to make a difference among the underprivileged.

She finally reached for the letter the butler had handed her. It was a letter from the school she had written to asking for a place for Blinker.

They had politely declined. They said they might have an opening in three months, but until then, they encouraged her to try somewhere else.

The trouble was that she had already been rejected from all the other places. This was the final school she had been pinning her hopes on. She flung the letter away and let her head fall into her trembling hands.

If only she could write to the schools under her real name, they wouldn't have dared refuse her. And if she did … it would cause a scandal. No matter how innocent the situation was, tongues would wag, and wild stories would float. The ton would conjecture if the child were hers from a previous lover or Huxley's bastard … mayhap Sophia's illegitimate child?

Cruel, cruel gossip could ruin Sophia's prospects.

And what of Blinker? How long could she go on hiding him? And if Huxley found the boy ….

So many pretences and half-truths. What was she going to do?

"My lady," Rosie rubbed her hands nervously. "It seems the rumour we spread was unnecessary since we already have a resident ghost."

"Eh?"

"The servants say that the chamber you sleep in was where Lord Huxley's mother died, and her ghost haunts this place since that fateful night."

Dorothy put the pot of Blooming Roses for youthful cheeks back on the dressing table. "Who said so?"

Rosie lowered her voice. "The oldest servants living on the estate. They say that Lord Huxley's father was cruel and killed his wife in this very room. The servants under the previous lord were tormented and murdered. When the current Lord Huxley took over, he hired budding artists as servants to replace the dead ones, but they heard about the entire ordeal from the local villagers."

Dorothy's heart began to pound. "Oh."

"Which is why the servants were not surprised and sympathetic to your plight when they saw all that blood. Like father, like son, they say."

"Oh," she said again, her fingers trembling and face pale.

"Anyhow, that is all." Rosie smoothed her skirts and dipped in a curtsy. "I will be going, my lady."

"Stay."

"I am hungry."

"Stay."

"Lord Huxley will be visiting. I couldn't possibly stay while you do this and that."

"I am not—oh, just hurry."

She watched her maid bounce away bitterly. Why must people eat?

Scrape, scrape.

A twig struck the windowpane, making her soul flee for a moment. Cold sweat trickled down her back as the twig continued to whip the glass.

Thud!

A piece of wood broke in half and tumbled onto the embers in the fireplace, sending sparks flying.

Her terror intensified, and her mind became clouded with panic. She half rose from her seat to run from the room when—

Rat-a-tat!

Someone knocked.

She opened her mouth to scream, but nothing came out.

"I am coming in," Huxley called out in warning.

Oh, it was a human being; she wilted in relief.

He walked in and froze. "Are you unwell?"

She weakly waved at him, her heart still in her throat. Oddly, even though the servants believed he was as cruel as his father, her heart believed otherwise.

She couldn't help but trust him.

He sat beside her and stared at her worriedly. "You are pale. Did you eat too much at dinner?"

"Nay." Her brows wrinkled slightly. Shouldn't he ask if she ate enough instead? She was a delicate young lady who did not stuff her face but lived on air and dew—

Scrape, scrape.

Blasted twig! The fear was back.

Her mother used to hold her hand at night when she got scared. Huxley was not her mother, but he did have hands.

Scrape, scrape.

She eyed his hand with a hungry look.

His hands were big and warm, with long, dependable fingers. If she held them, she would feel better, less afraid.

Her eyes darted to the window and back. "We should hold hands."

His eyes widened. "Pardon?"

Her brain worked at full speed, faster than it ever had to come up with a reason. "When we go out, people might notice my discomfort when we dance. If I practice holding your hand, we will appear more natural, like we are married."

His eyelid twitched.

Even after all the hard work, her skull had come up with something so stupid. She blushed but refused to cower. The hand must be held until Rosie came and took over.

He appeared confused at her reasoning but obligingly offered his fingers to her.

She stared at it and remembered how his stepmother had wanted to kill him. Her expression softened, and she reached out to carefully grip his fingers.

They both did not wear gloves, and the shock of touching a man's bare skin sent a tingle down her spine.

She stifled a gasp and looked away, feeling the warmth from his touch spread throughout her body as if she held little flames instead of fingers.

She was only holding his fingers because his hands were too big to grasp entirely.

But it was enough. Her heart eased, the fear lessened, and she tightened her grip.

"How long do we do this?" he asked in amusement.

"A while. Will you be able to work like this?"

"I can rest a bit."

She sat stiffly, with shoulders pushed back like a good girl listening to a sermon in church. Her face was flushed, and it seemed like she was being punished for doing something mortifying.

Her eyes darted to the window, the bed and the fire, flickering nervously.

"Are you afraid?" he suddenly asked.

She wanted to agree, but instead shook her head. "Would you like some tea?"

He nodded, but she failed to notice since her eyes fell on their clasped hands. If she had to give him tea, she would have to let him go and pick up the teapot.

She did not want to let go.

"Or," she amended, "you do not really want tea. You rarely drink it so late."

"Don't want," he amiably agreed.

She looked relieved. "Then shall we talk?"

"About?"

"What were you going to do today?" she bit her lip after asking. How could she pry into his work? Even the duke rarely discussed such matters with Penelope, and her mother was not even allowed to enter her father's study.

"I was going to look at a map," he replied, surprising her.

"The artists cannot stay here indefinitely. It is too dangerous for them and for us. With so many people, someone is bound to rebel. And now the matter is urgent."

"Why?"

His thumb stroked her skin absently. "Sophia would have married and left. Thereafter, I had no one to protect, but... now I do."

She understood his meaning, became flustered and tried to retract her hand. He held on firmly and continued, "I am going to build a place for them in the countryside."

She tugged again, and he released her this time.

"Can I see?" she asked.

He spread open the map he had brought along. "This forest seems suitable. I can clear out this space, and they will be hidden from view."

She pored over it for a moment before pointing to another place. "This here, with the mountains protecting them at the back and the river in front, is more suitable. They can use the water, and the land will be fertile. They may be hidden in the forest, but so will the enemies."

He stared at the map thoughtfully. "The villagers will find a group of loony men staying together strange."

"Turn it into a school. The artists can teach the local village children. It is better to be open and honest than to create an environment of suspicion. The more controversial works can be hidden away."

He smiled at her, and a spark of warmth was lit between them.

Thud!

A sound came from the adjoining parlour, and she hurriedly grabbed his hand again.

"We are going to continue practising?" he asked with a chuckle.

She nodded hurriedly. "Only for a bit."

And they stayed like that until their hands became sweaty, and it was time for him to leave.

She eyed him reluctantly.

He raised his brow. "Do you want something?"

She wanted to nod but shook her head. "My pillow is lumpy."

"Ah." He eyed the six fluffy pillows on her bed.

"Shall we exchange pillows?" She figured his scent and warmth would keep her company and hopefully chase away the ghosts. Surely, his mother will not want to kill the woman he was kind enough to lend his pillow to?

"We can," he nodded. "And the quilt?"

She brightened. "Can we?"

"We are married."

He went to his chamber, and when he returned with the quilt and pillow, she was already standing with her own quilt and pillow at the adjoining door, making him raise his brow.

She had moved very fast.

They exchanged bundles seriously as if performing a sacred ritual, bid each other goodnight and then paused.

She cleared her throat and asked in a very small voice, "Could you perhaps leave your door slightly ajar?"

His gaze softened. "Call out if you feel unwell or frightened. I will be there in a moment."

She felt a bit better and smiled gratefully.

That night, she was afraid, but every time she opened her eyes and found the door ajar, her heart became quiet, and she fell back to sleep.

Chapter Nineteen

Lord Hamilton's dinner party was underway. Dorothy sipped champagne with her head bowed. She looked like a delicate flower dusted with silvery flecks. Her exquisite dress shimmered every time she moved, catching the light most becomingly and highlighting her clavicle and long neck.

Alas, her quiet beauty was drowned out by the attractive, gilded women around her, and she was ignored even more than when she had been unwed.

The *ton* had not forgotten her speedy marriage, nor had they forgiven her for snatching such an excellent catch from under their noses. Besides, she no longer had Kitty by her side or her sisters to attract eyes.

Her usual positive temperament faded, and she felt a strange, melancholy rise in her stomach like a coiled snake. A gnawing loneliness and feeling like an unwanted impostor filled her up. She did not deserve to be here in this glittering gathering of blue bloods.

Helpless, she retreated farther into the dark corner of the room, her invisible tail drooping most unhappily.

A giggle had her glance up and spot a tall, young woman, Mrs Prunner, wrapped in black velvet, approaching Huxley.

Dorothy tensed, and the discomfort she had been feeling all evening became something deeper, darker and more violent.

Her heart felt heavy as if she were a pup sitting beneath the table laden with a grand feast, and the fragrance of food was teasing her nostrils, making her stomach growl, but her legs were too short to climb up the chair and have a nibble.

Mrs Prunner's beautiful nose hovered near the hollow at the base of Huxley's neck while her gloved fingers twirled the ivory-boned fan and tapped his arm.

Dorothy's lashes dropped again, and she took another sip. Perhaps this sinking, unhappy feeling was due to her having slept fitfully over the last few days, consumed by fear of the ghost and on tenterhooks that Blinker would be discovered.

Huxley moved closer to where Dorothy stood, and their conversation drifted over.

"I am thirsty, my lord," Mrs Prunner whined.

"I will get you a drink," Huxley responded politely. "Lemonade or wine?"

"Nay, I could not bear to see you fight through such a crowd. Perhaps I can sip from your glass?"

"No."

"Why not?"

"I don't share what is mine."

"Ah." Mrs Prunner, being a little dense, failed to notice the chill emanating from him and sidled closer still. "I hear you were tricked into marrying. Pity."

The gossiping ladies near them picked up their ears.

"You heard wrong," he said, moving away from the offending woman. He flicked his sleeve as if dirt had marred where she had touched it.

Dorothy inwardly scolded him, although her mood became lighter. He was being shockingly rude. The poor woman had turned puce as she finally understood that her overtures were unwanted. Honestly, he needed to be nicer—

"Here," he thrust his glass of champagne into Dorothy's hand, cutting short her mental chatter.

She stared at the two glasses in her hand, then at the shocked eyes of the women surrounding her.

"Drink," he urged her.

Dorothy obediently took a sip.

"Nay, from my glass."

She blinked in confusion but followed his quiet order.

Satisfied, he took her glass and walked away.

Eh? Dorothy could not make head or tail of what he was up to. If he wanted to drink, then why not continue drinking from his glass? Why did he exchange glasses?

She sniffed the champagne. Was it smelly? Nay, it was the same as hers, but perhaps he was more sensitive and discerned something?

Befuddled, she drank a little more, unaware of the speculative gazes thrown her way. The once dismissive eyes turned cautious, and soon, she was surrounded by the older, wiser women who reeled her into a dull conversation.

On the way home, the slow, rocking carriage, the copious amount of champagne in her belly and the sleepless nights finally defeated her, and her eyes began to droop.

Huxley watched her fighting sleep and tsked. "Will you confess?"

She looked at him, her eyes red and stinging. "Hmm?"

He sighed and moved to sit next to her.

He was very broad and tall, and the carriage seat, although spacious, was still not big enough to hold the two of them comfortably without touching one another.

Thus, the moment he sat beside her, his entire left side pressed against her right.

Naturally, her sleepiness flew the moment they touched.

"You have not been resting well." His arm came around to hold her, and with a little pull, he forced her head to lie on his shoulder. "What's the matter?"

"Ah, Ah-I am fine," she tried to wrestle away. Her chest suddenly felt tight, as if a tiny elf had sat atop it.

"Stay. Think of it as getting used to it... for the sake of appearing close in gatherings." His tone was mocking, but his fingers resting on her arm were gently patting her.

His warmth frightened away the late-night chill, and after a moment, her tensed limbs gave up the fight and relaxed.

Her shallow breath eased, and the blocked feeling began to alleviate.

His deep voice was low and rumbly next to her ear when he continued, "My mother died in her maternal home. You need not be afraid of her ghost."

"Oh." So, he had noticed her odd behaviour and discovered the reason.

Perhaps he had asked her maid.

So kind.

A tear leaked from her eye as his heat warmed her skin and travelled deep into her heart.

He continued speaking, "The servants were not tormented to death by my father, either. He was cold and harsh but not so cruel to outsiders. The artists are imaginative and prone to exaggeration. Do not believe their nonsense."

The tears now dripped down both her eyes, and she bit her lip to stifle her sob. His coat was getting soaked, she thought desperately; she needed to stop crying.

The two of them were kindred spirits. Lonely, aching and unloved. It was only right to curl into one another and seek comfort.

Nay, that was not entirely true. She had tasted familial love and friendships, while he seemed burdened with duty and surrounded by thankless people who fawned all over him simply because they wanted to nibble away at his luxuries.

No wonder he had a fence around his heart. How would he ever know if someone loved him for who he was and not for his vast wealth or influence?

Even his stepmother was despicable.

Despite his lonely upbringing, he was wonderfully considerate of her needs and comforted her often. He was also polite, gentle and exquisitely handsome.

A man like this deserved the world, but instead of finding love and living happily ever after, she had hurtled into his life and trapped him in a marriage that he did not want.

And yet, he had shared that blame, too.

Ah! She shattered and wailed aloud. She could no longer stifle her aching heart and gave up all pretence.

It startled him into holding her closer still and making soothing sounds.

He was so sweet and tender.

Waah!

She no longer cared about her misery and troubles; it was his plight that hurt her the most. If only she could grasp the strings of fate and twist them to give him every joy on earth. She wanted to see him laugh and smile, be surrounded by people who adored him, and see his eyes soften and light up with happiness.

She sobbed heartbrokenly, her figure shuddering against him while her hands gripped his coat as if she wanted to bury herself underneath it.

He stroked her arm silently for a moment, and when her sobs refused to quieten, he began to sing. His deep voice reverberated through the carriage in a soft, gentle song that stunned her into silence.

> Good night, my lassie, my sweet, sweet lassie
> Let the world fade away....
> Let me kiss your lips, share your breath and your dew,
> Draw every torment away from your heart.
> Like the shade of a lamp, let my hands encircle your soul
> Shielding you from the hurtful winds of the past.
> Good night, my lassie, my sweet, sweet lassie
> Let the world fade away....

A short while later, he gazed at her sleeping face, his expression soft and gentle.

She was endearing, he thought with a smile, and a little bit foolish. A clean, good heart, which should be happy, deserved to be happy, and he would do his best to make her so.

If only he could grasp the strings of fate and twist them . . .

Chapter Twenty

Dorothy reached her bedchamber, slammed the door shut behind her, and leaned against it. Her hand gripped the pearls hanging on her chest, and her eyes squeezed shut. She wanted to erase the memory of Huxley's shoulders brushing hers and his deep, dark, sinful voice rising and falling in musical rhythm.

The song had felt more intimate than that kiss in the library.

Her cheeks flushed pink at the memory of his mouth softly singing in her ear, his warm breath sending shivers down her spine. He had meant to soothe her, to make her forget her woes.

She had forgotten her woes and even fallen asleep, but was far from soothed.

"Are you well?" a soft, hesitant voice asked.

She forced her eyes open and found Blinker staring at her worriedly.

"I am fine," she said with a forced smile. "I ate too many fruitcakes and have the collywobbles."

He did not believe her; his eyes were still worried. Children who grew up in complex environments were often more sensitive than others, discerning the undercurrents and grasping the mood faster than most adults.

She broadened her smile and beckoned him to come closer. "Truly, I am fine. Just tired from dancing all night."

He finally bought her explanation and relaxed.

"I was waiting." He rummaged in his pocket and held a piece

of paper towards her. "I made something for you."

"What is it?"

"A picture," he responded shyly.

The short, dreamless nap had done wonders, and she felt refreshed. If only she could sleep next to him every day... her face flushed.

Pah! What nonsense was she thinking?

She focused on Blinker, reeling in her naughty thoughts.

This was just the thing she needed to brighten her dark day. This is why she wanted to help the boy, and the little hiccups were nothing but a temporary inconvenience. She reached out and stroked his head.

He didn't flinch. He was getting used to it.

She took the painting from him and eagerly opened it. She squinted at it for a moment and then asked hesitantly, "What's it meant to be?"

"Lor'! Can't you tell?" he asked, offended.

She squinted harder and finally said, "Oh, I can see what it is. You are ... very good. This ... is a very big man?" She continued at his encouraging nod, "This is a very small man."

"The big man," Blinker replied importantly, "is me, and the small one is Lord Huxley. See this here; that's a dagger."

"So, you have drawn a painting of you killing Huxley?"

Blinker nodded.

Good lord! Dorothy stared at the painting again, feeling a bit queasy. She knew what it meant, and the fault was hers. She was the one who had made Huxley sound like an evil monster. But she had no choice. She had wanted to ensure Blinker stayed out of sight when Huxley was around.

She eyed Blinker from the corner of her eyes, feeling uncertain. Had she turned an innocent soul into a murdering criminal?

He blinked back contentedly.

"At least," she mused aloud. "You haven't drawn me dead."

"I couldn't kill you. If I did, I would never get the cakes."

"Surely you want me to live for more than cake. You do love

me a little bit. Admit it."

Blinker frowned and scratched his head. "This morning, I promised you that I wouldn't tell any falsehoods."

She nodded encouragingly.

He took a deep breath and continued. "It's the cake … not the love thing."

∞∞∞

"I wanted to talk to you about the invitations," Dorothy said.

Huxley looked up from his desk, eyed her new gown that was cut dangerously low, and moved his eyeballs towards the ceiling. "Damnation! Can't it wait?"

She shook her head regretfully.

He put the quill down and stood up. "Let's go for a stroll."

"Now?"

"Now."

"Fine." Dorothy made her way towards the door.

"Wait," he called after her, "Fetch your pelisse."

She shook her head, making the pins in her hair glint charmingly. "The sun is strong."

He narrowed his eyes. "Then change your dress."

"I will wear a shawl," she compromised.

He clicked his tongue impatiently. "I don't like waiting. Be quick."

And just for that, Dorothy took her sweet time getting ready, enjoying the thought of Huxley fuming at the entrance.

When she finally joined him, his face was thunderous.

Dorothy was not an imbecile. She was not trying his patience because of some absurd, twisted desire for conflict.

No, she wanted to test him.

Just because he was big and strong did not mean he was a brute. That tiny remnant of fear in her heart that believed he would turn violent if angry had to be resolved. She needed to understand the man she had married, and this was one way to do it.

Vex him to death to see how he reacted.

She linked her arm with his and smiled brightly.

His irritation dampened at her smile, and he led her outside.

They sauntered around the oriental garden. Although the sun was blazing, the breeze stroking her skin was cool and heavily scented with jasmine.

She watched his face while he lectured her on which invitations to accept and which to refuse. He thought it necessary to explain why he was refusing certain people so that she wouldn't bother him in the future.

He appeared annoyed, his tone sharp, yet she noticed he had slowed his steps to match hers. Many times, she had held on to a man's arm, too impatient to slow down. She had run while they had walked, or the truly insensitive ones had dragged her speedily down garden paths, leaving her shoes scuffed beyond repair.

On the other hand, Huxley looked hardened, yet his actions seemed to show a different truth. The way he took care of the artists … the way he had softened at her tears and sung that beautiful half-song— and now he walked at a reasonable pace as they strolled around the glistening pond and carefully steered her away from a puddle, all the while shooting orders at her.

He wanted her to meet certain people and maintain a distance from the artists. He didn't want her to wear bold colours. He thought her current morning gown was far too deeply cut. Yet, all through his cold, arrogant instructions, she saw beneath the surface. She saw the heart thrumming with warmth and passion.

"You will burn all the new clothes," he finally said, turning to face her.

They stood under a large tree, and the sun filtered through the leaves, creating dappled shadows on the ground.

Dorothy smiled at him. "I will wear what I like, do what I like and speak to whomever I please."

Her defiant display was ruined when a servant came racing up to them.

"My lord," he hurriedly bowed. "A missive. Tis' urgent."

Huxley glanced at Dorothy and moved a few steps away before quickly opening the letter. His eyes widened, and his skin paled as he read to the end. "That blasted man!"

"Is something the matter?" Dorothy asked in concern.

He crumpled the missive and half turned away before changing his mind and striding up to her. His mood was black in contrast to the floating clouds and clear sky.

"Stop what you are doing," he warned her quietly. "I know you are trying to create a rosy picture to make the best of the situation. I can see it in your face. You are naïve and too young to hide your feelings. Sometimes people are what they seem."

Her cheeks flushed in embarrassment. Was she so transparent? As for his sudden temper... wasn't he simply taking out his displeasure at the contents of the letter on her?

Her heart thumped. One did that with family, knowing they would not mind their close ones unburdening themselves in such a way.

She stared into his stormy eyes uncertainly. Should she be pleased that he now thought of her as one of her own or be vexed by his demands?

Pah! Marriage was a difficult, convoluted business.

"I will do as I like." She wrenched her shoulders away from his grip and strolled back to the house, her mood entirely rebellious and stubborn.

Dorothy wore one of her new gowns again to dinner that evening ... a blue gauze over satin trimmed with white pearls. She had more bosom on display than she had ever dared in her life.

Lady Huxley gasped when she spotted Dorothy hovering

near the door.

"And I thought the abundance of flowers in the house was the only change," Sophia smirked.

Dorothy frowned. Didn't everyone like flowers? She eyed the big, round vase on the dining table filled with sweetly scented summer blooms and thought it looked lovely. It was one of the many vases she had placed around the house, bursting with scent and colour.

Huxley turned his head from his seat at the table to see what the matter was. He stilled at the sight of her.

His eyes raked her from top to toe. Slowly.

She baulked at the doorway, wondering if she had gone too far.

He rose gracefully and approached her. He handed her a glass of wine and said in a low voice. "You are trembling, my dear. Forgot your courage up in the chamber?"

She plucked the glass from his hand. "I am trembling not from fear but happiness. I love this dress," she lied.

His mouth tightened, but he moved aside to let her enter the room.

Dorothy went and sat down in her seat, and the bodice inched lower still, making her gulp nervously. Why had she thought it was a good idea to wear this dress just to irk Huxley?

"You look lovely," Lady Huxley muttered into her wine.

"Enchanting," Sophia giggled, tipping the entire contents of the champagne glass down her evil throat.

"Thank you," Dorothy responded, pulling at the lace over her bosom.

A servant poured her some wine, and she took a generous gulp.

Sophia suddenly leaned forward and said with a wicked gleam, "By rights, the estate should be run by you. I hope you do not mind my overseeing *everything*?"

Dorothy gave up on the dress and draped a napkin on her bosom. She finally responded to Sophia, her eyes wide and sincere. "I have recently married into this home and handling over a hundred servants, the kitchens, accounts, taking care of the needs of my husband and other family members, not to speak of the guests and artists, ah! It is too much. It is nice to rest until I have no choice but to take over when you marry and go away."

Sophia's face darkened. Why did it sound like she was working like a maid while Dorothy was enjoying herself, living a carefree life?

Dorothy sighed. "I do not do well when I have too much to think. It is not good for my complexion. Thank you for your hard work."

Sophia threw her spoon into the soup bowl, sending bits of vegetables flying over the rim. "You take over from now on."

Dorothy beamed. "You trust me with such an honour? I will do my best."

"I—" Sophia caught her mother's furious glance and closed her mouth. She had handed over the reins like a fool, and now, how was she meant to take them back?

Meanwhile, Dorothy continued to thank her profusely, even throwing in some fervent flattery. The more florid her words became, the more Sophia appeared as if she was chewing on a lemon, while Lady Huxley grew graver and graver. Finally, she leapt to her feet and strode out.

"Collywobbles?" Dorothy asked after her in confusion. "Shall I call for the physician? Miss Huxley? Miss Huxley!"

Lady Huxley pushed away her food and followed her daughter. What was the point of going a round of fisticuffs with a cushion? The punches landed in the air, making it an utter waste of time.

Huxley refused to look at Dorothy and focused on the meal. His mouth twitched suspiciously every now and then as if he was holding back his laughter.

Befuddled, Dorothy slumped in her seat and spent the rest of the evening poking at the cabbage and feeling like a tart, unaware that a battle had been fought and won by her that day.

Chapter Twenty-One

The following day, Dorothy conceded defeat and gave away the scandalous dresses to a few delighted maids. Ruffling Huxley's well-groomed feathers was not worth the embarrassment of wearing a dress that threatened to fall off her shoulders at any moment.

She kept the slightly more respectable ones but dyed them in more intense colours than she was used to wearing. The deep jewel tones made her eyes sparkle and her hair shimmer in a way that was becoming, making her feel grown up.

She breathed in the glorious sunny morning air and sighed happily. Despite all that was wrong in her world, she felt a sense of hope. Perhaps it was the music that was uplifting her mood.

Steibelt's 'Grand Concerto floated down the corridors of Ansley Hall. The artists in the garden hammered blocks of stone in time with the music, and the men in tree houses cheerfully crooned along.

Dorothy danced from the music to the small family room. She was slowly coming to adore this vibrant, passionate, capricious house.

She paused near the entrance to admire the humorous caricatures of government officials, aristocrats and even Huxley hanging on the wall. It was a surprising addition, considering the more serious art pieces scattered around the rest of the house.

She traced a finger down Huxley's exaggerated aquiline

nose. The artist had captured his essence wonderfully in a few brief ink strokes.

Huxley was brave, she thought warmly. Brave to have these placed in the house so openly. And the ability to laugh at himself, to let the artist make a jest of him alongside the royals and politicians, made him all the more endearing.

She turned away from the sketches and flung open the window, letting the sun stream in. The faint strain of musicians practising somewhere in the house grew louder and filled the room.

"What are you doing?" Blinker asked from the doorway.

"Putting up these lovely cream lace curtains. Aren't they delightful?" Dorothy replied, balancing precariously on top of a tufted chair.

"Why don't you let the servants do it?"

"It will take only a minute. Why bother them over such a trifle? Besides, I enjoy doing my work," Dorothy said, leaping down from the chair and looking at her handiwork.

"The window in your room rattles," Blinker grumbled. "Everywhere you go, things get noisy and bright. Too bright. And you leap about like a wild hare."

Dorothy hugged Blinker, ignoring his squirms. He sounded like Huxley. The thought made her grin.

It would be nice to see what Huxley's child would look like. But if he had a child, she gulped, she would have to give birth to it.

She had seen a cow give birth back home. A shudder went through her, and cold sweat beaded her forehead.

Nay, it was better to pour all her maternal love on Blinker; after all, he had already been squeezed out into the world by someone.

"And you cuddle too much," he grumbled.

She kissed him just for trying to wriggle out of the hug.

He scowled.

"Look," she put her hand out, letting the rays sparkle on her skin. "The sun has painted everything in tawny gold. See the dust dancing on the beams as if they are fey? Don't you feel as if you could call out to the glittering bits, and the right words would transform them into magical beings?"

Blinker eyed the sunlight and harrumphed like an old, wise man. "The 'eat," he told her regretfully, "'as gone to your 'ead. All those open windows," he shook his head, "spinning tales about magical creatures. Lor'! You tell me not to lie and then spout the most lusty clankers. I will ask the cook to give you some strong tea to revive your senses."

Dorothy sighed and allowed him to run away. Her eyes became misty as she watched his departing back and recalled her childhood. She suddenly missed her sisters and wanted to see them. She wanted them to forgive her and behave as they had before.

Her eyes strayed to the window. A short walk away lay Blackthorne Mansion, and yet it felt impossible to reach. She rubbed her temples, trying to come up with a plan that would make everyone forgive her and adore her again.

This chasm between her and her sisters could not continue to exist indefinitely; she would not let it.

Surely, it wasn't impossible to win back her family and fill Huxley's days with happiness?

Late that night, Dorothy was still conflicted over how to win over her sisters and couldn't sleep. Finally, she rolled out of bed, grabbed a candle, and strolled around the dark, sleeping mansion.

Should she pretend to go on a fast to death, bang her head on the stone steps of Blackthorne Mansion's entrance until they forgave her or grab her sisters' legs during a social gathering, threatening never to let go until they promised to love her again?

She paused when she spotted two figures standing together

in the narrow hallway that led to the East wing.

Huxley's excellent form threw a large shadow over the Aëdon hanging on the wall. The candle in his hand illuminated the young, newly arrived dauber who stood listening to him with his mouth open and paint dripping down from his brush onto the carpeted floor.

Dorothy inched closer, hoping to prevent any more damage.

"It must evoke an emotion," Huxley was saying in a low, earnest voice. "I must feel terror, horror, wonder, love, anger … something when I look at your work. You are skilled, but to be a true artist, you must delve deeper—"

Dorothy plucked the brush from the young man's hand, startling them both. They stared at her incredulously.

Dorothy nodded towards the blue paint puddle soaking into the rose carpet.

"Lawks!" the artist squeaked. I'm sorry. I will get something to clean it up." He didn't wait for Huxley to respond but darted towards the kitchens.

"I would like a word," Huxley said when Dorothy made as if to leave.

She turned back, trying not to notice how narrow the hall was, how close they were forced to stand, or the soft grey cotton shirt stretched across his muscled chest.

"I know women like flowers," he began, "and I am not objecting to the profusion of overfilled vases that have suddenly erupted all over the house, but the bright yellow sashes in my study—"

"They look lovely with the green brocade."

"They make the room … different. I don't like different. Nor do I appreciate that you have asked all the maids in the house to wear ribbons in their hair."

"It makes them chirpier. The grey livery is so dull—"

"They are meant to render the servants invisible."

Dorothy shrugged. "I like the ribbons."

"Does every single curtain have to be opened in the morning?"

"I like the light."

He let out an exasperated sigh. "Fine."

She watched him in amusement. He was so easy to twist every which way and so different from the ruthless face he presented to everyone else.

Why was he so accommodating to her? She had been trying to irritate him for days, but although slightly vexed, he quickly gave up the battle and let her do as she pleased.

She could no longer feel any fear when facing him. It was impossible.

In fact, now she saw him as incredibly sweet, his insides soft like clouds.

And handsome.

So handsome.

His dark lashes, contrasting with his pale skin, and a slight flush on the top of his cheekbones made him appear alluring, like an enchanting creature bathed in the golden light of the burning, flickering candles.

She stared at the shadow on his cheek and wondered how it would feel against her skin.

He raised his brow. "You are staring."

She flushed. "I was just wondering … Shouldn't you be a little careful? All those caricatures and comical watercolours of politicians and royals lying so boldly in the house … The six acts have been passed and … and you could be booked for sedition."

"Are you coming to care for me?" he mocked.

Dorothy took an involuntary step closer to him. "Why do you give so much of yourself to these artists? Why risk your life to save them?"

He sucked in a breath, caught her chin and turned it towards the light coming from the burning torch. He searched her face for a moment. "Ah, you really want to know."

She nodded, not daring to speak. She was certain her voice would tremble as it did every time he touched her. And he would know … and she couldn't bear for him to know about the devastating effect he had on her.

He turned his face towards the shadows. "When I was a child, my mother taught me to sing. My father disapproved of this feminine hobby. He thought it would make me less of a man if I learned such frivolous things. He made certain that if he ever caught me with a song on mine or my mother's lips … we would regret it."

"Regret it? How?"

"He beat us." His eyes darkened in memory. "And it wasn't long before my mother conceded defeat and even stopped humming secretly. The light in her eyes began to dim soon after. It was as if my father had taken away her desire to live by demanding that she stifle her voice."

He paused for a moment, clawing his way out of painful memories. "No talent should be reined in, discouraged, stifled … It can crush one's soul. I can't let the world bury true artists beneath poverty, rules and archaic laws. I want to find, nourish, and give them what they need to focus on their art. I want to set them free, free to do what they love … It's intoxicating watching them grow under my roof … become successful and independent."

"I see."

He looked down at her, his eyes ablaze, "Does it terrify you that my father was a violent man? Violence, they say, is in the blood."

She rose on her toes without a thought and placed her lips on his cheek. "But you have far more of your mother's gentle blood. You still sing and never gave up," she whispered.

He stilled while his hands gripped her shoulders, tightening almost painfully. "You—."

She dropped her lashes, suddenly realising how bold her actions had been. Had she gone daft?

Damnation, she had kissed him for no good reason. What must he think?

He dipped his head, and his hot breath splayed on her mouth. "You—" he said again as if his tongue had frozen and could no longer form a sentence.

He moved closer still and nuzzled the bit just below her ear as if he couldn't help but seek her warmth.

She instinctively trembled, shrinking her neck at the feather-light touch.

"Tickles," she whispered unsteadily.

He smiled and rubbed his stubble against her skin. The prickles made her heart itch, the sort of itch that begged for more. It was an odd, foreign sensation.

Her body arched towards him, and her mind turned to mush. Her fingers desperately held onto his shoulders, digging in as her knees threatened to give in.

His mouth began nibbling and kissing her neck, nipping at her collarbone and grazing the swell of her bosom.

She gasped when he pulled part of her gown lower still and exposed her breast to the cold air. He took her nipple in his mouth and sucked, making her bite her lip to stifle her cry. They were in the hallway, anyone could walk by and hear them, see them.

She could not make a noise.

His teeth grazed her swollen, pink nipples, sending tingling down her spine. This sensation was unbearable; her entire body felt tense as if it was on the verge of breaking. She could not take this teasing much longer.

He moved from one breast to the other, continuously pleasuring her, making her feel as if she was about to swoon from need and want.

One of his hands held her nape while the other kneaded her hip. She quivered and trembled in his arms, trying to hold on to her senses. She must remain aware of her surroundings to separate in time before anyone sees them.

He seemed to sense her slight resistance and fight to stay aware. Taking it as a challenge, he began to work earnestly to make her forget the world.

His hands left her nape and began exploring the rest of her. His fingers danced over her skin, reached her breast and moulded it firmly, his thumb stroking one nipple while his tongue and teeth were still teasing the other.

Her body trembled in pleasure, giving away all its secrets, and her eyes turned red as the sensations began to overwhelm her.

Her nipples had hardened some time ago, and now heat began to fill her lower belly, spreading outward, wanting something she had never had.

It suddenly became impossible for her to stifle her moans, and afraid she was about to lose control and give in to her instincts, she panicked and tried to wrestle his mouth away from her skin, but he gripped her waist and held her still.

"Do not move." His voice was low, hoarse and commanding, and his eyes were blurred with desire.

She stilled.

He lightly pinched her chin and raised it. "I am unpleasant, tyrannical and harsh in bed. Cruel, I am told, so be good and do not tease."

Her eyes were blurred and slightly teary. She barely comprehended his words, her mind still hazy and wanting more.

"My lord," she softly called out, her hands slipping down to his waist and lightly pinching it, wanting him to go on. Why did he stop?

He nipped her mouth, trying to make her come to her senses through the slight, sharp pain. "No more."

A pulse fluttered at her neck, and her lips were slightly parted as she took in shallow, rapid breaths.

"My lord," she called out again in an unsteady voice filled with desire. A faint pleading whine that tugged at his heartstrings.

He closed his eyes, adjusted her dress and leaned his forehead against hers. "Hush," he warned and ran a soothing hand down her back.

"I got the rag," the artist staggered up to them. He failed to notice the two of them standing close enough to kiss. His eyes were on the stain on the carpet.

Huxley stepped back, bringing Dorothy tumbling back to earth.

Chapter Twenty-Two

It had been two days since Dorothy learned why Huxley needed to nurture budding artists. Since then, she had dwelled on every word and nuance of that conversation and felt as if she had been allowed to peek into his closely guarded heart.

The passion and hurt she had witnessed churning inside him had taken her breath away.

And the intimate caress... she was still embarrassed and stuffed the entire moment in the back of her head. If any bit of it threatened to peek out, she would mentally pummel it and bury it once more.

Although at night, it was impossible to do so.

The more she ignored the matter during the day, the more it haunted her at night, creeping into her dreams until she woke drenched in sweat and quivering. Her body had also started aching in a strange way ever since, wanting to be wrapped in his arms so badly that it felt like she was suffering from an illness.

The butler cursed, pulling her back to the present. He had knocked his knee against a chair while chasing Blinker around the parlour with a bowl of vegetable soup.

Blinker wiped his nose on the sleeve as he ducked under the butler's arm and fled to the other side of the room.

Dorothy looked up from her embroidery to smile at Blinker's cheerful face. He seemed to have recovered from his fall. She smiled again when the butler held the soup tray high above his head and pirouetted gracefully when Blinker almost barrelled into him.

She caught sight of her smiling face in a mirror and froze. Her eyes seemed to echo Huxley's appearance while lecturing that young artist last night.

Perhaps she and Huxley were not so different.

She turned back to Blinker and found him wiping his nose once again.

"Come here, Blinker."

"Nay," Blinker said. He was still in a rebellious phase.

Dorothy eyed his runny nose and watched a bit of it drip onto the floor. She winced.

"Come here and blow your nose," Dorothy ordered in a firmer voice.

"Nay."

"Come, it will take but a moment for you to stick your nose into this handkerchief and blow. Be a good boy."

"Dorothy?" Lady Huxley's plaintive voice floated in from the other side of the door.

Blinker smoothly rolled under the bed and hid.

Dorothy picked up the embroidery and gestured for the butler to open the door.

Lady Huxley entered the room and looked around warily. She finally eyed Dorothy and the butler in confusion.

"Is something the matter?" Dorothy asked.

"You were asking ... I mean ... who were you talking to?"

"Nobody," Dorothy replied.

"But I heard voices."

"Oh, that was me instructing the butler."

Lady Huxley paled. "You were asking the butler to blow his nose with your pretty white handkerchief."

Dorothy pursed her lip and tilted her head. "We were discussing the dinner party. Nothing to do with noses."

"But I heard ... about the nose and the blowing," Lady Huxley said in a high-pitched voice.

Dorothy set her embroidery aside and approached Lady

Huxley. "Are you feeling all right?"

"Yes!"

Dorothy put an arm around her and asked in concern, "Have you heard things lately? I heard this house was haunted ... but—"

"No, no. I clearly heard you telling the butler to come closer and blow his nose—"

Dorothy looked down at her pityingly. "Don't you see how absurd that sounds?"

"Well, yes, but I did hear it—"

"Yes, yes. I am sure you heard what you did. Still, I think you should go to your room and rest a bit. I will send over a cup of tea and some brandy," Dorothy said soothingly and led her out of the parlour.

"I am fine. I demand to know what that was about—"

"All in good time," Dorothy said gently. "Now, don't worry about a thing. Nay, I insist you must lie down. We will discuss this later. Ah, here is my maid. Rosie will take you to your room, and if you feel funny again, please let me know. After all, it is my duty to take care of you from now on."

"I suppose," Lady Huxley blinked nervously. "Wait, I came to say that I have noticed how close you have become to your husband. Perhaps you can ask him to send the artists away?"

"I couldn't do that."

"You must. They are all over the house scuttling about like rats."

Dorothy watched her and recalled the evil words she had spouted. Had the estate not been entailed, she would have drowned Huxley. She allowed the woman to rattle on, pretending to be agreeable, all the while murdering the woman in multiple ways in her head.

"All in good time," Dorothy said again; her words were not in response to Lady Huxley's demands but a secret vow that promised retribution.

Whoever hurt her husband would, from now on, suffer at her hands.

∞∞∞

That evening, Dorothy glared at Miss March's long, pale fingers as they dug into Huxley's shoulders. Before marrying her, Huxley had never bothered to dance, and now all he wanted to do was dance.

Perhaps it was because he no longer had to marry any of them; thus, dancing imposed no danger, but still, even if he did feel inclined to dance, he should have chosen one of Lady Whitehall's daughters. After all, she had seven of them, and this was her dinner party.

All her good feelings towards her husband were metaphorized into anger. The blasted, flirty nincompoop!

Her inner turmoil was well hidden behind a composed mask, and she smiled and nodded at the eldest Miss Whitehall, a lovely, young creature with teeth a tad bit big, not so much that one would notice, and somewhere under that fold of skin was undoubtedly a pair of lips. She would have danced like a dream, she was sure. He should have chosen her as his partner.

Dorothy's eyes, once again, strayed towards Huxley. Miss March was whispering in Huxley's ear, letting her promiscuous ringlet brush his cheek.

She turned her back on her husband, feeling a little sick. It was the awful elderberry ice that was making her feel ill; after all, she had eaten three of them in the last hour alone.

"I hope you are not claimed for the waltz?"

Dorothy looked up at Aron Selwyn and smiled brightly. She had hoped Huxley would dance the waltz with her, but he hadn't asked. Instead, he was spinning around the room with the woman whom he had kissed on the balcony the day before their wedding.

She had not forgotten Sophia's words.

She glanced towards Huxley again and found him striding towards her. He tilted his head towards Selwyn and shook his head.

She tossed her head in defiance and took Mr Selwyn's offered arm. "I would love to dance with you."

He smiled in delight and led her across the room, away from Huxley's livid gaze.

Mr Selwyn twirled her around the dance floor, keeping her laughing with silly anecdotes. It had been a long time since she had had so much fun.

He looked down at her laughing face, and his expression turned rueful.

"I wish things had been different," he said with a catch in his throat. "I know it is not appropriate for me to say so … but I admired you greatly, and had you not married Huxley—" He left the rest unsaid.

She looked up at his embarrassed face and felt her face flame in response. For a brief moment, she wondered what it would have been like being married to Aron Selwyn. A life filled with love and laughter … He would have treated her well.

"What was he saying?" Huxley asked her the moment she returned to her seat.

"What was she saying?" She jerked her head towards Miss March.

"Dorothy," he said in an exaggerated, patient voice. "As my wife, you should avoid men like Selwyn."

"I think Miss March is waspish, and if you don't want to be stung, then you should stay away from women like her."

He narrowed his eyes. "You will no longer entertain Selwyn."

"I have to."

"Why?"

"I promised him the supper dance."

"That dance is mine."

"You didn't ask."

"Today is the last day you will dance with him."

"No." She stuck her tongue out at him.

His eyes blazed, and he took a few deep breaths to control his temper. It didn't work, and he finally gave up all pretence.

"We are going home," he caught her arm and hauled her up.

"I don't want to go," she stared at him in shock. This was the first time she had seen him so angry.

"You have no choice."

He kept a firm hold of her, ignoring her furious whispers. He led her to the hostess, explained that Dorothy was feeling rather unwell and then led her out of the townhouse and into the carriage before she could do so much as stomp her feet.

Chapter Twenty-Three

She didn't speak to him the entire way, and he didn't attempt to converse with her either. Their mood was volatile enough to ignite at any moment.

Pah! She had thought the man was sweet, easy to twist and amiable. More fool her! He was an unreasonable, hypocritical brute.

As soon as the carriage reached Ansley Hall, he leapt out and escaped to his study.

Her eyes flickered with a dangerous gleam. Blasted man! He flirted the entire night, and the one time someone wanted to dance with her, he flew into a temper.

Damnation!

She could no longer restrain the tumultuous emotions in her heart and, bubbling with anger, barged into his study. Today, only one of them would come out alive.

He was sitting behind the desk, swirling an amber drink in a crystal glass.

"How dare you!" she growled at him.

"I am your husband. You have to follow my orders."

"I will do no such thing." She yanked off a glove and flung it at his head. She missed the mark, which made her even more incensed. "You cannot expect me to follow your orders and treat you like a husband when you refuse to treat me as your wife."

He leaned back in his chair, his eyes now pinned on the delicate white lace glove draped over the arm of the dark leather chair. It stood out, stark, against the shadowy masculine room.

"Why are you angry?" She slammed a hand on the table to get his attention. "I danced with Mr Selwyn, a thorough gentleman. Surely that is not a crime?"

"I am not angry."

"I can see that vein pulsing on your forehead. The one that appears every time you are seething silently. I call it the aristocrat!"

He ignored her and began searching the contents of the desk.

"Oh, for goodness's sake, what are you looking for?" she asked irritably. "I am trying to talk to you."

"Tinderbox," he replied.

"Why?"

He held up a cigar.

"You don't need it."

"What?"

"You don't need it," she repeated. "The anger raging inside you is fiery enough. Just pop the damn thing in your mouth and see the tip go up in flames."

He chuckled and then looked surprised that he had.

Her anger melted away at the sight of his adorably confused face. He laughed so rarely that when he did, it made her feel all warmish. She took an involuntary step closer to the table.

"This is absurd," she said, waving a hand between them. "Why are we squabbling?"

"Indeed, why are we squabbling?" His lips tilted up in a half smile, and he came around the desk and leaned his hip against it. "To tell the truth, I can no longer remember."

Dorothy remembered, but his mood had changed. His eyes now held a tender expression while the soft, warm evening breeze flowing in from the half-open window caressed his hair.

Her anger dissipated like snow in the blazing sun.

"Your skin looks golden in candlelight," he said, watching her. "Did you know?"

Her eyes widened, and she shook her head mutely.

He leaned forward, caught her wrist and dragged her closer.

His eyes were unfocused, and a strong scent of sweet, warm liqueur emanated from his skin.

He was a good bit sozzled, no wonder he was acting so strangely.

"People," he began in that wise tone that drunk men often adopt, "are not good. There is darkness in people, Dora, a darkness so opaque that even the sun cannot pierce it. Your thoughts are light, innocent ... filled with sweetness and warmth. You refuse to believe in the existence of a violent, depraved mind. You refuse to see the truth."

"What truth?" she asked, barely daring to breathe. He had never called her Dora before, and the name, which only those closest to her had used all her life, felt like a dart coming from his lips. The way he said it sounded foreign to her ears ... more intimate, like a fleeting caress.

"I will not have you ... I cannot," he said in a ragged whisper.

His face was filled with intensity, and he looked as if he wanted to devour her. His need was so transparent it should have frightened her; instead, all she felt was a shiver of anticipation. She barely heard his words as her head spun with his scent.

"Go to your chamber," he said, yet he dragged her into his arms until she could feel his warmth seep through the bodice of her dress. His fingers began stroking her hair, slowly pulling out the pins and letting them drop silently onto the thick, lush carpet. He softly hummed the song he had sung to soothe her tears not so long ago.

She clutched his broad shoulders and swayed closer still. Her lips parted, and she tilted her head back invitingly.

The air felt as if it was infused with sparkling champagne. Intoxicating, bubbling, and bursting with sweetness.

The heady atmosphere slowly sapped their capacity for thought, replacing it with a delicious, swimmy sensation that weakened their knees.

She leaned into him, unable to stand on her own, silently urging him to hold her closer still. Her shy demeanour splintered in the face of overwhelming desire and need.

When he continued to gaze at her and do nothing, she lightly nipped his ear and then licked to soothe the spot.

His fingers, holding her waist, trembled, giving away the delicate control he had over his senses.

His breathing became uneven.

Delighted and emboldened by this discovery, she bravely kissed the hollow of his neck and began to pepper his skin until her teeth grazed his collarbone.

He hissed and slightly panted.

Her eyes widened as she realised he wanted her.

Huxley wanted her so much that her touch had made him quiver. Her head spun at the thought, and a quiet joy exploded inside her.

She had danced countless times with earls, viscounts, and lords of all sorts, but she had moved none of them. None of them had reacted as if her touch would undo them.

Learning that someone as coveted as Huxley could melt because of her made her feel strange, as if she were an impostor who had tricked him.

But this need in his expression... surely it was not just because of the champagne?

He seemed to sense her spiralling thoughts, or perhaps he had enough of her hot mouth nibbling and sucking his skin.

The next moment, he spun her around and pushed her down so her bottom sat on the desk while her upper body lay over the strewn letters.

Her hair spread out like a dark shimmering lake over the cream pages scattered on the desk, while her mouth was red, skin flushed, and waist arched.

The cool breeze caressed their bodies but failed to alleviate the throbbing heat. It raced around the room, making the candles flicker and threaten to go out.

Her heart began to beat harder, harder than ever, while her

eyes became unfocused.

He leaned over her, pressing his hardness against her and nipped her ear in retaliation. "I wish someone could capture you like this in a painting."

"You can have me sit for a portrait," she said with a quiver in her voice.

"Nay, the thought of someone else seeing you like this—" His fingers dug into her flesh almost painfully while his mouth began tracing the same path that she had traced but a moment ago, except he did not pause at her collarbone but continued lower still. His nose followed the slight swell of her bosom, inhaling her light, floral scent and kissing when he so pleased.

She moaned as he suddenly ground his hip against her

It was startling and sudden.

She gasped in shock and pleasure, her cry caught by his lips.

He smiled against her skin and continued to rock against her, making her dig her nails into his arm.

"Stop," she hissed as something surged up inside her, followed by panic. Ah, this was too shameful; she could not go over the edge, not with him staring at her so, not with people just a wall away.

What if someone heard her cry?

"Nay," he muttered, his voice slightly hoarse as if he had drunk something harsh and gritty. "I cannot bear to."

He ignored her desire to flee and held her hips more firmly; the heat of his fingers burned through her skirts and flowed into her skin, bones and marrow, making her tingle all the more.

The candle flames trembled and dimmed as if ashamed to watch the two embroiled in an erotic haze while Huxley's shadow suddenly seemed to roar out and merge with hers on the wall.

In a few heartbeats, he had had her soft and pliant like a handful of rain-soaked earth ready to be moulded however he pleased.

"Please, no more, not here," she said, shuddering against

him. Her body felt weak and defenceless, and she knew if he wanted, he could go on and devour her.

It was not that she did not want him; every bit of her yearned to break all walls between them and fuse body and soul. But this was the study; anyone could walk in. The artists were awake at all hours, roaming the hallways like ghouls.

This bit of rational thought nudged her to protest.

Her soft, gentle, insistent request made him pause. He closed his eyes, hiding the roiling raging passion, and raggedly sucked in air.

Their breaths mingled and entwined, their bodies flushed red and warm, and their hearts beat at an incredible pace.

After a moment, he opened his eyes and stepped away.

She hurriedly smoothed her hair and looked down at herself. Remarkably, her dress still covered her modestly, and yet, she felt like she had undressed and rolled around in bed with him, bare as the day she was born.

He gazed at her mouth, reluctant to move aside and let her escape entirely. If nothing else, surely a kiss was not too much to ask for?

They still had not kissed properly tonight.

He dipped his head, inching closer to her lips—

"Eek," she exclaimed, slapping a hand on her cheek.

"Eek?" his head snapped up in surprise.

"Ugh!"

The pink atmosphere shattered, the candles stopped spluttering like horrified chaperones, and the breeze slowly left the room now that there was nothing to see.

Huxley sighed and rubbed his chin. "Not a response I have gotten before, but women make all sorts of odd noises at all sorts of times. Blasted inconvenient but—"

"No, no, it is not you. It's this."

"What?"

"This fish bone."

He shook his head, looking dazed. "Is this some odd hobby of yours? Collecting fish bones? Did you procure it at dinner tonight? Shall I admire it, or what one does with fish bones?"

"It just hit my cheek," she said, waving it before his eyes.

"It's wet," he shuddered in disgust. His inebriated head rapidly cleared up. "Where did it come from?"

"Here," Woodbead said apologetically.

They turned towards the small door in the corner of the room.

Philbert's head was poking out of the hidey hole; his head was resting on his palms, and a dinner plate sat in front of him, along with half a glass of wine.

"I was eating boiled fish, and it had a lot of bones," Woodbead said regretfully. "The one that landed on your blushing cheek looked remarkably like a wishbone. I was attempting to make a wish when it slipped from my oily fingers, flew across the room and interrupted what would be a fascinating scene."

"How long have you been here?" Huxley growled.

"From the moment she said please, no more," Woodbead shrugged. "The two of you were so lost in one another that I hated interrupting. Also, I was entertained. Nothing like a spot of good entertainment to digest a good dinner."

"I would like a word," Huxley snarled.

Woodbead baulked. "I say, fish bone, wishbone ... I feel a poem coming on. This sort of thing needs to be squeezed out of the upper story as soon as possible, or it gets lost in the wilderness. We should palaver in the morning when the sun is bright, and moods are soft, gentle and forgiving."

"I heard you were fasting," Huxley growled. "Why have you started eating again?"

Woodbead smirked. "Did you want me to starve to death so I would not spoil your romance? Surely you get enough of it in bed every night?"

Dorothy squirmed in Huxley's arms and stepped away. The romantic atmosphere was thoroughly ruined.

She cleared her throat and asked nonchalantly, "Why were you fasting?"

"I wanted to torture my soul so the words ooze out of me like a leaky pustule."

"Did it work?" Huxley asked, still clutching one of Dorothy's fingers as if reluctant to let her go.

Woodbead pretended not to see the clingy side of his drunk benefactor. "I realised some truths about life."

"Like?" Dorothy asked curiously.

"We eat birds, we eat pigs."

"Yes," she nodded.

"We eat fish. We eat snails."

"We do."

"Then why, pray, do we not eat everything in between?"

"Eh?"

"Mosquito is also meat."

"Oh."

"If slimy snails can be eaten, as well as partridges and hens, what is wrong with munching on a good ol' bumblebee?"

"Ah."

"And how about the moths and butterflies? Why do they not make an entrance during our feasts?"

"I- that is odd."

"I thought so. For a starving man, it is all meat. You are meat, I am meat, the ants and the ladybirds are meat." Woodbead eyed her fondly.

"Go to bed," Huxley rubbed his head and ordered Woodbead. "I am too foxed for this nonsense."

Woodbead bowed and obediently retreated.

"I suppose I should also go to bed," Dorothy mumbled.

"I suppose you should," Huxley responded, looking not at all pleased with the thought.

She turned and slowly walked away while he bore holes in her back as if he wanted to fling sharp hooks towards and yank her back and tie her to his side forever.

A part of her wondered if he would finally give up the battle and visit her chamber tonight.

Chapter Twenty-Four

Last night, Huxley did not visit her chamber. She had scrubbed her cheek and waited for him to arrive and finish the kiss ... but the knock on the connecting door never came.

She berated herself for spinning windmills in her head. He had been liquored up to his splendid ears. He didn't know what he was doing. And once he came to his senses, he prudently stayed away.

Perhaps he thought she was unworthy of him, just like his mother and sister did.

He could have picked any woman in the world, and yet he had been forced to wed her, and none of it was his fault.

It was all hers.

"Your eyes have gone foggy again," Blinker complained.

"Do you like the painting?" Dorothy asked, staring up at the Aëdon.

Blinker pursed his lips and shook his head. "She could do with a bit of soakin' in moonshine."

"Hmm."

"Foxed is what she needs to be," Blinker continued sagely. "Drunk as a wheelbarrow."

"I see."

"A bit of gin or 'umming liquor will set her right. Along with the gin, she should eat a bit of—What's that fruit on the ground?"

"Pomegranate."

"Eat a bit of pommy—what you said—and she will feel less watery-headed."

Dorothy could see what Blinker was trying to say ... she, too, found the painting a tad mopey. She couldn't understand why Huxley loved it so.

"What were you going to show me?" she tugged Blinker's hand.

He led her down the hall towards the back of the house.

The evening sun had bathed the sky in pink and gold. She would have rather strolled outside on such a beautiful evening, but Blinker had other ideas, and she couldn't bear to break his heart.

"'ere," Blinker said, standing before a tapestry. "I saw one of the artists disappear behind it."

Dorothy frowned. "Don't be silly. How can an artist disappear into a wall?"

Blinker grinned, took hold of the bottom of the tapestry and whipped it upwards.

Dorothy gasped. There was a door. This house was full of never-ending surprises.

Thrilled, she stepped in through the door, and Blinker followed.

Her mouth dropped open at the sight that met her.

The room turned out to be a stark white grand hall with a dome-shaped ceiling filled with giant statues and sculptures.

There were statues of elephants, horses, warriors, mermaids, sculpted trees, birds, and flowers. Some statutes were explicit. She covered Blinker's eyes when she found him ogling one depicting a man and woman entwined in a passionate embrace, and it was clear neither of them was wearing any clothes.

"We have to leave," Dorothy scolded in a prim voice. This was no place for curious children to wander.

"But I want to show you the bear," Blinker said, tugging her hand. "It's this way."

Dorothy's eyes fell on yet another statue. It seemed as if a couple had turned to stone amid lovemaking. Her face flamed, and ignoring Blinker's loud protests, she moved towards the exit. She pushed Blinker out first.

Blinker grumbled and whined in protest.

She had just entered the hallway when she spotted Rosie hopping up and down.

"Lady Huxley heard the boy. Hide," Rosie whispered urgently.

Dorothy had just shoved Blinker back into the room of statues when Lady Huxley was upon her.

"I heard a boy," Lady Huxley said, looking around the hallway. Her brows knitted in confusion when all she could see was Dorothy standing by a tapestry and blank walls, with not even a window close by.

"A boy?" Dorothy frowned. "In Ansley Hall?"

"I heard him distinctly," Lady Huxley insisted.

"What was he saying?" Dorothy asked.

"I want you to see the bear. Please, it will only take a minute," Lady Huxley replied.

"A bear? In Ansley Hall?" Dorothy looked at her worriedly.

"You," Lady Huxley turned to Rosie. "You heard the boy, did you not?"

Rosie, bless her, widened her eyes and shook her head. "I heard nuffing."

"But … I heard it clearly."

Dorothy eyed Lady Huxley pityingly. "Perhaps you have developed a skill."

"What skill?"

"The sort that thins the veil between two worlds."

"Eh."

"Ghosts. You could be hearing the voice of some poor little chimney sweep who died long ago."

Rosie gasped. "A chimney sweep did die here, miss, twenty years ago."

Lady Huxley paled. "I remember," she said faintly.

"A cup of tea, Lady Huxley?" Dorothy asked soothingly.

Lady Huxley nodded dazedly. "Are you certain you heard no voice?"

Dorothy shook her head regretfully. "I would like to request you to keep this a secret. You are, after all, family ... and if word got out that you hear voices—"

"Bedlam," Lady Huxley whispered in horror.

"Take her to her room," Dorothy told Rosie, then gently assured Lady Huxley, "Your secret is safe with me."

Lady Huxley smiled weakly and allowed herself to be led away.

Dorothy felt not a hint of guilt. After all, Lady Huxley had confessed she would have gotten rid of her stepson if Sophia had been a boy.

As soon as Lady Huxley was out of sight, Dorothy slipped back into the room of statues.

Blinker was nowhere to be seen.

"Where are you?"

"Find me," Blinker laughed.

"This is no place to play," Dorothy scolded.

Blinker remained silent.

Dorothy sighed and began looking around. She spotted him hiding behind a statue of Athena. She lunged, but Blinker was too quick. He slipped through her fingers and raced away.

"Come back here, or no cakes for you," Dorothy threatened. When that didn't work, she said coaxingly, "Come, show me the bear. I am keen to see it."

"I am here," Blinker's guilty voice echoed around the room.

"What did you do?" Dorothy asked, cautiously approaching the beautifully carved, giant pineapple.

"I broke this," he said, peeking over the fruit. He handed her a basket made out of stone.

Her mouth turned dry.

Before she could scold, he slipped under the tapestry and disappeared into the corridor.

She looked around wildly, wondering which statue the basket belonged to.

She walked towards a beautifully sculpted statue of a couple where a handsome man had his hands splayed across the tiny waist of an equally handsome woman. Both of them were unclad.

She was inspecting the woman's hand lying limp and empty by her side when a voice startled her.

"I heard two women," a thin voice said.

She turned in horror to find Huxley approaching her with a plump man who was covered in splotches of paint.

"There," the man pointed a finger at her accusingly.

"She is my wife," Huxley said quietly. "She has the right to be here."

"I am sorry—"

"It's an understandable mistake. You can return to your work."

"I don't see the other girl," he hesitated. "I heard two women."

Dorothy quickly shook her head. "I was alone." No doubt he had taken Blinker's young voice as that of a girl.

The artist frowned but kept his doubts to himself. He nodded to them and disappeared into the back of the room.

Dorothy inched away from the scandalous statue, her face aflame.

"My stepmother and sister have never discovered this place despite living here all their life," he said, pulling out a cigar. "You are resourceful."

"Why keep it hidden?" she asked. Her voice sounded high-pitched to her ears.

"Do you think I would like my sister to set eyes on this?" he asked, pointing towards the marble couple making love, the one she had been peering at so intently a few moments ago.

She turned her face away, and a blush spread all over her body. "You didn't come from the corridor?"

Huxley shook his head. "There are two entrances to this room. One is in the library."

She was surprised he had told her that.

"What is that in your hand?" he asked sharply.

She looked down and remembered the basket. "This broke ... I am sorry ... I was trying to fix it."

His eyes narrowed in anger. "I have allowed you to go where you please, but if you do not respect the art pieces, then I will have to limit your movements."

"You cannot imprison me in my room!" she exclaimed.

He snatched the basket out of her hand. "I can, and I will."

"Your inanimate sculptures are more important than me?" she asked, pushing his chest angrily. Why did he always have to stand so close?

He stumbled back in surprise, and an object flew out of his fist and skittered across the stone floor. The noise was deafening in the silent hall.

Her eyes widened when she realised what it was.

The eagle embossed snuff box.

The same one that had pierced her skin after a too-brief kiss in the library. Her eyes flew to his face to see if he remembered.

He did. He was staring at her mouth.

She clutched her chest as an odd, sweet pain shot through her limbs. "Don't ... don't look at me like that," she whispered.

"You are my wife. I can look," he said, taking a step closer. "I can touch," he said, tucking a curl behind her ear.

She shivered, and her lashes fell to caress her cheek.

"I can kiss," he murmured as he placed his lips against her neck.

She arched her back and let out a shuddering breath.

"You are mine," he repeated. "Sweet, warm ... obedient."

Her eyes snapped open, and she broke away from his embrace.

"Obedient?" she asked irritably. "Not while I live and breathe."

"I am your husband. Do not look or dance with other men. Go where I say, do what I say. Always stay a few steps away from me. You must always behave like a lady and keep your voice and eyes down when talking to me—"

She widened her eyes and stuck her tongue out at him.

He turned red in anger. "I will have to punish your insolence—"

"You will have to catch me first," she said and took off in the direction of the corridor.

Chapter Twenty-Five

He ran after her.
She raced down the corridor and slid down the bannister of the grand staircase.

The butler's mouth dropped open while the housekeeper swooned.

Huxley took the steps two at a time. "Stop," he roared. "I am ordering you to stop."

"Order away, Your Highness," she laughed and hurtled towards her chamber. If she could get to it before he caught her, she could lock him out, slither out of the window and escape into the gardens until his anger cooled.

"I will cut off your allowance," he threatened.

She froze and slowly turned to face him. "You wouldn't dare!"

He smirked. "I think it's the best way to keep you in check. You have been running around the house like a disobedient pup. What's more, you had me chasing you but a moment ago. Too many times have I forgiven you for your insolence, but not anymore, my dear, not anymore. I will cut off your allowance completely, and if you need money, you must come to me and petition your case."

She stared at him in shock. She needed the money to plan for Blinker's future. She couldn't send him to an orphanage of bad repute.

Her heart clenched at the thought of Blinker being beaten and fed burnt gruel. She couldn't do that. Not to Blinker. His spirit would be broken.

She had to keep him until one of the better schools had a place for him, and those schools cost a fair sum. And clothes ... Blinker would need new clothes ... some of the servants had to be paid for keeping silent about him ... and ... Oh! She would have to do something to prevent Huxley from cutting her off so cruelly. She just had to.

∞∞∞

It was mid-afternoon. The sun had popped out to boil the Thames and cook the delicate English folk until they turned an unsightly salmon pink.

Dorothy lay on her bed feeling awfully sorry for herself. The heat seemed to have affected her ability to think. She had to get her allowance back, but it had been two days, and she had yet to come up with a plan.

A faint scratching on the windowsill had her sit up. Was Blinker attempting to climb down the ivy again? She flung aside her fan and leapt towards the window.

Instead of Blinker's sweet little face, she found a tall, muscular man with black hair streaked with silver staring back at her.

"Ack!" she exclaimed.

"Oh dear," the fellow on the other side echoed.

"Who are you?"

"Pardon. I didn't expect to find you in your rooms or for you to catch me dangling off the ivy," the man said. "You never laze about in your room in the afternoon—"

"Who are you?" she repeated firmly, cutting him short.

"I am the Black Rover."

She blinked uncomprehendingly.

"The Black Rover ... The pirate."

"Eh?"

"Blast it," the man muttered. "Going respectable is no good.

Why did the blooming king have to pardon me? No one reels back when I announce my name anymore, the breeze continues to blow, and the tea no longer jumps out of cups in my presence—"

An ivy branch snapped under his weight, breaking off his tirade.

"Come in," Dorothy said hurriedly, even though she didn't think it was a wise thing to let a sinister-looking fellow enter her bedchamber. But he was hanging fairly precariously onto the delicate tendrils, and she didn't want him to plummet to his death.

He gratefully climbed into the room and took off his hat. "I am a pirate of some repute."

"So you said," she answered sceptically.

He bared his teeth. "See the gold tooth?"

"I see three of them."

"Well, that proves it, doesn't it? I am a pirate."

"Do all pirates have gold teeth?"

"Only the good ones."

"I see."

"Do you believe me?"

"That you are the Black Rover, a sinister, bloodthirsty pirate with three gold teeth? I do. But we are on land, and Ansley Hall is not a ship. So the question is, what are you doing here?"

"Been keeping an eye on you. It was to be a secret, but now that you have seen me, there is no point in hiding the rest of it."

"Please do carry on."

"You see, some years ago, I had kidnapped George—"

"Lord Elmer?" she gasped.

"Correct. Your sister, Celine's, husband. You are a bright one. Well, as it so happened after the Duchess gave birth to her firstborn on my ship, I couldn't help but melt a little."

"Penny gave birth to her firstborn on a pirate ship?" Dorothy squawked in disbelief.

"Not the sort of thing you mention to a younger sister. I can understand why she kept it to herself."

"Huh."

"After that, I became sort of friendly with the Duke and Lord Elmer. And Lord Elmer happened to mention that he needed a dependable fellow to keep an eye on you. What with your rushed wedding to Huxley … He wanted to know if you were well-fed and cheery. I happened to be lazing about in London for a while. Mother wanted to shop. So I decided to do the job myself."

Her lashes flickered with suppressed emotions. Her family had not abandoned her, and they still adored her just as much. Her heart lightened, and she had to swallow a few times before being able to speak without tearing up. "H-how long have you been keeping an eye on me?"

"Since the day you got married. Which brings me to why I am here. You have been uncommonly mopey the last two days. Is it Lady Huxley? Would you like me to do away with her?"

"No! Lady Huxley is fine, and I don't want anyone to be done away with. It's nothing. It's the heat. You really don't have to look out for me anymore—"

"If you need anything, just poke your head out of the window and crow. I will arrive within moments. I can steal, threaten, blackmail, chop off limbs—"

"I think you should return to your mother. She must be missing you," she interrupted hurriedly.

"A few more days, and I will splash away," he replied politely.

"A week and no more," she said firmly.

"If you insist."

"I insist."

"Wonderful," he smiled, showing off his sparkling gold teeth. After a quick, elegant bow, he departed through the window.

He popped right back up a few moments later. "Forgot to say. Another young lad's been keeping an eye on you. Want me to send him up?"

"Another one? I don't know—"

"Caught him kissing your maid, Rosie."

"Send him up."
"Aye, aye, picaroon."

∞∞∞

It took the Black Rover an entire day to locate the other young lad. He found the fellow taking refuge in a recently vacated tree house on the grounds of Ansley Hall and promptly sent him up the ivy.

"Tommy!" Dorothy exclaimed in surprise when she saw a nervous head appear at her window. It was the chimney sweep she had wanted to keep as a pet all those years ago.

A tall, thin man who looked remarkably like a reed nodded sheepishly.

"I thought you were apprenticed to Pickering," she scolded.

"I am."

"The Black Rover says you have been lurking in my garden."

"I have. That's the job."

"Eh?"

"You see, the duke wanted a reliable man to keep an eye on you—"

"To see that I was happy and cheery after my hasty wedding," she sighed in resignation.

"Just so. And I, being your devoted servant since you saved my life—"

"I did no such thing."

"Gave me a better life than I would have otherwise had … I couldn't let anyone else do this job."

"I see."

"So I have been hopping about—"

"Kissing Rosie?"

He blushed. "Lawks! She was keeping an eye on you, and I would meet her every day to learn how you were, and she was lonely, and I was alone—"

"You planning to marry her?"

He blushed harder and nodded.

"You don't have to keep an eye on me," she said once he had turned back to his usual pale self.

"But—"

"You will return to Blackthorne mansion and say everything is fine."

"But you have been mopey."

"It's the heat," she said with gritted teeth.

"If you insist—"

"I insist."

He ducked his head in acquiescence.

"Anyone else keeping an eye on me?"

"A few young lads you had helped in the Blessington orphanage and the butcher whose vicious cat you had saved."

"Please, ask everyone to leave. I am touched by everyone's concern, but truly, I am fine. If I need any help, I will let them know."

"They won't listen—"

"Tell them it's an order. And if they don't comply, I will never speak to them again."

Tommy saluted smartly. "I will see that it is done."

"It's good to see you," she finally smiled.

"Take care, miss."

After Tommy had departed, Dorothy collapsed on a chair with a big smile on her face. Her family had never stopped loving her, missing her or worrying about her. Oh, they were still angry, but beneath that anger was pure, unconditional love.

Soon after Dorothy dismissed the spies her sisters had set on her, the opportunity to get her family to forgive her presented itself.

Penelope was hosting a ball, and Dorothy, along with her

family, had been cordially invited. The Duke of Blackthorne usually gave Lord Huxley the cut direct, but now that Dorothy was married into the family, the gossiping *ton* had to be silenced.

She chuckled at the memory of Penelope and Celine pretending not to care about her. No more, she decided. She wouldn't let them pretend any longer. She needed her sisters, for without them, she felt adrift.

Dorothy clutched the blue beaded reticule in one hand and the brown, patterned, rough cotton skirt in the other as she prepared to descend the stairs. She was eager to see Blackthorne once again and greet familiar faces.

Huxley took one look at her and charged up the stairs. He pulled her into the hallway, his face thunderous.

"What are you wearing?" he hissed.

"A dress," she replied, batting her lashes.

"That thing is hideous. Take it off."

"It's my maid's best going-out dress," she replied, affronted.

"Are you ready?" Lady Huxley called. They heard her make her way up the grand staircase. Her foot thumped heavily on the stairs. "William!"

His eyes grew large in panic. "Why are you wearing your maid's dress? Surely, you have dozens of your own."

"You told me my new dresses were too risqué, and Penny has seen all my old dresses, and since you have cut off my allowance, I had no choice but to wear my maid's dress," she replied innocently. "Don't you like it?"

He glared at her.

She dropped her lashes and tried to look demure, all the while trying not to grin. He couldn't afford to have her appear at the Duchess's ball looking like a badly rigged mopsey. The dress was truly ghastly.

"William, Dorothy, we will be late," Lady Huxley called. She was but a moment away now.

"Please, change," Huxley begged in a strangled voice.

"First promise, you will give me an allowance."

He scowled.

"The carriage is waiting," Lady Huxley hollered.

"Yes, yes. I will give you an allowance," he growled.

"And never cut it off?"

"No. I will never cut it off. Now, quickly take this hideous thing off."

Dorothy began unbuttoning her dress.

He eyed her in horror. "What are you doing?"

"Taking the dress off. I am practising being obedient."

"Good god, woman! My mother will be upon us. The servants will see—" He turned purple, and his breathing came in shallow gasps. "Do not be obedient. Do what you please. I was wrong—"

Dorothy continued to unbutton her bodice calmly. She pulled the final string.

He turned his face away.

"You can look."

He peeked at her reluctantly.

She stood resplendent in a beautiful silver muslin gown. She held the maid's dress out to him. "I wore the maid's gown over this dress. Isn't it lovely? "

He looked like he wanted to throttle her.

She shoved the gown into his arms just as Lady Huxley huffed and puffed into sight.

Lady Huxley stared at the maid's dress, which Huxley was clutching in surprise. "What's this?"

"I was asking him the same thing," Dorothy said, folding her arms.

Huxley dropped the bundle. "It's not mine."

Lady Huxley picked up the dress and eyed it in disgust. "Of course, it is not yours, dear. It's a maid's dress. Why were you holding a maid's dress?"

"Yes, why were you holding it?" Dorothy echoed.

"She was wearing it not a moment ago," Huxley accused Dorothy. "And she changed into this."

"In the corridor?" Dorothy asked in horror. "I changed my

clothes here? Why would I do such a thing?"

Lady Huxley patted her sympathetically. She had decided to be as nice to Dorothy as possible since one word from her about hearing voices would send her to Bedlam.

"Now, now," Lady Huxley admonished. "How could Dorothy do such a thing? Besides, look at the lacing at the back of this gown. It is too intricate for her to manage on her own."

Dorothy sniffed and leaned her head against Lady Huxley's sympathetic shoulder. She allowed tears to shimmer in her eyes. "He is blaming me when he is the one holding a maid's dress. What?" she asked with a dramatic sob, "may I ask, is a maid's best dress doing cuddling your bosom? And what," she wailed, "is the maid wearing when the dress is in your arms? Where is that rotten, scheming maid? I understand it is fashionable to keep a mistress or two, but to canoodle in my very home, and that too with one of the servants," Dorothy howled and stuck her head back into Lady Huxley's shoulder.

"This is terrible," Lady Huxley said, patting Dorothy's head. She glared at Huxley. "You must make it up to her."

Huxley's mouth dropped open. "But she ... you don't understand ... she is a scheming little—"

"He should double my allowance," Dorothy hiccupped into Lady Huxley's ear.

"Double her allowance," Lady Huxley ordered obligingly and walked away with Dorothy's unhappy figure in tow.

Dorothy looked back to find Huxley purple with rage. She winked.

Chapter Twenty-Six

Blackthorne Mansion was lit with so many candles, torches and gas lamps that it appeared almost as bright as daytime.

Dorothy raced up the steps eagerly. This was her chance to pounce on her sisters and make peace.

Huxley followed at a more sedate pace, his expression carefully masked.

The moment he was announced, curious heads swung his way. Whispers flew from ear to ear. Everyone wanted to see how the duke would treat his former archenemy.

The Duke and Huxley kept their conversation brief and polite. They discussed the King's declining health and the Regent's unfortunate separation from his wife so soon after his wedding. Thereafter, the two men parted ways and stayed away from each other for the rest of the evening. The numerous ears straining to hear every word the two exchanged wilted in disappointment.

Dorothy, on the other hand, bounded over to Sir Henry and admired his moustache, hugged the dowager with all her might and greeted the butler enthusiastically. She even slipped down to the kitchens to give the cook's florid cheeks a loving pinch.

"Penny, Celine!" Dorothy approached her sisters, chatting with Lady Grim. "I missed you."

The two sisters shuffled uncomfortably. They couldn't be rude to her in front of a guest. Whatever was said and done, their issues were a family matter and should not be aired publicly.

Dorothy grinned and squeezed their hands. "Do say you missed me too."

Celine and Penelope mumbled a reply.

"I didn't hear you," Dorothy said with a broader grin.

"Missed you—" Celine and Penelope reluctantly clarified.

Dorothy linked her arm with Celine's and rested her head on her shoulder.

Celine tensed.

"When will you visit?" Dorothy asked, smiling widely at Penelope.

The Duchess tried to pretend she didn't hear the question

Lady Grim obligingly repeated it.

"I am not certain—" Penelope muttered.

"You should go soon," Lady Grim admonished. "I remember when I had just gotten married, the strange house full of strange faces was overwhelming. A familiar face visiting did me a lot of good. And calf's foot jelly."

"I will come soon," Penelope reluctantly promised.

"Within a fortnight?" Dorothy pressed.

"Yes," Penelope sighed.

"And you too, Celine?" Dorothy asked.

Celine nodded with a smile, though her eyes sparked in annoyance.

Dorothy grinned like a cat who had demolished a bowl of stolen cream.

"How is married life, my dear?" Lady Grim asked, her fluffy grey curls bouncing around her round face.

"Wonderful," Dorothy replied.

"I can see how marvellous he is," Lady Grim remarked, her eyes pinned on Huxley's tight breeches.

"Why don't you have some more wine?" Penelope cut in hurriedly. "I see someone Dorothy must meet."

"I don't want to meet anyone," Dorothy complained. She wanted to hear more of what Lady Grim was about to say.

Penelope grabbed her arm and pulled her across the room. Celine followed.

Dorothy had a distinct feeling Penelope didn't want her to see something … or someone. Celine was trying to block her view. She squirmed in Penelope's grip until she was able to look over her sister's shoulder.

"Are you all right?" Celine asked quietly.

"She saw?" Penelope asked worriedly.

Celine nodded.

"We didn't think they would come," Penelope said.

"I told you not to send the invitation," Celine scolded.

"It was a mistake. I had asked—"

"I need to speak to her," Dorothy cut in.

"What?" Penelope gasped.

"I need to speak to Kitty just once," Dorothy repeated. "I have to know why—"

"Do you want me to come with you?" Celine asked.

Dorothy shook her head.

"But—" Penelope gripped Dorothy's arm.

"I love you," Dorothy said, kissing her cheek. "And I am sorry."

Penelope dropped her arm with a resigned sigh.

Dorothy squared her shoulders and made her way towards Kitty.

Kitty took one look at Dorothy's face and fled.

Dorothy found her friend cowering in the coat room.

"I was hoping to catch you alone," Kitty said.

Dorothy refrained from rolling her eyes.

"I wanted to apologise," Kitty said hesitatingly. "I should have told you."

"Yes, you should have."

"But it all worked out in the end," she said brightly. "You got Huxley, and I got Lumley."

"I didn't get Huxley. I had to marry him because I went to look for you in his house, thinking he had imprisoned you. I went to save you but ended up having to marry him."

"I heard," Kitty bit her lip. "But he is an excellent catch. Women are envious. You couldn't have done better."

Kitty's words stung her like a slap. When had her friend changed so much? Or had she always been like this?

Kitty grabbed Dorothy's hand and held it tight. "I was confused, Dora. The more time I spent with Lumley ..., the more I wanted him. His devotion, his little sweet gestures ... they stayed with me long after I left him for the day. I was filled with guilt, love, and turmoil ... I knew Father would never approve of Lumley. I knew he would think Lumley was after my dowry ... so I had to elope. Don't you see?"

"You could have told me."

"How could I? I knew you loved him, and I couldn't break your heart. He admitted he did not care for you ... and never would. He said he loved me instead, and, oh, the difference between his tender affections and Huxley's indifference was stark. I realised I never loved Huxley. How could I? He is such an awfully rude man. That day at the park, it became all too clear to me that I had never loved anyone until Lumley toddled into my life—"

"I see," Dorothy said curtly.

"I am glad you understand. I knew you would!"

Dorothy's mouth twisted wryly.

Kitty took her silence as consent that all was forgiven. "Enough about me. How are you? And, oh! You poor dear, you have to see Sophia's face every day!" She shook her head sympathetically. "Is she still ogling that foreign prince? Rumour has it he is eyeing someone younger, fresher ... but I hope he marries Sophia. I heard they keep women locked away in his kingdom, and once she is gone, you can build on your romance with Huxley—"

"Lord Huxley," Dorothy corrected her crisply. "As for Sophia, I would appreciate it if you refrained from insulting my family."

Kitty's face fell. "I didn't mean to . . . I suppose you are right. It was thoughtless of me. Well," she paused and tried again.

"My father just procured the most beautiful silk. You would love it. It's cream and gold and would look marvellous on you. Not a single shop in England has it yet. He got it off the latest shipment. I wanted you to come home and take what you need—"

Dorothy took a step back. She had had enough. "Kitty, I loved you as a person. You were my friend not because you could lend me your dresses and jewels but because you were loyal, kind and generous. You stood up for me more than once and made me laugh ... I thought you cared about me. And your betrayal has hurt me more than you can imagine."

Kitty paled, her eyes shimmered with tears. "Can we ever be friends again? I miss you."

Dorothy eyed her and realised for the first time in all these years she didn't trust her. The betrayal had torn apart the trust, and she wasn't sure if she could gather all the bits and sew them together again. It was as if, instead of her beloved childhood friend, a stranger stood before her whose thoughts, actions, and feelings she could no longer understand.

"We can try," Kitty pressed. "I miss you more than you can imagine. I want to share so much. Lord Lumley ... he treats me so well—"

"I have to go," Dorothy spun on her heel and strode out of the room. Her eyes were full of unshed tears when she reached the ballroom. She felt like something precious in her life had died.

"Come," Huxley's voice arrested her tears. He caught her hand and tugged.

She allowed him to lead her towards the dancing couples, too emotionally spent to care about what she did anymore.

She didn't know when or how Huxley wrapped his arms around her. She hid her face in his shoulders. Her ears felt stuffed with wool. She couldn't hear the symphony echoing in the room or remember the simple dance steps. If it hadn't been for Huxley's support, she would have made a fool of herself in front of the *ton*.

He gathered her closer still, his arms a warm anchor. His

hands nudged her now and then, leading her from one step to the next, reminiscent of the morning after their wedding.

The difference was the gentleness with which he held her now as opposed to the anger that had prompted his actions then.

"I can't hear the music," she said, clutching his shirt desperately.

He dipped his head and began singing softly,

> Let me kiss your lips, share your breath and your dew,
> Draw every torment away from your heart.
> Like the shade of a lamp, let my hands encircle your soul
> Shielding you from the hurtful winds of the past.
> Good night, my lassie, my sweet, sweet lassie
> Let the world fade away.
> My heart stops a moment,
> Time splits and lengthens,
> A moment becomes a day.
> Your breath begins to flow,
> Easy and free, your lips tilt up in a smile.
> I weep and I weep o' sweet lassie of mine.

His deep, melodious voice resonated through her body. It was familiar, comforting and a soothing balm to her hurt. The heavy darkness that had enshrouded her a moment ago began to fade.

"Don't let them win," he said quietly. "Show them how happy you are."

Dorothy dashed the tears from her cheek and looked up at him. "Sing once more. Finish the song."

He began singing again. They twirled around the room, and she let herself drown in his voice. She surrendered herself to him, trusting him to lead her completely.

Fingers flew over the piano keys, moving closer and closer to the climax.

Her face softened, and she focused on the warmth of his

palm splayed on her back and her hand engulfed in his. She leaned into the scent of sweet, warm liquor emanating from him.

All she could see and feel was Huxley. She needed his strength tonight. Needed to be held and kissed.

She lifted her heavy lashes and stared at his mouth. It hit her like lightning. Knowledge so deep and sure that she was surprised she hadn't realised it before. She wanted no other man's lips descending on hers.

She wanted only Huxley.

"Dorothy," he said huskily.

"Hmm?"

"Too many people."

"I don't understand."

"I do," his jaw ticked. "Only too well. People are looking. You are going to fall if I let you go—"

"Don't let me go—"

"You have to look away. Compose yourself."

"What?"

"You look … like you want to bed me," he growled in her ear.

Her stomach clenched. "I want a kiss."

He inhaled sharply at her words and then, as if giving up the fight, steered her towards the balcony.

The cool air did nothing to snap her back to her senses.

It was raining. She reached out, captured a few drops of summer rain in her palm, and flung them at him with a laugh.

He looked stunned for a moment and then spun her around, and she found herself pressed against the wall, out of the rain.

She stared at the droplets of water suspended on his long, thick lashes.

"Did you drink too much wine?"

She shook her head … at least, she didn't think so. "I feel a little drunk when you come close to me," she confessed. "I don't know why."

He cursed. "Stop saying everything that comes into your head. We should go home."

"And kiss?"

"No kiss."

"Please?" she batted her lashes and pouted.

He made an annoyed sound and dipped his head, intending to give her a chaste peck.

She threw her arms around him at the first contact and held on firmly. She wanted a proper kiss from her husband, and she would not let go until he complied.

He muttered against her lips and then suddenly took control. He gripped her chin and tugged until she opened her mouth and deepened the kiss.

Sweet, painful darts shot through her body.

They had kissed before ... and it had been nice. This was not nice ... this was dark, roiling passion that assaulted her senses in a way that left her trembling.

He did not hurt her or punish her as she had expected from such a large, powerful man, but stroked her tenderly, expertly, coaxing a response from her until she slid her hands up his chest and gripped the back of his neck and curled her body to fit his.

He sensed her melt against him and growled deep in his throat in what sounded like a mixture of impatience and triumph. His kiss, which had begun as a delicate assault on her senses, became rough ... demanding ... almost feral in intensity. His hand began moving up her bodice, and she tightened her hold on him, kissing him back with a desperation she had not thought possible.

The slight tug on the lace of her bodice made her bring her hands up to his chest and push half-heartedly. She didn't want him to stop, yet a voice at the back of her head whispered warnings ... begging her to run.

He gripped her fists, locked them behind her back and pulled her even closer. His lips shifted, trailing heated kisses against her jaw and flushed neck. It wasn't long before he had her completely pliant once again ... deaf to all voices of reason.

His tongue flicked over the top of her collarbone, and his

hand began stroking her stomach and between her thighs through the dress.

It was always him touching, she thought dazedly. One day, she wanted to tie him and feel every inch of him, tease him until he teared up just like her at this moment.

Her mouth nipped his neck in half, in half-agitation, half-grievance for holding her captive and not letting her hands run free.

He captured her unruly mouth and kissed her deeply. His tongue pushed against her teeth and delved in, eagerly tasting the remnants of champagne.

Soon, she was limp against the wall, her eyes tinged red and heavy-lidded, while his desire throbbed against her belly, hard and blatant.

She softly whimpered, her hot breath brushing his ear in quick bursts.

The sound of rain became stronger and stronger still.

The wind, heavy with the scent of rain and night jasmine, now carried the fragrance of desire. Thick, luscious and intense as it swirled around them, binding them with invisible threads, whispering in their ears to get closer and closer still.

The pitter-patter of rain and their ragged breathing mingled with the low sounds coming from her throat, pushing him close to losing his reason.

A woman shrieked in laughter somewhere nearby, breaking into their passion-filled mind like a discordant note.

His head shot up, and he eyed her in shock.

Her eyes were half-closed, her lips pink and swollen, her head tilted back, exposing her nape, and her silver dress had slipped off one shoulder.

His eyes cleared, and he swiftly fixed her dress and her hair.

She blinked in confusion, and then her eyes widened in horror.

They were at the duke's home.

She had forgotten rules, propriety, and the room full of teeming guests. A kiss had intoxicated her so much that she had forgotten the world. She stared at him wide-eyed, and something like fear crawled up her spine.

How could anyone have the power to make her feel so much?

She stared at him, fingers pressed against her swollen lips. Had he been swept away, too? Had he been deluged with chaotic feelings as well? But he was an experienced man ... and while she had been unprepared... he had surely known what to expect.

Yet, she spotted the wild, shocked expression on his face mirroring her own before it was expertly concealed behind a mask.

She eyed the vein ticking on his forehead, the telltale Aristocrat ... and wondered if her husband was not as indifferent towards her as he claimed.

He seemed to go up in flames every time they kissed, skirting the edge of giving in entirely every time as if his control over himself was tentative around her, as if he held a handful of fine silk that began to slip out of his grip whenever he held her.

It made her wonder...

Could she hope for a loving married life after all?

Chapter Twenty-Seven

Dorothy's first thought the moment she woke up the next morning was that Huxley had not finished the song last night, and her next was that she should kiss him again.

It was the only way to confirm that it was the kiss that had made her feel so foggy and swimmy and not the champagne, the food, or the presence of Kitty and Lumley at the ball last night.

She crawled out of bed, went over to the dressing table and stared at herself in the mirror. Her cheeks were flushed. Other than that, she looked healthy.

Still, she would have to kiss him to know for certain that it was him and not the gumballs or the cheese wigs that had made her act so barmy. Now, all she had to do was find him alone, glue her lips to his and see what happened next.

An hour later, Dorothy was still in her bedchamber, with the remnants of pound cake, hot rolls and tea staring back at her accusingly. She had opted to eat her breakfast in her room since the prospect of running into Huxley made her feel awfully shy.

This went against her resolve to run into him and kiss him.

Lud! She was all muddled.

Blinker snatched the last of the rolls and sped out of the room to play with Rosie in the garden.

She watched him leave enviously. Ah, to be so young and have not a care in the world!

No more stalling, she scolded herself and took a deep breath, adjusted her cream muslin gown and stood up.

A heartbeat later, she was sitting down again, her skin flushed in embarrassment as the memory of last night blazed in her mind.

Forget kissing, how could she even face him?

It was the arrival of a few guests that forced her to move from the fainting couch and venture downstairs. She dealt with them, prepared baskets for some tenants who were ill, wrote a few letters and cuddled grumpy Blinker.

She also learnt that Miss March was expected for dinner. The prospect made her feel ill, but she drew up a splendid menu for the evening.

It was late in the afternoon when she ran into Huxley during her stroll in the garden. She quickly turned away, hoping he hadn't seen her. She wanted to kiss him, but not just yet. Perhaps, in a few days, weeks, or even months.

They were married and were bound to be together for a long time. And in the years to come, surely they would kiss again, and it didn't have to be her kissing him. He could take the initiative. Yes, in fact, he should be the one to kiss her—

"Dorothy," he called out.

She stopped but kept her head ducked and shadowed under the wide-brimmed bonnet.

"I—" He paused and cleared his throat. "You sent food for the tenants?"

Dorothy nodded.

"I see. The butler has been giving me tea and a bite to eat every morning when I wake up. I suppose you asked him to?"

"You wake up early, and it is still a good few hours before breakfast is ready. I ... I thought you may be hungry."

"My cigars had been ordered, the ink replenished, the snuff box filled... You don't have to think so much about my comforts—"

"I am your wife," she replied, finally lifting her head and showing him her lightly flushed cheeks and quivering lashes.

He stared at her, his expression uncertain.

Her heart broke a little. She realised no one had ever done anything for him before. It was always he taking care of his mother and sister, as well as the artists and servants. No one had ever paused to wonder what he wanted. Throughout his life, people had taken from him without ever thinking to give back.

"I am here to share half the burden," she reminded him gently. "You no longer have to do everything alone."

He gave a short nod, but his eyes were still wary.

She wanted to assure him that she only wanted to help. To ease some of his stress and take on some tasks that were unpleasant for him. Why did he feel no one would do anything for him without wanting anything?

Did he not know how wonderful he was?

She began walking back to the house, her thoughts heavy. His father had beaten him, his mother was dead, his stepmother didn't love him, and his sister was a spoilt, selfish child.

She stared up at the stone walls of Ansley Hall. Every single living being in the house respected and needed him, but how many of them truly loved him?

Dorothy had taken pains with her appearance tonight. She wanted Huxley's eyes on her and not Miss March, and she was hoping to lure him into kissing her again.

She took her place at the dining table and found Sophia's eyes on her.

Instead of the usual disdain in her face, Dorothy found … uncertainty.

"Did you want something?" Dorothy asked carefully.

Sophia hesitated for a moment and then got up and approached Dorothy's chair.

"May I?" Sophia asked, reaching towards Dorothy's hair, which was neatly coiled and pinned to the back of her head.

Dorothy forced herself not to flinch.

Sophia pulled a strand of hair from Dorothy's temple and another from beside her ear. She was gentle. She wrapped a strand around her finger and released, letting the ringlet float around Dorothy's face.

"That's better," Sophia remarked, gesturing towards the large Venetian mirror hanging on the wall.

Dorothy walked up to it and peered at herself. Her eyes widened in surprise. The curls framed her face in a rather pleasing fashion.

"I—" She stared at Sophia, at a loss for what to think.

"He didn't kiss Beth the night before your wedding," Sophia said, fiddling with a vase on the mantelpiece.

"Eh?"

"Miss March. He never kissed her. I saw her fling herself at him and attach her lips to his. He ... he pushed her away," she clarified.

Dorothy eyed her suspiciously, not ready to believe a word of it.

Sophia pressed on, "I heard you and Kitty. You protected me. I may not like you ... but a family stands up for one another. Huxley always says so ... and it seems you believe the same thing."

"I do." Dorothy eyed Sophia in a more favourable light.

The girl was fiercely loyal, first to her friend Miss March and then to her brother. She seemed to be the only person who genuinely loved Huxley, not solely for his wealth. She recalled how Sophia had stood up for him against her awful mother. She hoped that, in time, Sophia would come to see her as a sister too.

For now, this awkward gesture of apology and friendship warmed her heart.

"I am sorry for the way we married," Dorothy offered her own apology. "I did not plan it. I know it's hard for you to believe, but I... I wanted to marry Lord Lumley."

Sophia looked shocked and then sympathetic.

They walked back to the table, each rethinking the other's character. The next time Sophia looked her way ... she didn't smile, but then she didn't scowl either.

The dinner went far more pleasantly than Dorothy had thought possible. Her heart had lightened after learning that Huxley had never kissed Miss March. Miss March, meanwhile, tried her very best to insult Dorothy throughout dinner, but this time, Sophia tempered her friend's harsh words.

After dinner, Huxley retired to the library and asked not to be disturbed. Dorothy dragged her feet back to her room, sorry to leave Huxley's presence. The world felt dull and empty when he was not next to her.

∞∞∞

When she returned to her room, she found Blinker racing about pretending to be a horse and carriage.

"Hush," she begged in vain.

He simply leapt from the bed to the couch and back again, making loud clipping-clopping noises.

Dorothy wrung her hands in agitation. It was becoming increasingly difficult to keep the boy entertained and quiet.

"I got paint!" she suddenly exclaimed.

Blinker froze.

"Fresh pots. Would you like to see?"

Blinker grinned and raced after her into the parlour.

She pulled out the paint pots, a pencil and some paper and set them on the table.

Blinker immediately set to work.

"Would you like me to help you get ready for bed?" Rosie popped her head into the room.

"No," Dorothy waved her hand. She was busy showing Blinker how to keep the colour within the lines. "I will do it myself. Goodnight." She failed to notice Rosie's concerned look or Blinker's bored sigh.

Finally, fed up with being told what to do instead of being allowed to smear paint where he liked, Blinker leapt up. "I am going for a walk."

"It's midnight!" Dorothy gasped in panic.

"A walk," he said with a determined expression on his face, "is what I require."

Dorothy didn't have long to feel pleased with his gentlemanlike turn of phrase, for he shot out of the door.

Dorothy raced after him. "Blinker," she whispered as loudly as she dared. "Come back this moment, or I will have to tie you up in the dungeon."

He didn't respond.

Dorothy increased her pace, trying not to stomp down the corridor.

"No more pudding!" she hissed, "or paint. I will send you back to Gin Lane without a darned penny, you little rascal!"

She heard a rustle in the library and smiled in triumph. Now she had him. Ooh, the boy would be severely punished. He was becoming increasingly out of hand.

She slipped into the library. It was dark, and the dim torchlight from the hallway was creating shadows on the wall. She peered into the shadows and made out a figure. It was curled up on the chair facing an empty fireplace. She had the boy!

She leapt on top of the chair, landed on top of Blinker, and held tight. "I have you now, you wicked little monkey."

"Do you make a habit of strangling people in the dark?" Huxley asked.

She screeched.

"Please refrain from screaming in my ear," he begged.

"I," she pushed against his chest, trying to get up.

He held her fast. "What were you doing?"

Dorothy opened and closed her mouth like a fish. What was she to say?

"Who is the evil monkey?" he prompted.

"Thief!" she gasped. "I thought I heard a thief."

"Ah, and this thief would have surrendered on account of your promising to never give him pudding?"

Dorothy's eyes widened. He had heard that? What else had he heard?

He lit a candle lying next to him on the table and turned to look at her.

"I..." She squirmed in his grip.

"You have paint on your face," he said softly, his grip on her waist lightened not one bit.

"Here," he said, stroking her cheek. "And here," he ran a finger across her forehead. "It has dried. You will have to wash it off."

She nodded.

His hand lingered at the sensitive spot on her nape. His finger went back and forth a few times, almost as if he were caressing her.

Her heart began beating faster.

"I can't get it off," he said, suddenly pushing her away and setting her back on her feet.

He reached for a book and opened it.

"Goodnight," she squeaked after a few moments of silence.

He waved two fingers at her, but she was too agitated to take offence at it.

She rushed back to her room and found Blinker curled up on the chaise longue. She sighed in relief and moved to the mirror. She wet a flannel in the basin and scrubbed at her cheek and forehead. But when she reached her neck ... she found not a speck of paint.

Her eyes widened in realisation. There was no colour on her neck ... he had simply wanted to touch her some more.

And that knowledge changed something deep inside her. She decided that she wanted a proper marriage. Surely, if he desired her, he could love her. And even if he never fell in love with her ... they could still share the marriage bed. She touched her stomach ... to give him an heir. Her heart warmed at the thought of giving him a child ... his very own, who would make him smile and laugh, love him unconditionally and melt some of that coldness in his heart.

She no longer wanted to battle Huxley. She wanted to love him.

Chapter Twenty-Eight

Dorothy walked speedily down the hallway, feeling a bit wistful. Vowing to give her husband a dozen or so children was easy enough, but accomplishing the fact without looking like an unseemly wench was much harder.

She popped a wild strawberry in her mouth and chewed furiously. She had thought Huxley was not averse to the idea of thrashing about in hay with her, but lately, his actions perplexed her.

If she entered a room he was in, he shot out of it so swiftly that all she saw was a vague, blurred image of his fleeing breeches.

"Dorothy." He manifested before her as if her thoughts had yanked him over.

The hallway was narrow, and he tried to squeeze past her.

"I wanted to talk to you," she said, blocking his way.

"Yes?"

"What did you do today?"

He blinked at her question. "What did I do?"

"Yes, did anything of interest occur?"

He frowned. "As a matter of fact, I was reading the Quarterly Review. It had a passage from Lord Raikes speaking of his dealings with the officials of the East India Company. It was an interesting read, and he focused heavily on the religious and political differences between Africa, India, and England. He further expanded—"

"Don't expand," she cut in quickly.

"Eh?"

"I would rather hear your opinions than Lord Raikes'."

"I see."

"Well?"

He squinted thoughtfully. "You should eat more."

It was her turn to blink. "Eat more?"

"You look—" He scanned her from top to toe, searching for the right word.

"Ethereal?" she suggested.

"Shrivelled up. Like a fruit left in the sun too long."

She scowled. "I assure you, I am no thinner than most of the ladies of the ton."

"No one else looks this leathery," he grumbled. "Eat some more of those berries … and have a biscuit or two, or make that twenty. The number of times you swoon, deuced woman, is not normal."

She smiled warmly. "You are concerned for my health … for me."

"I am concerned that someone in my household is starving herself for the sake of fashion. I hope you haven't been subsisting on clear broth like the other ladies of the ton?"

"I am doing no such thing," she replied, seeing past his sarcasm. He was worried about her!

"Now, I need to return to work," he said, trying to ooze by her.

Again, she blocked him. "I am on my way to Mayfair. Would you like anything? More cigars?"

"I wrote down what I need … it should be on my desk," he said. "Take a maid and a footman with you."

She nodded.

"Don't attempt to save any little boys."

She smiled and shook her head.

"That's that," he said.

She watched him for a moment, trying to wriggle past her once again without touching her. She refused to help him. Instead, she asked mischievously. "Would you like to kiss me goodbye, husband?"

He took a step back, looking stunned. "Kiss?"

"Husbands kiss their wives goodbye."

"You shouldn't be saying these things. It's not seemly," he spluttered.

"I thought men liked kissing women."

He placed his hand on his ears, "Stop talking, stop bouncing on your toes ... I have to go. I need to see the steward."

She puckered her lips and batted her lashes.

He glared at her, muttered something about impudent hussies and stomped away, this time returning the way he had come.

She watched him stride away, filled with mixed emotions. She felt touched at his concern, and yet ... she didn't want him to think her so delicate. Is that why he refused to kiss her ... he thought she would break?

He was a large man ... perhaps he was afraid of his strength.

Still deep in thought, she made her way towards the rosewood desk in the small library and began rummaging through the sheets and tomes.

"What are you doing?" Woodbead's curious head poked out of the small door in the room.

"He said he left a list for me on the table," Dorothy replied without looking up.

"I wonder ... I wanted to ask," Woodbead spoke hesitantly.

"Yes?"

"I really shouldn't ask."

"No, do."

"Truly?"

"Yes, go on."

"You won't be offended?"

"Not one bit."

"Is your sister happy?"

"Celine? Yes, she loves Lord Elmer very much."

"Oh," he wilted gloomily.

Dorothy felt sorry for the fellow. His sigh had been pathetic.

It echoed the unhappiness of her unrequited love. She quickly did what should be done in such circumstances.

She changed the subject.

"Mr Woodbead, I am concerned about something."

"About your husband," he responded shrewdly.

She inclined her head. "He seems irresponsible about his safety. What if he is caught?"

"Ah, what if they find me and the contentious artworks?"

"Yes. Shouldn't he be more careful?"

"The Regent may be a jingle–brained, maggot-pated, puff guts, but he is a great patron of art. The royal coffers are already depleted, what with all the wars, and the Regent is eagerly emptying what is left of them. Your husband and the Regent share a similar love for artists, but the difference is that your husband can maintain his wealth. This common hobby finds the Regent often at your husband's doorstep, asking for a few pounds for his latest artistic venture."

"In short, he has the Regent's royal protection."

"The Regent who will soon be king. This is an important fact that people often forget when making a jest of the blue-blooded creature. Apart from that, Huxley has used his vast fortune to uncover some remarkably unpleasant secrets of politicians and influential aristocrats. Hence, he is universally loathed, feared and admired."

"I see," Dorothy said thoughtfully. It did sound like her husband was too powerful to be trifled with. It made her feel a bit better. She turned back to the desk and began hunting for the list again.

Woodbead coughed delicately into a green silk handkerchief. "Do you think when Celine visits you, I can waft in for a bit of chat?"

"Yes," Dorothy said distractedly. Her fingers had brushed over a newspaper, and she had found a thick lump concealed between the pages. She pulled it out and froze.

"I suppose I really should call her Lady Elmer," Woodbead continued. "But it doesn't roll off the tongue naturally. It stalls repeatedly ... a bit like a carriage lodging into numerous potholes—"

Dorothy heard no more. Her eyes were pinned on the envelope—a thick envelope addressed to Huxley and smelling of roses.

She carefully opened it and took out the sheets. It was from Diana, Huxley's mistress. Her face flamed as she read the contents. It was long, torrid and explicit ... it mentioned a lot of nibbling. Where he should nibble her and where she should nibble him sort of thing.

That man! She raged silently. He didn't kiss her because he didn't want to. It had nothing to do with her being delicate. Why this mistress, this famous opera actress, was just as fragile as her, if not more.

Tears pricked her eyes, and she dashed them away.

She would have her revenge.

If he could have fun ... then so could she. She would flirt at the ball tonight, wear her most scandalous dress and do the most unspeakable things. She would find a man, she vowed, and kiss him.

Any man.

"Oh dear, dear, dear," Woodbead warned belatedly. "You shouldn't have read that. You really, truly shouldn't have. I was going to stop you, but the artist in me rose and tied my tongue in knots. You see, your expressions were changing so swiftly, your skin turning all those lovely shades of blue, green and red, that ... I was enthralled. Enchanted. Entertained. Deep in my bones, I feel a poem coming on...."

The first person that Dorothy ran into at Lady Blake's ball was Kitty. She pasted a smile on her face and nodded briefly.

Kitty would have none of it. She caught Dorothy's hand as if nothing had ever gone wrong between them. "Isn't the chandelier marvellous? I have never seen one so big. And did you see Miss Chadwick? Her dress is outrageous. It looks like she is wearing nothing but flesh. From what I know, four women have already swooned."

Dorothy peered over Kitty's shoulder, desperately looking for her sisters to extract her from Kitty's clutch. "The duchess … is she here?" Dorothy muttered.

"I have not seen her today," Lord Lumley appeared next to them. "But I did see her yesterday at Lady Blueworth's dinner party."

Dorothy winced, wondering when he had procured such a booming voice. He looked a lot different, too. He had lost the emaciated look—his cheeks had filled out, and his belly was nicely rounded. He was clad in a beautifully tailored, gold-braided blue waistcoat, scarlet breeches and shiny buckle shoes that made her eyeballs sting.

"I even saw the duke," he continued, "and had a word with him. I told him how wonderful his ball had been. I was very firm on that point. No one knows how to throw a ball quite like him. But one little thing plagued me. I forgot to mention it to the kind Duchess, and you must do so on my behalf."

"Did someone cause a scandal?" Dorothy asked obligingly.

"The servants were smiling," he said disapprovingly. "I saw the butler bare his teeth at one point. Not something one would expect from the duke's household."

Dorothy stared at him.

"As for the food, the ices were melting."

"He does like things to be perfect," Kitty gushed.

Lord Lumley nodded in agreement. "If one must do something, then one must do it right. I was about to tell Lady Blake that this room is beautifully done up, but the lemonade … needs more lemons."

Dorothy eyed Lord Lumley in delight. She had never known a man could transform into something so despicable simply because he was a few pounds richer.

"I will convey your message to the Duchess when I see her,"

Dorothy grinned.

Lord Lumley puffed up even more with self-importance.

Dorothy saw the man's head expand rapidly, and it bothered her. It irritated her like fruit flies vexed her when they hovered over a bowl of perfectly ripe peaches. She wanted to take out her hatpin and jab him hard to wipe that smug look off his face.

She did the next best thing. She offered him a great big smile and said loudly, "Your neckcloth is marvellously crisp, sir, but a trifle crinkled."

And then she walked away, leaving him gasping and turning all shades of puce.

She knew nothing vexed an aspiring dandy more than having the condition of his neckcloth questioned. She chuckled quietly. It had been an awfully childish thing to do, but she hadn't been able to help herself.

He was just so … windy!

How had she ever imagined that she loved him? She shuddered at the thought of being married to the stiff-rumped Lord Lumley. To permanently turn a blind eye to his faults, smooth over his boastful words and placate offended guests sounded ghastly.

Her anger towards her friend thawed a bit, turning into pity at the edges.

She spotted Aron Selwyn near the refreshment table, and her thoughts changed course, becoming darker. Her shoulders drooped unhappily as the torrid letter Diana had written to Huxley blazed in her mind.

Her mouth tightened, and she pretended to knock her fan against Mr Selwyn's arm a tad more sharply than she had intended.

He turned apologetically and, noticing who it was, smiled in pleasure.

"Miss Fairweather … I mean, Lady Huxley," he bowed.

She curtseyed in return.

He took her arm, and they began strolling through the room. "I haven't seen your sisters tonight."

"I don't think they have arrived yet."

"The Fairweather sisters," he smiled down at her, "are a lovely lot. Each one is remarkable and uniquely fetching."

"Why, thank you," she replied, fluttering her lashes and then wondering if she was doing too much. She had lost the art of flirting since she married Huxley.

"Any more sisters hidden away in Finnshire?"

"You remembered the name of my village," she said, pleased. "None of marriageable age."

"How dreadful," he said, touching his heart. "Be gentle when you snatch away a man's hope."

She laughed at his absurdity.

He looked down at her and softly stroked the underside of her arm that he was holding. It was a delicate, secret brush of fingers that no one could possibly see, yet Dorothy's face flamed, and her heart began beating uneasily.

"Would you like to dance?" he asked.

His tone was different. She had never heard his speech so rough. The uneasiness returned, and she looked up into his pale face uncertainly. She had heard the implied question in his tone. Did she want to dance, or what?

"Dorothy," Huxley appeared by her side. "Our dance is about to begin."

Selwyn smiled charmingly and a little regretfully before relinquishing his hold on her.

Dorothy slipped closer to Huxley and gripped his arm.

"You will not argue with me for unceremoniously detaching you from Selwyn?" Huxley asked as they headed towards the dancing couples.

Dorothy waited until he had placed his hand on the small of her back before saying, "I am surprised to see you here. I thought you were not coming." She kept her eyes fixed on his shoulder.

He stepped away from her as they briefly switched partners, and when he came back, he changed the subject and kept up a string of mundane prattle.

She replied quietly, feeling subdued and miserable.

Once the dance was over, she escaped to the balcony. She needed to think. Selwyn had wanted to bed her. She was not so naïve as not to see it. And her staged approach had encouraged him.

But it was Huxley and the letter that played most deeply on her mind. She wanted to hurt Huxley as severely as he had hurt her.

She gripped the railing, feeling a wave of anguish that was almost physically painful.

"Are you ill?"

She hadn't heard her husband approach.

"Nay," she whispered.

He pulled her around to face him.

"You look ill," he said, brushing aside a ringlet and placing his palm against her hot cheek.

She couldn't help it. She closed her eyes and leaned into his touch.

He stilled.

The summer evening suddenly turned dense, and she had trouble breathing.

"So beautiful," he whispered, tilting her chin up.

Her eyes flew open, and she caught the blazing desire evident in his eyes.

He dipped his head and kissed her hard. A moment later, he flung her away, looking furious.

Tears pricked her eyes as she watched him stride away.

Was it so terrible to want to kiss your wife? What was holding him back?

Chapter Twenty-Nine

Penelope and Celine came to visit the following day.
Dorothy hugged them both longer and tighter than usual.

"Yes, well," Penelope grumbled, trying to straighten her hair to look more dignified after the hug. "We came to see the famous painting."

"The painting," Celine nodded firmly, "is what we came to see."

Dorothy soundly kissed their cheeks.

They pretended to be annoyed.

Dorothy patted the sofa. "You will see the painting right after you have some tea and these delicious cakes."

"Lord Huxley keeps you well," Penelope remarked, looking around the opulent room.

Celine nodded and wiped invisible crumbs off her lips. "Mrs Drew was asking Lady May how a man like Huxley could bear to be married to you since you tricked him so cruelly. He overheard her and told her that you did not do such a thing. The affection was mutual, and so was the decision to marry. That shut everyone right up."

"Well, we know it wasn't affection," Penelope said. "But it was good of him to say otherwise."

Dorothy nodded, her heart too full to speak.

The sisters sat in silence for a few moments. Penelope absently plucked at a tassel of a green silk cushion while Celine ran a finger around the rim of her teacup over and over again.

Dorothy watched them quietly.

Finally, Celine broke the silence, "I suppose you are well."

"I suppose I am," Dorothy replied in an equally flippant tone.

"Is he … your husband… as cruel as they say?" Penelope asked, forgetting to veil her concern.

"Didn't your spies tell you?" Dorothy asked innocently.

Her sisters gasped. "You know?"

"About the pirate, Tommy and Rosie?" Dorothy shrugged. "Aye, I do."

Penelope looked guilty for a moment, and then she let out a long sigh as if she had been holding her breath since the day Dorothy married Huxley. "Now that we know you know, we can stop this silly game. Hush, Celine, I have been trying to look morose in front of her for weeks. I can do it no longer."

"But—"

"No, Celine," Penelope cut her. "I cannot lurk on the borders of Blackthorne in this heat anymore, hoping to catch a glimpse of my sister." She turned to Dorothy, and the familiar, friendly warmth was back on her face. "I tried to get the Blackthorn servants to befriend the servants of Ansley Hall to get news of your welfare, but it didn't work. And as for Celine, she may protest all she wants, but I have seen her watch you at every gathering. She stares at your expressions, trying to determine if you need to be rescued from Huxley. Her eyes oscillate between you and all the escape routes in the room, waiting for Huxley to make one wrong move, and if he ever had, she would have bundled you into her carriage and taken you home."

"Yes, well," Celine thawed. "I … we were concerned."

"Huxley is wonderful," Dorothy said, her eyes shimmering. "You needn't have worried. If only you had asked—"

"Well, well, well," Celine's eyes widened. "You have gone and fallen in love with your husband. How awfully unfashionable and, yet, just the thing for a Fairweather to do."

Penelope sat up in her seat in delight. "Oh, it's true! I can see it in your face, Dora."

Dorothy looked from one sister to another and finally

shrugged. "I don't think so."

"Do your toes curl when he comes close to you?" Penelope asked. "That is love."

"Try imagining a carriage hurtling towards Huxley and someone else you care about. Who do you want to save first?" Celine queried. "If you choose Huxley, then you are in love."

"Do you tremble like a blade of grass on a breezy day when he holds your hand?" Penelope sighed.

"Or do you feel like you have run into a stone wall every time he kisses you, and your vision goes dark like a starry night?" Celine prompted.

"Love, love, love," Penelope and Celine sang, "we wonder if you are in love at laaaast!"

Dorothy frantically shook her head.

"Do you shake, and do you shiver?" Penelope warbled. "Does he make you all aquiver?"

"Do you smile like a loon?" Celine trilled. "When he enters the room?"

"Do you chuckle at his every word," the butler crooned from the doorway, "Even when they are badly slurred?"

They all screeched together, "Love, love, love, our little Dora is in love at laaaast!"

"I am not," Dorothy scowled.

"I think you love him," Penelope said firmly.

"I concur. She has that addlepated look of a woman in love," Celine agreed.

"Have you forgiven me?" Dorothy asked abruptly. She was tired of being scrutinised like a novel insect.

Penelope stared down at her lap. "I had forgiven you the very next day of your wedding and, thereafter, fretted about you staying here in Ansley Hall."

"I am well, truly," Dorothy assured her.

"And happy?" Penelope asked a little apprehensively.

"You didn't have to stay angry with me for so long," Dorothy grumbled. "And I know it was Celine who kept you away."

"Well, now," Celine frowned. "You need to learn discipline."

"And you need to learn to be more tractable," Dorothy snapped back. "And to make it up to me, you must spend this afternoon with someone special."

"Who?" Celine asked.

"Me," Philbert Woodbead squeaked apologetically from the door.

"Oh, dear lord," Celine paled. "Not him."

"I have a poem I would like you to hear," Woodbead said shyly. "I wrote it for you ... on a pair of brown breeches. For old times' sake."

Penelope burst into peals of laughter, and Dorothy smiled. It was good to have her sisters back.

∞∞∞

Dorothy felt like a wave, ebbing and flowing, rising and falling on a stormy summer day. One moment she was pleased that her sisters were speaking to her again and all had been forgiven, and the next she recalled that horrid Diana and her letter.

"You shouldn't have set Woodbead loose on your sister like that," Huxley said.

Dorothy continued to walk up the stairs.

"Are you listening?" he asked testily. "I am speaking to you, my lady."

"I am speaking to you, my lady," Dorothy mimicked under her breath. "Bah! Bloody fathead."

"What did you say?"

"I said I am tired."

"You called me a sapskull."

"Nay, I called you a fathead."

"Ha! I knew it."

"Hmmph."

"You have been acting peculiar," he said patiently. "Are you angry with me?"

"No."

"Come, don't be childish."

"I want to go to sleep."

He stared up at her, his eyes full of questions. When she refused to say anymore, he said coldly, "I will leave you alone then. Sweet dreams, sleep well."

"And I hope you are plagued with dreams of Diana turning into a scruffy teapot," Dorothy whispered under her breath and fled to her rooms.

Hours later, she burrowed deeper into the pillow and stared at the ceiling. She couldn't see anything since the candle had died out long ago, but she knew that in the light of the day, she would see a beautiful painting edged in gold of sleeping angels and puffy clouds.

She rolled over to face the wall. She couldn't sleep. All she could think of was Diana the teapot.

A small hand nudged her shoulders.

"Blinker?" She sat up and lit the candle on her bedside table.

"I want to show you sumffin," Blinker grinned.

"You should be in bed!"

"I made sumffin for you," he insisted.

She sighed and teetered towards the adjoining parlour room.

"Ack!" she gasped.

Blinker had decided to paint a beautifully carved antique table in vivid blue, green and yellow colours.

"I made it for you," he said, pointing at the monstrosity with a shy smile.

She was horrified and touched at the same time.

"How ... wonderful," she smiled weakly.

"I think I am going to paint the doors next," he mused.

"No! It's late. You can do what you like in the morning."

"I am not sleepy."

"Put the brush down," she begged him again in an exhausted voice. "You are dripping paint all over the silk cushions!"

It was a mistake. Blinker, Dorothy had learned, hated being

told what to do. And if one insisted, then he either decided to go for a stroll, no matter the hour or decided to hide.

He opted for the latter today.

"I am going to hide," he announced, coming to a standstill near the door. "Come find me."

"No!" she squealed in fright, but it was too late. Blinker was out of the room and racing down the hallway.

She quickly threw on a robe and snuck out of the room. She had to be careful. The best way to capture Blinker was to sneak up on him.

She crouched low, hiding in the shadows of the dying candles.

She crawled forward on her hands and feet, trying to listen for his footsteps.

All she could hear was a candle sputtering somewhere close by.

Moonlight streamed in through the windows in bars of translucent silver, and a soft draught of air trickled in from somewhere, cooling her warm neck.

She closed her eyes, thinking rapidly. If she called out to Blinker, he would only run harder. She had to be sneaky. She had to pretend she was a wolf and he was a swift little rabbit that she had to capture. She would have to be soft-footed, lurk in the dark, and attack when he would least expect it.

She hid a yawn and rubbed her tired eyes. How did her sisters manage all those children? Here, this one child was making her as nutty as a fruitcake!

Thud!

She froze. She had heard something.

She crawled down the hallway as fast as she could manage and paused at the top of the stairs.

There! A step creaked loudly.

She took a deep breath and lay down flat on her stomach. Next, she began slithering her body down the stairs like a snake. This, she thought, was ingenious. Blinker would never spot her in the darkness.

She quelled an urge that suddenly rose within her to howl like a wolf. A few moments more, and she would capture her wilful rabbit.

She chuckled soundlessly at the thought and slid down a few more steps.

"What are you doing?" Huxley's voice boomed up the stairs.

She bit her lip and stared at the carpeted step grazing her nose.

"I am not going to let you escape without an answer this time. That is a highly peculiar position." He stood at the bottom with a candle held aloft in one hand and his mouth open in astonishment.

She swallowed nervously, at a loss for how to explain why she was slithering down the stairs on her stomach instead of walking down like a normal human being.

"Err, I am not sure." That was the best she could do.

"Do you know your name?" he asked.

"I haven't lost my memory."

"If not your memory, then your marbles," he muttered. "Are you going to remain in that position the entire night? Surely, it is uncomfortable. Stand up and explain yourself."

Crash!

Dorothy's head whipped up towards the stairs.

"It came from the hallway," Huxley said, taking two steps at a time.

"A thief," Dorothy replied, gripping his hand as he moved to pass by her. "I heard something and thought it was a thief, and that is why I was slithering down the stairs."

"And that would have helped you catch the thief? Let me go; the man will escape!"

"No, the thief may kill you. He must be frightening. Do not leave me. I am terrified," she babbled, hoping to give Blinker time to escape to her room.

He made an impatient sound, extracted her fingers and hurtled down the hall.

Dorothy followed resignedly.

They arrived at the place where the Aëdon was hanging.

Dorothy sighed in relief. Nothing had happened to his precious art.

And then Huxley brought the candle closer to the painting, and they both stilled.

Dorothy stared at the Aëdon and gulped. She leaned forward, narrowed her eyes and looked again and was unhappy to note that what hung before her was still the Aëdon painted by the famous recluse Raziel.

"It has a—" he gasped.

"Oh dear," she squeaked.

"I am not dreaming?" he asked.

"You could be?" she offered in an overly bright voice.

"I am not dreaming," he said, pinching himself. "The woman … Aëdon has a moustache."

"And squiggly flowers in the poison pot," Dorothy replied nervously. "An odd sort of thief."

He leaned his head against the wall and let out a low moan, followed by terrifying gasps and gurgles.

"It's a lovely moustache," she soothed him. "Full and dark."

He continued to gurgle.

"See, it turns up at the corners," she added hurriedly. "A proper moustache, a little crooked but … admirable."

He shuddered and shook alarmingly.

Concerned, she placed a hand on his shoulders and turned him around.

There were tears in his eyes … tears of laughter.

"You have gone mad!" Her hand flew to her mouth.

"That boy of yours," he said amid splutters, "I knew he was trouble."

"You know about Blinker?" she asked in shock.

He wiped his eyes. "I don't know why you tried to hide him. I adopt artists, and you adopt orphans. You and I are not so different."

"Children make noise. They can't be controlled," she replied. "You don't like noise."

He looked back at the painting thoughtfully, the smile not yet faded from his lips. "Artists are moody too, and controlling them would be restricting their creativity. Have you ever heard a painter bawl in frustration? And the sculptors with their constant chipping at stones, musicians on a bad day …. Children run around, artists dance around, children howl and cry, artists wail and shriek."

He took a step closer to her. Now, the candle's golden light illuminated her face, leaving the painting in shadows once again. "You draw the line and hope they stay within limits, but occasionally they, too, break the rules. We are the same at our core, Dora. I want to help starving artists, and you want to help hungry orphans. We both feel the same compassion."

"But this painting … Blinker ruined it."

Huxley softened. "He has changed the painting. The fear in her eyes now appears dramatic … unbelievable. She is now a comical actress; the tragedy is lost. The painting made me restless before … that was the beauty of it. Now, it makes me smile, and in that, I see beauty too."

He took another step closer.

She gulped. "Err, can it be restored?"

He leaned forward, his shoulder brushing her arm. He dripped wax on the ledge, jutting out from the wall behind her head, and glued the candle in place. "Raziel will be here in a few days. I think he can restore it. But … I am not sure I want him to."

"Want to what?" she asked dazedly. She stared at the dark shadow on his cheek and the tiny freckle under his right eye. She placed her hands on the wall behind her to brace herself.

He shifted his weight, and she watched the muscles ripple under his thin blue robe. Her eyes strayed to the rope tied at his waist.

"What are you thinking?" he asked huskily.

"Are you wearing anything underneath?" she spoke without thinking.

His eyes widened, and his muscles tensed. "You want to

seduce me," he accused in a mocking tone.

She bobbed her head up and down. "Take advantage of your vulnerability."

His lips turned up in a half-smile. "I am no innocent."

She boldly cupped his cheek; the rough stubble grazed her palm, making her toes curl. "Prove it," she whispered.

In a trice, she was pinned against the wall, his body pressing into every feminine curve and hollow.

"Your head barely reaches my shoulders," he observed softly.

He was too big, she thought. He was engulfing her from all sides. His scent was heady, his warm breath almost unbearably sweet on her sensitive nape.

She felt his strength in every sinew of his body, and yet the hands circling her wrists were gentle.

Her chest rose and fell; breathing became difficult. She felt like the tightened strings of a violin; her body tensed to an extent where she felt as if she would break any moment.

His thumb grazed her lips. "Did I prove it?"

"Hmm?" Her lips parted in anticipation.

He chuckled softly and stepped away.

She stared at him in confusion.

"Go to bed," he said gently.

Her eyes widened in indignation. He was not going to leave her without a kiss.

He had no time to prepare before she leapt into his arms, wrapped her legs around his waist and glued her lips to his.

Propriety and rules be damned. She wanted this kiss, and she was going to get it.

He froze for only a moment before he kissed her back just as desperately as she was kissing him.

"I can't," he groaned into her hair.

She gripped his robe, trying to get as close to him as possible. Every inch of fabric between them felt like an unwanted barrier. She reached down and tugged the rope at his waist.

"I say," Woodbead coughed apologetically. "Am I interrupting?"

Dorothy turned a blazing eye towards the poet. "Are you interrupting?" she growled low in her throat. "Are you?" Her voice rose in pitch.

"I heard a noise. Came to save Huxley. Can't have him dead now—"

"When you saw he was well, why didn't you slink away?" she hissed.

Woodbead took a hasty step back. "I should go. You see, I feel —"

"A poem coming on?" she cut in. "Not yet, Mr Woodbead. You can write your poem once I am done with you." She extracted herself from Huxley's embrace and yanked a spear from armour nearby. She had not even had a glimpse of bare skin before Huxley had tightened his robe, and for that, Woodbead would pay.

She charged.

Huxley caught her around the waist, and she flailed in mid-air.

Woodbead took the hint and fled.

"Despicable, horrid, frosty-faced villain," she howled after him. "I will feed you boiled trotters from now on. No more apple pudding! Do you hear me, you interrupting cad!"

"Hush, people are sleeping," Huxley dropped his hands from her waist.

She trembled on her feet, still furious but quiet.

He gave her a moment to compose herself and said, "This must not happen again."

She jerked her chin up. "My attempt to kill the unlaundered poet or—"

"Neither," he warned.

Dorothy watched his angry back disappear into the shadows, wondering who he was angry with.

Her or himself?

Chapter Thirty

Dorothy braced herself and knocked on the connecting door.

The door swung open almost immediately, and Huxley stood before her in the same lush, blue robe he had on last night.

"I–" Dorothy swallowed the sudden lump in her throat.

Huxley clutched the lapels of his robe closer together and peered at her suspiciously.

"I am not going to pounce on you again," Dorothy hissed. Loudly, she added, "Someone would like to apologise." She moved aside to let Blinker come into view.

Blinker looked up at Huxley with round, fearful eyes. "Sorry, sir, for rooning Eggon."

"He means the painting," Dorothy clarified.

Huxley stared down at the tiny boy and shifted from foot to foot. He darted a helpless look at Dorothy.

"Don't throw Dora out," Blinker continued. "It was my fault. You can send me back to Gin Lane."

Dorothy teared up at his words. She had only asked him to apologise and never thought he was concerned about her.

Huxley looked deeply uncomfortable. Clearly, he had never dealt with anyone less than four and a half feet tall. He finally said, "You both can stay. I am glad you acknowledged your mistake. It shouldn't happen again."

"It won't," Blinker swore. "I won't even give the 'orned devil in the 'allway a flower crown. I am awfully tempted to do so, but I won't."

"Good, good," Huxley said gruffly.

"Nor will I fill all those funny vases around the 'ouse with the leftovers from my dinner," Blinker continued eagerly.

Huxley turned a trifle green.

"And the statue in the Greek garden—" Dorothy placed a hand over Blinker's mouth.

"He won't ruin anything anymore. No paintings, vases, statues, tapestries, nothing," she promised on his behalf.

Blinker bobbed his head in agreement.

Huxley eyed the two of them warily for a moment. "I trust you," he said, looking not at all trusting. "I had better get dressed."

Once Huxley left, Dorothy patted a subdued Blinker on the back. "You did well."

Later that day, Rosie burst into the family room.

"Blinker has refused to eat his pudding," she announced.

"He did what?" Dorothy slammed the quill on the table and shot to her feet.

"Refused the pudding," Rosie confirmed. "Apple, it was too."

"Was it burnt?"

"Creamy and sweet and perfectly cooked."

"Is he flushed? Feverish?" Dorothy asked, speeding down the hall.

Rosie shook her head. "I think his liver is depressed. Missing the gin, I reckon."

"His liver is doing no such thing," Dorothy snapped. She entered the parlour and found Blinker lying on the sofa, looking gloomy.

"What is it?" Dorothy asked.

"Gin," Rosie said.

"Nuffin," he responded, but his lips trembled.

"Is it the gin?" Dorothy forced the words out.

He shook his head.

"Whiskey?" Rosie asked.

Dorothy ignored her maid. "Are you missing your mother?"

"No."
"I see. Would you like to visit her?"
Blinker nodded.
"Your mother never scolded you, did she?"
Blinker shook his head.
"And when I did this morning—
"I didn't like it much," he confessed.
"If you do as I say, I won't scold you."
"I don't like doing what you say much either."

She chuckled and led him to the bed for his afternoon nap. "When you are all grown up, you will realise that what I am telling you to do is for your own good."

He scowled in response.

She smoothed his forehead until the lines disappeared. She recalled the song Huxley always sang to soothe her. Perhaps if she changed it a bit, she could soothe Blinker, too?

So, she climbed into bed next to Blinker and began to sing,

> Good night, my lassie, my sweet, sweet lassie,

Blinker's eyes flew open, "I am not a lassie!"

"Oh, hush and close your eyes," she said and began the song again.

> Good night, my lassie, my sweet, sweet lassie
> Let the world fade away.
> Think of sorbets and soufflés,
> Blue lilies and sea sprays.
> Of windows and doorbells,
> And green trees and bluebells.
> Good night, my lassie, my sweet, sweet lassie
> Let the world fade away.

"Think of dames with red rashes and maids with no lashes?" Blinker sat up.

"Of Miss March and her twitches and Miss Gray and her

itches?" Dorothy giggled.

"Think of them scratching." She leapt out of bed, "Of all of them matching."

"And dancing all funny," he caught her hand and twirled. "Allll daaay. Hurrayyy!"

"Lawks! That was beastly rotten," Rosie moaned in a sing-song voice, "Beastly rotten it was."

"Good lord! The sun has not even risen," Penelope groaned.

"It has. The duke is already at his desk; Celine is in the morning room. Wake up," Dorothy tugged Penelope's braid.

"Wake in an hour," Penelope groaned.

Dorothy whipped the curtains aside, letting the sun stream in.

Penelope dug her head further into the pillow.

"Please," Dorothy begged. "It's urgent."

Penelope opened one red eye and groaned in resignation.

Dorothy's shoulders sagged in relief. She handed her sister a cup of tea and headed to the morning room, where Celine waited.

The table was already laden with steaming pots of tea, coffee, chocolate, cakes and biscuits, but no one felt particularly hungry this early morning.

"What is it?" Penelope blearily stumbled into the room and knocked over a vase. She had thrown a robe over a nightgown and was barefoot.

"Sit," Dorothy patted the cushion.

Penelope sank into the sofa and squinted at the shiny silver teapot as if trying to move it with the power of her mind.

"It's to do with Huxley," Celine guessed shrewdly.

Dorothy nodded. "I need your help. I want to know how to seduce my husband."

"Gack," Celine choked on her tea.

"Wonderful," Penelope replied, stifling another yawn.

"You mean you want to know what happens when men and women are in bed," Celine asked in horror.

Dorothy clicked her tongue impatiently. "Oh, I have seen enough sheep and horses to know that. What I want to know is how to get him into bed?"

"An excellent question," Penelope said.

"That is unseemly," Celine spluttered.

"Unseemly or not, you will help me?" Dorothy asked.

"Of course I will," Celine replied, affronted. "I adore unseemly things."

"Likewise," Penelope said.

"How do I begin?" Dorothy leaned forward in her seat.

"Kiss him," Penelope suggested.

"I have. He always pulls away," Dorothy moaned.

"What an odd thing to do. Men adore kissing women," Celine mused. "Did you try wearing a scandalous gown?"

"Leaned forward to present your bosom to your best advantage?" Penelope asked.

"Flirted with your fan?" Celine wondered.

"Showed him a bit of ankle?" Penelope sighed.

"Wriggled your bottom when you walked," Celine queried.

"Peeked at him seductively?" Penelope demanded.

"I have done it all!" Dorothy said. "I know he desires me; I see it in his face." She blushed. "I know he has had mistresses in the past and perhaps still has them … so his … err—"

"Go on," Penelope encouraged.

Dorothy blushed harder. "You know that poor sheep we had in Finnshire who couldn't mate."

"We had named him Beau," Celine recalled.

"Then Father killed him, and we ate it, and it was only later that he told us we had eaten our beloved pet," Penelope said dreamily.

"We all cried," Dorothy said. "I wondered if perhaps … Huxley—"

"Ah, you wonder if he is like the sheep," Celine grinned.

"Well, he is not."

"How do you know?" Dorothy demanded.

"We know," Penelope replied guiltily, "because when it became clear that you would have to marry the man, I set my dear bosom friend, Jimmy, the highwayman, also known as the Falcon, the task of finding out all he could about Huxley."

"George asked the pirates and did a little nosing, too," Celine added.

Dorothy's mouth fell open. "I thought you had only set the pirate and Tommy loose on Ansley grounds! You had my husband investigated, too?"

"We couldn't let you marry a man who could have been abusive, a criminal, dangerous—" Penelope retorted in indignation. "We were angry, Dorothy, but we still loved you. We can't help it. However vexing you are, we have no choice but to love you."

"What did Jimmy find out?" Dorothy leaned forward eagerly. "Tell me everything quickly."

Celine pulled out her knitting. "The best way to find out a man's true self is through his mistresses, clubs he frequents, friends he keeps and the way he treats his servants—"

"And? Penny! What did Jimmy say?" Dorothy groaned impatiently.

"Jimmy happens to be visiting. Let him tell you himself," Penelope said, ringing the bell.

Jimmy 'The Falcon' arrived in his cape and mask. He took them off out of respect for the ladies present and bowed low.

"Dorothy wants to know what you found out about Huxley," Penelope said, gesturing to the empty seat beside her.

Jimmy turned pink and took the offered chair. "Err, this sort of thing is rather unseemly. You are like my sister, and to speak so bawdily—"

"Oh, hush. Celine and I have produced a dozen children between us. We know all about this sort of thing. Speak freely."

Jimmy stared at his shoes. "Huxley," he cleared his throat and continued, "never slept with unmarried women or genteel women. Never visited brothels. The man has working bits. Very fine working bits. His mistresses were sorry to see him go. The clubs respect him for his honesty in cards, and his friends are loyal."

"It was very sweet of you to find all that out," Dorothy patted his hand.

Jimmy smiled. "If it weren't for Penelope, I wouldn't have gotten my wife back."

"The falcon dance," Penelope recalled fondly. "You won her over with the falcon dance."

"How did it go?" Celine asked. "Bob, flap, flap, bob flap, flap."

"No, it was thus," Jimmy responded. "Bob, flap, bob, flap. Bob, bob."

"Bob your head a tad bit more and flap harder," Penelope added.

They all bobbed and flapped correctly for a few moments.

Jimmy eyed Penelope in admiration. "How do you think of such things?"

Penelope cast her eyes down modestly. "It comes to me naturally."

"About Huxley," Dorothy reminded them apologetically. "Is there anything else I should know?"

Celine lifted her head from the knitting. "He travelled abroad for a few years. George had asked the pirates about it. Huxley led a wild life but was by no means cruel."

"None of this helps," Dorothy threw up her hand. "What you are telling me is that Huxley is a good man. I know that! But it doesn't help me seduce him."

The Falcon swooned at this pronouncement.

"Men are so delicate," Celine tsked.

"Have patience," Penelope soothed. "Love will bloom, and you will come together when the time is right. It will be like spring ... everything will fall into place, and love will blossom into a beautiful flower scented with romance, passion, and joy."

"Wear a thin muslin dress and fall into a pond," Celine said practically. "He is bound to notice you then."

Chapter Thirty-One

Dorothy stood on the edge of the artificial pond. It was early. The sun had just popped up and not even begun to take the chill out of the air. Blinker was fast asleep, none of the gardeners were about, and the servants were busy preparing the house for the day.

She fingered her thin white muslin dress and shivered in the cold. She prayed Huxley would arrive quickly. She knew he walked this way daily to greet some of his tenants.

She side-eyed the pond. It looked deep and cold. She had already positioned a rock near the edge. Everything was ready.

Her maid suddenly turned and gestured frantically.

Ah, Huxley was almost here. It was time.

She tilted her face to the sun, forced a smile on her frozen lips and began walking towards the lake.

She heard his footsteps slow and stop behind her. Pretending not to hear him, she floated forward like an ethereal creature who was one with nature.

And just as she had planned in her head, she struck her ankle with enough force to make her wince in genuine pain, and then she let out a gentle screech and plummeted into the pond.

When she popped her head back up, Huxley was eyeing her curiously.

She swam towards the edge of the pond, intending to emerge from the blue-green lake like a beautiful nymph, shaking off the droplets while letting his eyes feast on her figure, clad in a soaking, transparent muslin dress.

And once he had seen her … his love would bubble up, and he would shed his inhibitions and sweep her up in his arms and nibble her like he had nibbled that Diana—

A loud shriek on her right broke her reverie.

Her maid, her dear, dear maid, Rosie, unwrapped her shawl and flung it over Dorothy's shoulders the moment she began to surface.

"You will catch yer death," Rosie scolded.

Dorothy's shoulders drooped.

"And look at the dress," Rosie continued. "Why, it's transparent. I saved yer modesty."

Dorothy limped out of the water and shook herself like a disgruntled dog. She had not wanted her modesty saved, and it was beastly of her maid to try and protect it so thoroughly.

She caught Huxley trying not to laugh.

She glared at her maid and him before stomping back to the house.

Dorothy picked at her dinner that evening. Huxley had not joined them. She wondered if he was dining out and with whom. Was he meeting Diana? Her heart squeezed in dread at the thought.

This seduction business was not going as planned. She wished she were a siren, a dangerous mermaid who could lure men to their deaths by merely sprawling on a rock. A succubus who could enthral men with her beauty and capture their souls. A beautiful witch who could whip up a love spell in a trice … alas, she felt as seductive as the salted eel on her plate.

After the disaster at the lake, she had tried to flash her ankle at her husband in the library. She had subtly rustled her skirts, kicked the dress harder than usual when walking, and let out a delicate shriek while pretending to have twisted her ankle.

He had ignored all her attempts until she had given up all guise, planted herself in front of him, hiked up her skirts, and showed him both her bare ankles.

He had laughed and laughed and laughed.

Not a response she had expected. Her sisters had assured her that a bit of bare ankle always excited men.

Instead of excitement, her husband had been tickled. Tickled into uncontrollable laughter.

It left her wondering if her ankles were frightful. Were they too fat or too slim? What did an attractive ankle look like?

She peeked under the table to inspect the offending part once more. It looked just the same as anyone else's—bony and unremarkable.

Perhaps Diana's ankle was pearly and fragile and tender with gossamer wings....

She stabbed the mushroom in anger, sending the vegetable flying across the room until it hit the wall at the opposite end of the room.

No one noticed. The dining room seemed to have lost its vitality with Huxley's absence. Everyone looked dull, the conversation lagged, and even the candles seemed dimmer.

Dorothy watched the mushroom slowly and sadly slide down the wall. She knew just how it felt.

"Where is Lord Huxley?" one of the guests finally asked, expressing what was on most people's minds.

"In his rooms," Sophia said.

"How is he now?" Lady Huxley asked, gesturing towards the salt.

"How is the salt?" Dorothy frowned.

Lady Huxley laughed like it was the wittiest thing she had heard all year. "No, I meant my stepson. How is he now?"

"He was ill this afternoon," Sophia clarified. "He is no better, mother."

Dorothy pushed her plate away. "I wasn't informed."

"I didn't want to worry you," Lady Huxley said, sipping her wine. Her intent was clear. Dorothy may have taken control of the servants, but as long as she was around, Huxley was her and her daughter's responsibility.

"I am his wife. I should have been informed," Dorothy snapped, uncaring of the shocked faces around her.

"I am sorry, I thought you knew," Sophia said, looking distressed.

"A man wants his mother, not his wife, when he is ill," Lady Huxley shrugged. "He ate something funny. Nothing to bother your little head about."

"His mother," Dorothy said, standing up on trembling feet, "is dead." She strode out of the room as quickly as she could without breaking into a run.

"Where is he?" she demanded of the valet.

"In his room, I think it was something he ate," the valet replied.

She hurtled up the stairs, not waiting to hear more. She barged into Huxley's room and raced to his side.

He lay on the bed, his face ashen with droplets of sweat beading his forehead. She gently wiped them away using the edge of her dress.

"I thought I told you to stay away from my room. I knew you had unseemly thoughts about me. And now you have arrived to take advantage of my weakness," he said, tugging the quilt up to his chin with a smile.

She didn't smile back. He looked extremely ill.

Deathly ill.

Her hands shook as she placed them on his forehead. He was burning up.

"Something you ate?" she asked with a tremor.

"What if it isn't? You shouldn't come near me. Could be catching," he said, turning his head away.

She leaned over and kissed his forehead to show what she thought of his suggestion.

He closed his eyes and didn't respond. Nor did he move away.

"I will be back," she promised and charged out of the room.

"Has the physician been called?" she demanded of the butler.

The butler nodded. "Came in the afternoon. Said it was something he ate."

"Was it poison?" Dorothy snapped.

"He didn't say," the butler replied apologetically.

"Why wasn't I informed?"

"Lady Huxley told us not to say anything to you. Didn't want to worry you, she said."

Dorothy wanted to scream in frustration. Instead, she squared her shoulders and decided to take charge.

Firstly, it was to find a physician she could trust.

"Get the carriage ready," she begged. "And after that, stay with my husband or outside his room until I return. Don't leave him alone, not for a moment."

The butler softened and nodded.

Dorothy left for Blackthorne Mansion as soon as the carriage was ready.

"Penny," she wailed, racing into her sister's bedchamber.

Penelope opened a sleepy eye. "Is it morning already?"

"No, it's almost midnight."

"Where is the duke?"

"He was coming up to join you. He escaped to the library when he spotted me racing up the stairs."

"What are you doing here?"

"Huxley is ill."

Penelope shot up in bed. "Is he dying?"

Dorothy paled.

"I am sure he is not," Penelope soothed hastily. She leapt out of bed and flung on a robe. "Go home, stay with him. I will haul the physicians out of their beds if I have to and send them across to Ansley Hall within two hours."

"Physicians?"

"One will not be sufficient. You need at least two to examine him and a third to examine you. You look ready to swoon any moment."

∞∞∞

Four hours later, Dorothy was pacing Huxley's room. The physicians had confirmed her fears.

Huxley was deathly ill.

One of the young doctors had agreed to stay overnight in case Huxley took a turn for the worse. She had put him up in the next room. As to what the matter was with her husband, the doctors couldn't decide.

Huxley mumbled something in his sleep.

Dorothy jumped out of her skin. She still wasn't used to his delirious mumblings. He had called her name a few times ... but she couldn't be certain if it were a moment of lucidity since he fell back to intelligible mumbling shortly after.

It was one of the most frightening nights of her life.

At around two in the morning, the artists started trickling in. One by one, they came to ask about Huxley. Dorothy could not help but see the genuine concern and love they had for him.

No one slept that night except Lady Huxley.

The staff, Sophia, painters, sculptors, and musicians kept Ansley Hall lit with candles burning in their rooms. A few restless folks headed towards the gardens, and every time Dorothy peeked out of the window, she could see the comforting light of bobbing lamps as people strolled by.

How had she ever thought no one loved her husband? He was admired, respected and needed by far more people than she ever would be. If only he were awake and well enough to see it all....

At some point in the night, she fell asleep sitting on the floor with her head lying on his bed.

A light touch on her hair woke her a few hours later.

It was morning, and Huxley was lucid and staring at her. He looked better, still grey, but some colour had begun returning to his face.

She leapt up and wiped the sleep from her eyes. "You were ill last night," she informed him.

He grunted in response.

"Did you—Would you like me to inform anyone of your illness?" she asked, avoiding his eye. It was a question that had been plaguing her all night.

"Eh?"

"Would you like anyone particular to come and see you?" she insisted.

"What do you mean?" he rasped.

"Diana," she blurted out. She was exhausted from worrying about him, constantly thinking about his mistress and wondering if he wanted her by his side when he could be dying. She was tired of secrets and unspoken things between them.

"Diana?" he asked, looking confused. It took him a moment to realise who she meant. "The Opera actress? Why would she come and see me? Is she going to sing me back to health?"

"Don't you love her?"

"I think you were the one who was ill last night," he said grumpily. "Are you certain you didn't catch what I have?"

"I think not."

He licked his dry lips and eyed her disbelievingly.

She gave him a glass of water, which he drank thirstily, followed by a spoonful of medicine. He gulped it down and then looked surprised at himself.

"Dr Johnson said you need to take this tonic every four hours. You need to stay in your room and sleep as much as you can," she said, fluffing his pillows. "I am going to go get breakfast and send Dr Brown up to look at you. He stayed overnight, so be kind to him."

"How many doctors did you call?"

"Not enough," she muttered. "They couldn't even make up their minds as to what was wrong with you, what to dose you with and whether you would recover at all." Her voice shook at the last bit, and she quickly turned her face away.

"I will be back," she threatened before asking Sophia to mind her brother.

At noon, she stormed back into the room.

She caught him pushing his hand through his coat, preparing to begin work for the day.

She walked over, took the coat from him, and put it back in the cupboard. Then she took the medicine bottle, poured some of the contents into the spoon, and turned towards him.

"I am not—" he began.

She popped the spoon into his open mouth before he could finish.

Next, she picked up the sheets of paper strewn across the bed and placed them on the mantle.

"If he attempts to leave the room or refuses to take his medicines," she told the shocked valet, "come and get me. I will be in my room."

Two hours later, she was back in the room.

He crossed his arms and eyed her stubbornly. The papers were once again strewn across the bed.

She picked them up and handed them over to the valet. "You can leave now."

"I want the papers," he ordered the valet.

"Leave," Dorothy ordered him right back.

The valet stood looking torn.

"I have to work on some important matter," Huxley snapped.

"He needs to rest, or he will die. Do you want him to die?" Dorothy asked.

The valet shook his head frantically and quickly left the room.

She rounded on Huxley, "Take the medicine and go to sleep."

"You cannot order me as if I am Blinker," he said irritably. "I am your husband. I demand that you get the valet back along with my papers."

"Take your medicine and go to sleep," she repeated, waving

the spoon before him.

"I am not going to take it. Leave."

"Oh, keep quiet," she snapped. "You are ill. You cannot go ordering people about and endanger your health by acting like a child. Do you know how many people depend on you for their livelihood? You have to begin listening to people, especially your family. We want what is best for you."

"I am not one of your little orphans. Call my valet now. Or I will—"

She shoved the spoon into his mouth.

He helplessly swallowed the medicine.

"I will go to the library and work," he threatened.

"I will lock you in the room, or better yet, begin burning your precious papers one by one if you do not behave. In fact, I will burn a few right now—"

She was flat on her back with her hands pinned above her head before she could finish the sentence.

She stared at his face, hovering inches above her own. His breath fanned her cheek.

"Why don't you want me to leave the room?" he asked suspiciously. "Has your boy destroyed yet another painting or broken a precious vase?"

"You were ill. Awfully ill. Delirious, burning up with fever." Tears pricked her eyes. "I thought you were going to die. I don't want you to die."

"What does it matter to you if I die?" he snapped.

"I care," she whispered. "I can't see you ill. I want you to order us around, but with the pink back in your cheeks, your eyes bright with health. I want you to rest, to eat, to get well soon. I hate feeling so helpless. I want you well. I need you well for my peace of mind."

His eyes widened in shock at her admission. He swiftly rolled away from her, allowing her to get up.

And, thereafter, meekly submitted to her ministrations without a single complaint.

Chapter Thirty-Two

The sound of music filled the air. Irish jigs and Scottish airs, sonatas and sonatinas by Haydn, Beethoven, Piccinni and Arne bounced off the walls of Ansley Hall in joy. Huxley had recovered, and every single resident, from the scullery maid to the grumpiest artist, had tried in some small way to show their relief and happiness.

Dorothy had filled the house with flowers, and the cook had outdone herself at mealtimes, creating mouth-watering roasts and exquisite dessert gardens too pretty to eat. Meanwhile, Blinker had shyly presented Huxley with his present—a frog, two worms, and an oddly shaped twig.

The celebrations lasted two whole days, and then the weather turned. The sun, which had shone so delightfully over the past few days, was now hidden behind clouds. Its brightness dimmed like a candle burning through a grey cloth while the breeze turned cold and thick as if weighed down by a sinister omen.

And as it so often happens, spirits that had soared after Huxley's recovery came crashing down once the celebrations were over. A blanket of boredom and dullness floated down on Ansley grounds, coating every creature and blade of grass with its blandness.

Along with the change in the weather came a missive. A missive that threw Dorothy into turmoil.

She stared out of the window in her chamber, wondering how the world outside could look so pale and flat when her mind and heart were in such turmoil.

She wanted the rain to cascade down like a waterfall, the wind to hurtle across England and uproot plants and trees.

She wanted it to storm.

She bowed her head and stared at the letter clutched in her lap. It shouldn't have come as a surprise after all this was what she had been working towards for so long … and yet now that it had—"

"Is something the matter?" Huxley asked, pausing at the door outside her room.

Her mouth trembled, and she jerked her head in a half-hearted nod.

He hesitated a moment before entering her room. He was well now, apart from a little lingering weakness that time would cure.

"Dorothy?" he prompted softly. "Tell me."

She looked up then, her eyes filled with tears. She flung the letter aside and barrelled into him.

He had just enough time to open his arms to catch her.

"The school has accepted him, the school you wrote to," she sobbed into his shirt.

"These tears don't appear happy," he observed calmly. "And here I thought you wanted him to be accepted. Wasn't that what you have been trying to do all these months?"

"I do. I did. It's not an orphanage … he will be well looked after. Thank you for paying the fee—

"Then why are you soaking my shirt with your blubbering?"

"He leaves in a fortnight. So soon."

"If you don't want him to go, then keep him."

She stilled and looked at him, "But what will we say? Where did we get him?"

"We will say we adopted him. He showed artistic talent, and I decided to give him a home and train him."

She gripped his shirt and said honestly, "But he has shown no talent. His flowers look like pigs."

"Apart from mischief," he smiled down at her. "No one will

recall what reason we give in a few years. We can get tutors for him, treat him like a son—"

"Oh, you wonderful, wonderful man!" she cried, throwing her arms around him. She stood on her toes and kissed his cheeks, "Your heart is so big."

His cheeks turned red in embarrassment.

Her heart filled with a warm, soft emotion. The emotion bubbled over, and she couldn't help but tighten the embrace and begin showering him with more kisses.

He was just so big; her arms barely reached around him. A moan of frustration escaped her. She wished she could squish him into a tiny ball, cuddle, kiss, and hold him close forever.

"I love you so much," she whispered against his lips.

They both froze as the words murmured so low but sounded louder than church bells on a quiet morning.

"What?" he cleared his throat, "what did you say?"

"I love you," she repeated in wonderment. The sentence spoken in gratitude and passion was true, she realised. She did not want to improve him like Lumley or fatten him like a starved dog or a cat. She loved him for himself.

She loved how kind, generous, and considerate he was. She loved how he lived his life on his terms, how improving creative minds was more important to him than the opinions of the shallow ton, and how wealth had not turned him into an arrogant, windy imbecile.

She adored his gentleness and the bashful expressions he wore when she teased him. She loved how he made her feel when he held her in his arms, how his kisses sent her senses reeling, and how his deep, dark voice soothed her no matter how disturbed she was.

She loved him. Loved him more than anyone in her entire life, even more than her family with whom she had grown up. He had crept into her heart in such a short time and taken over it completely.

It was the oddest, most astonishing feeling.

"Dorothy," he snapped.

She blinked up at him.

He gripped her arm and set her aside. "I did not expect this to happen."

"I don't understand."

His face was full of pain and regret. "You were not meant to fall in love with me. Say it isn't true. You were jesting."

She smiled, "Oh, I do love you more than—"

"Stop. I don't want to hear it."

She grabbed his arm when he moved to go. "Do you love me?"

"I can never claim you," he responded after a moment. His eyes dimmed as if all light had been sucked out of it, leaving it an empty shell. "I can offer friendship and no more."

"You can bed Diana, but not me?"

He saw the hurt and bitterness in her face and cursed under his breath. "Diana was my mistress, Dora, before we were married. Woodbead told me about the letter you found. She wrote it, hoping I would weary of my new bride and take her back. I did not."

The relief at the news was short-lived. All these days, she had someone to blame for her apathetic marriage. She had thought Huxley cared for Diana and hence could not bring himself to love her. She had assumed she was competing with a woman, a distasteful but tangible reason.

And now … she flung his arm away in annoyance. "I don't understand. I am tired of your games and not knowing how to play. I am tired of not knowing why you turn hot and cold like a temperamental spring day. Please, give our marriage a fair chance. If nothing else, I may be able to give you an heir, and you might come to care for me … love me—"

"Love," he spat the word out in disgust. "Love is akin to madness in our family. My father loved my mother. He beat her to death, Dora. I heard him hit her until she had no choice but to escape this house and succumb to her injuries in her mother's home. I couldn't stop it. He never loved his second wife, and she was safe from him. He never raised his hand to her. But my beautiful, gentle mother ... he couldn't believe someone like her had married him. He wanted to keep her at all costs. He wanted to lock her away from the gaze of every man in the world. He was mad ... love drove him to madness."

"But you are like your mother."

He looked away. "They said my father had never been a violent man until my mother came into his life. The love he had for her was all-consuming and yet tainted with dark, roiling madness that appeared one day suddenly and inexplicably. He would beat her and then cry in regret. And as you well know ... if my father was mad, then I am most likely to be mad too. All the physicians say so."

"You will never hurt me," she replied, undaunted. "Your father was a cruel man. He may not have been violent before he met your mother, but the duke told me how harsh he was in his business dealings. You are nothing like him—"

"You didn't know him. You have only rumours to go by. Do you want to risk your life based on rumours?"

"But if you don't try, we will never know. What if you never go mad?"

"Ifs and buts and maybes!" he spat. "I will not take a chance—I am no gambler."

"I am. I am willing to risk it—"

"If you insist on continuing that thought, then, unfortunately ... we would have to live separately."

"We must try—"

His expression turned hard. "So be it. I will retire to my country home while you can dwell in London as long as you damned well please!"

She watched him turn his back on her, but refused to give up hope. She wanted him to love her with his entire being.

She didn't believe for one moment he would hurt her. She had provoked him enough times to know this. Now, all she had to do was prove it to him.

Chapter Thirty-Three

Dorothy looked into the crack in the study door and admired her husband for a moment. His hair was mussed, his eyes tired, and his mouth pinched, yet he looked remarkably handsome.

He dipped the quill in ink and continued writing furiously. The candle stubs scattered on his table indicated he had barely slept last night, if at all. Whatever he was working on must be important and urgent.

His valet stood before him, speaking earnestly. "Does my lord not trust his wife? Is that why he wants her to be followed?"

Dorothy's heart shook, and she unconsciously stepped closer to the door to hear better.

Huxley dusted his writing with sand and spoke with his head down, "I do not trust the *ton*."

"The *ton*?

"I am afraid someone will kidnap her."

Both the valet and Dorothy stilled at this odd notion.

The valet spoke after some thought, "You think they will try to blackmail you for money?"

Huxley glared at him. "Nay, because she is the prettiest young woman in all of England."

The valet and Dorothy stuffed a finger in their ears and wriggled it about.

"Eh?" the valet couldn't help but frown.

Dorothy did not blame him. She knew she was pretty

enough, but the prettiest? Lud! She was not so swollen-headed as not to see the truth.

"What is wrong with your blasted eyes?" Huxley growled. "Any man over eighteen and under ninety will covet her. Naturally, I must do all I can to protect her. Hire some capable shadow guards and have them follow her whenever she leaves home."

The valet suddenly smiled. "Are you sure you are not in love, my lord?"

"Love?" Huxley looked up, his eyes dazed. "Simply because I noticed that she is beautiful? Admiring beauty does not equal love. Don't be daft. Most of England must want her. Does that mean they love her?"

"If all of England wanted her," the valet asked carefully, "then why did she remain unwed for so long?"

"Because the duke frightened her prospective grooms away. He cannot allow just any wishy-washy creature to marry the duchess's beloved younger sister."

The valet's head reeled, and he stared at him in shock. What had happened to his intelligent master? He had turned blind and woolly-headed after his marriage. He suddenly felt very lonely. Ah, to have someone look at him with stars in their eyes, oblivious to the truth, wouldn't that be delightful?

Dorothy was self-aware and knew the duke had done no such thing. Therefore, she, too, was stunned. Did her husband think she was so lovely that the entire *ton* wanted to kidnap her?

A burst of happiness and love bubbled up inside her, and she suddenly wanted to annoy him for some reason.

She wanted to pounce on him, chew his ears, pull his hair, and nuzzle his neck.

Ahhhh! She was going to die from her husband's adorableness.

The mischievous turmoil could no longer be contained, so she took a deep breath, shot into the room, snatched the papers he was working on, and shot back out.

He chased after her through the halls, out into the back gardens, and then back into the house until he finally cornered her in the dining room.

She sat cross-legged under the table, clutching the papers in a deathly grip behind her back.

He crawled in after her and, after a heated but silent struggle, extracted his precious work from her grip.

He did not scold her.

The following day, she dried and pounded colourful flowers from the garden, mixed them with water, and poured them all over Huxley when he was wearing his new coat for a walk.

The man clearly wanted her, but he refused to give in due to some misguided notion. It infuriated her, and she wanted to infuriate him in turn.

When that didn't stoke his temper, she tried tickling his ears and nostrils with a paintbrush while he slept. She also leapt out at him from dark corners to frighten him, kissed him on the cheek every time she saw him and called him darling and husband simply because it made his brows furrow.

The man did not lose his temper, nor did he acknowledge that he had not lost his temper. She had made an absolute pest of herself, yet Huxley continued to prepare to move to his country home. He had already sent a carriage ahead with some of his necessities to the house and informed the housekeeper and butler of his inevitable move.

After two weeks of silence from Huxley, her spirit began to brood. She stared out of her bedroom window at the long-stemmed crimson roses as they bowed down under the onslaught of heavy rain.

The weather had taken a turn for the worse. Turbulent clouds had crept over England that morning, plunging everything into darkness.

The storm she had hoped for not so long ago had finally arrived.

She watched the wind dash about in a temper and wished Huxley, too, would let free the tempest raging inside him.

She could see the carefully contained turmoil in his eyes, yet his face remained hard, stoic …, and impenetrable.

He was leaving soon. Leaving for the country home. Was this the end of their relationship? Would she have to live her life like so many other neglected women? A life filled with loneliness and needlework, while Huxley took mistress after mistress, his heart turning colder as the years flew by.

She watched the roses struggling to stay upright against the heavy raindrops. It was only a matter of time before they conceded defeat and broke.

She arched her neck and straightened her shoulders. She would try one last time. Something drastic … and if that didn't work, she would bow down and concede defeat.

And that something drastic was Aron Selwyn—the only man who had managed to rile up Huxley in her experience.

She would start tonight. She would bury her fears and flirt outrageously with Mr Selwyn at Countess Marianne's dinner party.

She would work on Selwyn all through dinner until Huxley arrived, and, thereafter, Huxley would see her being overly familiar with a Selwyn, and hopefully be jealous enough to confess his feelings.

She set the plan in motion immediately upon arriving at the party. The fear of losing Huxley made her reckless. She giggled at everything Selwyn said, flirted with her fan, allowed him to stroke her bare arm, and let her ringlets brush his cheek.

If anyone thought her behaviour odd, she didn't care. She ignored the disapproving old women. Everyone flirted with everyone these days, so why shouldn't she? Besides, she was a married woman now, and as long as she avoided a scandal, she could do as she pleased.

She swallowed her third glass of wine, feeling unfettered and heady. As a single woman seeking a husband, she had been bound to follow the rules, to watch her every step, to pause and think before speaking to avoid causing offence.

And now, married to Huxley, with a powerful title and

enormous wealth, she was someone of note. Once she had been brushed aside, she was now being sought out, included and remarkably listened to.

This respect, independence, and security were all due to Huxley.

She sighed and set the glass down. Where was her husband? She missed him awfully.

Selwyn seemed to sense her rapidly deflating mood and steered her towards the balcony.

She gratefully gulped in the humid air scented heavily with petrichor.

"Soon, it will be too hot to stay in London. The season is almost over," Selwyn remarked, turning her so that the moonlight lit her face up.

A whiff of the familiar fumes of a cigar distracted her. She cast her eyes about and found Huxley standing a few feet away.

Her shoulders relaxed at the sight of her husband, and she turned towards Selwyn with a genuine smile for the first time that evening.

"Will you be leaving for the country?" Selwyn asked, taking a small step closer to her.

Dorothy peeked over his shoulder at Huxley.

He was watching them, his eyes glinting in the lamps' light like a deep lake glimmering in the moonlight.

Satisfied, she offered Selwyn another blinding smile. "Oh, no. I tend to stay right here in London. My husband might retire for a few months, though."

"Will you not miss him?"

She laughed. "I don't know if I will have the time. London, in all seasons, contrives to keep one busy."

"You don't love him?" Selwyn asked and touched her nape. A light, delicate caress that made her skin pebble in discomfort.

She stepped back. "What an old-fashioned question?" she smiled to take the sting out of her action.

Selwyn's teeth gleamed white in the moonlight. "A light-hearted miss who doesn't take life too seriously. The sort I like best."

Dorothy nodded agreeably and again looked over his shoulder.

Huxley had disappeared.

"When will he leave?" Selwyn asked, forcing her attention back to him.

"Who?"

"Your husband?"

"Within a fortnight," she replied, her heart sinking. Huxley had left her alone with Selwyn and turned a blind eye to her flirtations. He had not been jealous.

Her last resort had failed.

Chapter Thirty-Four

Huxley was leaving in two days.

Dorothy clutched the note Selwyn had written to her. He wanted to see her that afternoon, and her unhappy heart pushed her to take up his clandestine offer.

She dashed off a letter to Penelope, cancelling their previously planned engagement, and set out to meet Selwyn.

Alone.

As the carriage trundled through smoky, brown London, the anger and hurt clouding her mind began to fade a little. By the time she arrived at the meeting spot, she began to regret her rash decision.

Her thoughtless action had got her married to Huxley, but this time, she had a feeling she would not be lucky enough to escape unscathed. What did she think she was doing meeting Selwyn and that, too, unchaperoned?

Her heart began beating in dread.

What had she thought would happen once she met him?

Surely he would try to kiss her? Her lips curled up in disgust at the thought.

She was not ready to have an affair. This had been a mistake! But before she could rap the walls to indicate she would like to return to Ansley Hall, the carriage lurched to a stop, and Selwyn flung the door open.

"I think I should go back," Dorothy blurted in embarrassment.

"I agree. I didn't think this through." He appeared to be just as uncomfortable as she felt.

She nodded in relief. "Oh, I am so glad you see what I mean."

"We will be better friends than lovers," he said frankly.

She blushed and looked away. "Evenings in London fog up the brain. What seems so sensible by moonlight—"

He nodded in agreement. "Are not so sensible in the light of the day."

"I should leave."

"I think you should stay," he disagreed.

Her eyebrows shot up in surprise.

He took her gloved hand and said coaxingly, "You have come this far … surely we can spend some time together as friends?"

"What will we do? It's beginning to rain, so we can hardly stroll. Besides, I don't have a chaperone—"

"True, we can't sit in a stuffy carriage either." He frowned thoughtfully. "By Jove! I know; I have recently bought a house. It's not a mansion like Ansley Hall, but you might like it. I don't have many women in my life, and I would appreciate the opinion of a friend. About curtains and things."

She hesitated.

"I would like your help," he pressed. "It would be a good start to our friendship, but if you are uncomfortable with the thought—"

"No, I am … not uncomfortable," she lied. "I would like to see your new home."

What else could she do? Her manner towards him had been awfully encouraging; she had led him to hope… behaved horribly, yet he was kind enough to understand. Besides, he looked so hopeful….

She would dash in and dash out; it would only take a few moments since, thankfully, the cottage was not far away.

He asked his carriage to follow them as he slipped beside her for the drive. He chattered on about the house, telling her how big the garden was and how many rooms it had. It would have been a very dull conversation, but his pride and enthusiasm at having procured a home were infectious, and soon, she, too, was eager to see the place.

They arrived before long, and she peeked out of the window to find herself facing a sweet little place with ivy crawling up the walls and a small, well-maintained garden in the front.

"We don't have a chaperone," she hesitated at the wooden gate.

"My old aunt lives with me," he replied. "She is a stickler for propriety. She will do, won't she?"

She nodded, forcefully dampened her uneasiness and followed him indoors. She decided to stay for a moment, perhaps advise him on what curtains to buy and then hurtle out the door.

She would hop in, she assured herself as she crossed the threshold and hop out.

Hop in and hop out. It wouldn't take long—

The door slammed shut behind her.

She turned around to find Mr Selwyn airborne. He crashed into her, sending her flying back on the sofa.

"Mr Selwyn, what is the meaning of this?" she gasped, hands and feet flailing as she tried to push him away.

"Come, your sister didn't resist me at all."

Dorothy reeled back. "Sister?"

"Lily," he grinned.

Dorothy froze in horror as the truth dawned on her.

Lily? He was the man who had gotten her sister with child?

She felt sick with disgust. Disgust at the man before her, disgust at herself and her idiocy.

How gullible had she been? What an absolute fool! She had innocently believed every word poured out of his vile mouth! The story he had spun about procuring a house and wanting her opinion on the colour of curtains ... curtains, for goodness' sake! And she had swallowed it all like a naïve little lamb.

Dorothy stared at the handsome face hovering inches in front of her. A rush of indignant power built up inside her, and she punched his smiling face.

He looked shocked momentarily and fell back as if he

couldn't believe a woman would dare deny him. Then his face darkened, and he moved towards her with far more determination.

She kicked his stomach while he was mid-pounce, and he crashed onto the floor with a moan.

In a trice, she ripped off a bit of her petticoat and tied his arms.

"This," she snapped, thwacking him with her parasol, "is for seducing Lily and leaving her when she was with child."

"This," she twisted his ears until he squealed, "is for trying to do the same to me. You thought it would be amusing to seduce another Fairweather, did you?"

She grabbed his nose and yanked. Hard.

"This is for all the women in England whom you have tried to dupe or duped."

"And finally, this," she said, stamping on his hands until she heard the bones crack, "is a lesson for you to remember in case you try and attempt such foolishness in future."

"Don't touch her!" Huxley roared, crashing in through the door.

Dorothy straightened up, clutching a bit of her torn petticoat, while Selwyn peered at Huxley through one rapidly swelling eye.

All Huxley saw was the torn petticoat. He advanced on Selwyn with a roar.

The duke barrelled in next, assumed much the same as Huxley, and sprang upon Selwyn.

"He seduced Lily." Penelope flew into the room.

"Stay away from her," Celine swooped in.

"I have a gun," George warned.

"I am the Falcon," Jimmy shouted, crashing into George.

"Stop!" Dorothy cried, yanking at the duke and Huxley's arms. "I already clouted him and gave him a bruiser!"

Everyone ignored her, their hands and feet too busy taking care of Selwyn.

Once they were satisfied with the amount of thrashing

Selwyn had received, they turned to Dorothy to ascertain that she was well.

Dorothy, in turn, told them what happened.

Everyone agreed that Selwyn deserved the extra beating simply because of his evil intentions.

"How did you know where to find me?" Dorothy asked while the duke checked to see if Selwyn was still alive.

"You sent me a letter saying you were to meet Selwyn," Penelope reminded her. "I knew he was the man who had seduced Lily. She had confessed his name but sworn me to secrecy, but I know this one time she wouldn't mind me telling the truth."

"Your sister told the duke and me," Huxley said. "We thought it best if we came and saved you."

"We didn't know you didn't need saving," Celine agreed.

"Fairweather sisters never do," George smiled, looking down at his wife. "I knew you would be fine."

"Have you two become friends?" Dorothy asked, watching the duke and Huxley eagerly discussing ways to bury Selwyn.

"We have agreed on the disputed piece of land," the duke replied with a nod. "We have decided to give you the plot."

Dorothy clapped her hands in joy and then frowned. "I think he winced," she said, staring down at Selwyn. "Do corpses wince?"

"He is alive," Huxley said regretfully. "The duke thinks it best if we leave him. He will hopefully leave the country—"

"Or we will make him leave the country," the duke said, clapping George on the back.

The three men shared a smile.

Chapter Thirty-Five

Once Dorothy was back in her chamber with a cup of warm tea and a bag of sugared pineapples, Huxley entered.

"Why did you go with him?" he snapped.

"I wanted to make you jealous."

"Foolish, girl! What if something had happened?"

"I can take care of myself."

"Selwyn was weak; what if a stronger man had attacked you?"

"You mean like you?"

"Yes, I mean like me."

"Have you ever hurt a girl?"

"I have never fallen in love."

"Do you think Selwyn tried to hurt me because he loved me?"

"No, but in our family—"

"I have already heard you mention the mythical madness."

His lips pressed together in a tight line.

"You bedded your mistresses even though you didn't love them?" she asked after a moment.

"Love and lust are not the same."

"Then why won't you let me give you an heir? Is it because you are afraid … afraid you will fall in love with me if you do, or are you afraid of hurting me in the throes of passion since you already love me?"

He paled and stepped away from the bed. "Women should

not be so ... frank," he hissed.

She reached over, grabbed his hand, and pulled him down on the bed. She closed the distance between them and kissed him.

He groaned and kissed her back.

She crawled into his lap and snuck her hand inside his shirt to splay her fingers on his bare chest.

"I might hurt you," he growled against his lips.

She smiled. "You love me."

He froze.

She continued, "You could have lost your temper countless times with me. When Blinker ruined your painting, when I landed in your study and placed us both in a compromising position, all those times I annoyed you ... and yet you never hurt me. Doesn't that tell you something? You are a wonderful, gentle, kind man. My mother mistreated Penelope, but I know I will never be so cruel, nor will Celine. There are good and bad people. And you are one of the good ones, and I love you with all my heart."

He thrust her aside. "I don't love you," he snapped. "I won't bed you because I don't desire you enough. I didn't want to hurt your feelings, but you forced my hand."

Dorothy paled in shock.

He continued harshly. "You wanted the truth; I have given it to you."

"I can't bear to live under the same roof as you," she whispered. "Not if you love me and deny it, and not if you despise me either. Both of those situations are hell for me."

"Then leave. Leave for good."

The cold, leaden atmosphere was broken when Rosie raced into the room, interrupting their argument. "Blinker is missing."

Dorothy ignored Huxley as he sat beside her, interrogating

the servants. Her heart was full of worry, and her mind felt unusually blank.

Rosie wiped her eyes and repeated everything. "He had porridge and then wanted to play in the garden. I insisted he bathe before that and told the kitchen maid, Bella, to fetch hot water. But, Bella and I became busy with other chores and only returned to the chamber later in the day to find Blinker missing."

"Did you look for him?" Huxley asked.

Rosie nodded. "But not well. Since the grounds are vast and he hates bathing, I thought he was hiding from me. I knew he would be back for dinner—he never misses it—so I waited until then to catch him. He did not arrive, and I began looking for him again. And now . . . It is almost supper time, and he is still not found."

Huxley leaned back thoughtfully and glanced at his valet. "Where do you think he could be?"

The valet appeared startled at suddenly being addressed. "He must have fallen asleep somewhere. He will appear in the next few days; don't worry about it, my lord."

Dorothy shot Huxley an anxious look. A few days? Wouldn't the child starve?

Huxley waved his hand and dismissed the servants.

"My lord," Dorothy swallowed and continued, "I-if you find Blinker, I will leave for the country immediately. I can buy a small cottage with my dowry and live away from the gossiping *ton*. We can say my nerves are delicate, and I am too ill to continue staying in London. You can have your freedom back... please, find him."

He walked up to the window and flung it open.

A chill rushed in, along with a servant dressed in dark clothing.

"My lord, I found no trace of the child."

"Follow the valet," Huxley whispered his order.

The man nodded and disappeared again.

"I think I know what might have happened," Huxley still

spoke in hushed tones and returned to his seat behind the desk. "Get some rest. We are in for some excitement over the next few days. I hoped to send you away before this—but the other side was more impatient than I thought."

"What are you mumbling about? I can't hear you!" Dorothy wailed. "I want Blinker."

"And you will get him back," he vowed. "Now, go back to your chamber and sleep."

"Nay, I will sit here until he is found."

Huxley rubbed an index finger between his brows, sighed, and stood up.

She froze when he slowly approached her, his gaze intense and turbulent.

"Wha—" her words were cut short when he swooped, picked her up and walked out of the study.

She felt his hands burning through the layers and clothes and was inexplicably reminded of the time he had held her on Gin Lane.

He ignored her struggles, took her to her chamber, carefully placed her on the bed and then, using the quilt, wrapped her up. "If I catch you out of bed, I will stop looking for the child." Frightened, she obediently closed her eyes. Her eyeballs moved impatiently behind closed lids, but she obediently kept them shut.

He stood gazing down at her, his eyes tender and his expression soft. It belied all his harsh words from earlier, and it was a pity she couldn't see it.

A few hours later, Huxley woke her up. She sat up, dazed and surprised that she had managed to fall asleep.

Blinker stood by Huxley's side, but Huxley placed a hand on her mouth before she could squeal. "Hush. We must pretend he is still missing."

She nodded, and he released her. "What is going on?"

"Make a bed under your bed and get the boy settled. Do not tell anyone, except your maid, Rosie, about him. She will share her meals with him and stay in this chamber, pretending to be overwrought over the missing child since she thinks it is her fault that he went missing. Understood?"

"Yes."

"After that, I need to make certain arrangements. Can you write to the Duke and ask him to meet you now? Except instead of you, I will go."

"So many instructions, my head hurts." Dorothy shook her head in a daze.

"I do not care." He stuffed Blinker into her arms. "I am sending Rosie over; she is asleep in the parlour. Explain the matter to her."

She kissed Blinker's head and then kissed him a few more times. She paused when she noticed Huxley watching her and went slightly pink. "What time is it?"

He ruffled Blinker's hair, his fingers lingering where she had been showering kisses a moment ago, and answered, "Past four in the morning. I have to go."

After he left, Dorothy turned to Blinker and smacked his head. "Where did you go?"

"I had an adventure," the boy's eyes shone brightly. "I was kidnapped, isn't that blasted wonderful?"

Dorothy froze in shock. "You-what do you mean? Wait, tell me from the moment you woke up until now, hour by hour."

"I woke up, had porridge, then that harridan—"

Dorothy growled.

Blinker paused and then continued more politely, "The great and astonishing, fragrant lady Rosie wanted to bathe me, so I ran. I hid in the room with the statues behind the tapestry, remember it?"

"Yes."

"While I was hiding inside the large pot with those fruit carvings that I broke off last time, the valet arrived with another man."

"A servant?"

"Nay, I think one of the new artists. I did not recognise him."

The conversation paused briefly as Rosie entered the room

and burst into quiet tears at the sight of Blinker. At Dorothy's urging, she hugged him and sat down at the edge of the bed to hear the rest of the story.

"Then?" Dorothy poked Blinker.

Blinker scrunched his nose as he tried to recall the words. "The valet said everything was ready, and Lord Sedley had been alerted. He would come and arrest Lord Huxley on charges of sedition. The proof was all over the house, and he couldn't escape."

Dorothy gasped in horror.

Blinker nodded wisely. "I gasped, too, and was thus discovered. The valet stuffed a rag in my mouth and carried me out of the estate and to a nearby village. He placed me in a dark room above the village inn. He rushed away and returned late that evening to give me a cup of water and some dried meat."

"You must be starving," Dorothy rubbed his head worriedly.

Rosie pulled out a bag of sugared pineapple and, without asking Dorothy, stuffed the child's mouth.

Dorothy waited until he had eaten before saying, "After he left, Huxley arrived?"

"Lor', how did you know?" Blinker asked, widening his eyes. "He stormed into the room, snatched me up, and threw me on a horse waiting outside. I felt like a princess!"

"Prince," Dorothy corrected.

Blinker nodded and continued, "We only stopped moving once he reached his study. I told him everything I had overheard, and he brought me here."

"Were you very afraid?" Rosie asked tremulously.

"Afraid?" Blinker rolled his eyes. "It is the most exciting thing. I felt like an empress—

"Emperor," Dorthy said.

Blinker sighed and dramatically placed the back of his hand on his head. "An emperor who has been slapped to death, and then he wakes up, he is slapped again and wakes up again. So much excitement, I could barely contain my joy."

Dorothy stared at him; the tears she had shed for this child still created rivers down her cheeks.

This child's way of thinking... it was a little odd.

She wanted to smack some sense into him again, but held back. "Make his bed."

"What a strange creature," Rosie echoed Dorothy's thoughts as she crawled under the bed and threw quilts and pillows underneath. "Must be all the gin he drank that addled him."

Once Blinker was hidden and comfortably asleep under the bed, Dorothy lay back down, her head spinning with all the information. Huxley was in trouble; the valet was a traitor, and some men would arrive to inspect the estate and arrest him at any moment.

It would be impossible for Huxley to transport so many people, statues and artworks out of the estate in such a short time without being noticed.

He was trapped.

Chapter Thirty-Six

When the valet frantically knocked on Huxley's study door, the sun had just risen and dyed the sky pink and gold.

"Come in."

The valet swept in and started speaking immediately, "My lord, I could not find you in your chamber, but it is good that you are awake so early. Alas, Lord Sedley, the one who is close to the king, has arrived at the doorstep. He is demanding to be let in. W-what are your orders?"

"I see," Huxley calmly set aside the letter he was writing. "Woodbead!" he called, and the poet pushed aside the bookshelf and entered the room through the hidden entrance.

"My lord?" Woodbead took the letter and nodded. "I will personally deliver this."

The valet stared at the letter, his eyes flickering with curiosity. Huxley ignored him and leisurely stood up, stretching. "Ah, it will be a long day."

"You will be sent to the gallows," the valet stressed. His manner was perfect, that of a young servant distressed at the thought of a well-paying master being caught and sentenced. He even managed to squeeze out some tears.

Huxley ignored him and walked out in the same steady manner. He paused when he reached the entrance to Ansley Hall and blinked in surprise. He had expected to see Lord Sedley, with his grey hair, long white beard, and mottled skin, along with his armed men, but next to them stood, nay, sat the

Duke of Blackthorne holding a cup of tea and nibbling a piece of cake that his wife, Penelope was feeding him.

Apart from the duke, he also discovered a strange motley of people of all shapes, sizes and ages.

"Who are they?" Huxley asked the duke, gesturing to the people sitting on chairs behind him. Had they just returned from a ball? Why were they dressed for a dinner party?

The duke gave his cup to a servant and wiped his mouth. "You said you wanted witnesses, so I brought them. This is them."

"Where did you procure such witnesses?" Huxley continued to be befuddled while Lord Sedley and the valet turned darker and darker in hue.

"My relatives," the duke introduced them. "They are Aunty and Uncle Worthington, Cousin Grey, second Cousin Arthur Babbage, third cousin the Parringtons, and those two young men who look like delicate wafers are their children, that one with the moustache is Uncle Petunia—

"They are eating peanuts," Huxley cut him short.

The relatives appeared bright-eyed and had unmistakable gossipy heads on them. It seemed as if they had come dressed up to watch a play.

Huxley frowned and continued, "But so many people? One would have sufficed as a witness. And is that old lady at the back blind?"

The duke scowled. "At the end of the year, my relatives come to watch fireworks with me, but I thought this would be far more entertaining this time."

"It is not even August," Huxley snapped back.

"Am I a horsefly?" Lord Sedley finally exploded. He was being looked at as something more exciting than Chinese fireworks; this was unacceptable. "I am here to search your home, but I have a question before that." He turned to the duke and bowed politely since the duke, although younger, outranked him. "Your grace, why is he called Uncle Petunia?"

"He is my uncle."

"But, heh heh, Petunia?" Lord Sedley showed a row of missing teeth.

The duke narrowed his eyes. "What heh heh? How am I meant to know why he was named thus? Ask his mother."

Lord Sedley peered at the crowd that was sipping tea and eating peanuts. "Which one is his mother?"

"She is dead."

"Then how am I meant to ask her?"

The duke flicked a crumb off his sleeve. "By dying."

Lord Sedley paled and shook his cane. "If you were not a duke, I would have used some foul language."

"You are a nitwit, nincompoop, an extraordinarily nasty flea," the duke calmly retorted.

"Do you have no qualms? At least respect my age!"

"I do not respect anyone who attacks my family. Wait until I see you in the parliament."

Huxley's eyes softened at the duke's words while Lord Sedley raised his cane towards him and spoke with less conviction. "Let us enter and search amicably."

At some point, the commotion had risen in Huxley's household, and now they stood surrounding him. Dorothy, Lady Huxley, Sophia, his butler, valet and some guards faced the driveway, filled with confusion and fear.

Dorothy suddenly leapt out from behind Huxley and lay down on the step. "No one can enter my home."

Huxley and the duke were too stunned to speak for a moment.

"Why?" Lord Sedley asked with a glint. "Do you have something to hide?"

"The mansion has not been cleaned yet; why the scullery maid is still asleep. How can I allow guests in when every surface is covered in dust and soot is piled high in the fireplaces? My reputation as the lady of the house shall be ruined."

"I can simply step over you," Lord Sedley rolled his eyes and then flinched.

Someone had thrown a peanut at his head, incensing him.

While he searched for the culprit, Huxley tutted and hauled Dorothy up and away from the door. He whispered soothingly, "It will be fine. Let them in."

"You will be safe?" Dorothy asked, her nails digging painfully into his arms.

He nodded, allowing her sharp nails to dig in even more sharply until he almost bled. "If you do not trust me," he continued, whispering close to her sensitive ear, "then trust your family. Trust the duke. I will explain it all later."

She shrank her neck as his hot breath tickled and obediently stepped aside.

Huxley turned to Sedley. "You are most welcome. But if you find nothing, I will seek retribution."

Lord Sedley baulked for a moment, and his eyes flew to the valet and away so quickly that had Dorothy not been watching him, she would have missed it.

Sophia sidled over to Dorothy. "Will my brother—will he be fine?"

"I hope so," Dorothy took Sophia's hand, noticed it was cold and clammy and began rubbing it. "I do not know how he will manage this, but I have faith in him."

Although she said those words to assure Sophia, she did not believe them. Her heart pounded as she watched Lord Sedley, his guards, the duke, and his peanut-eating family stride indoors to search for artists and incriminating works.

The paintings in the hallway, the sculptures in the wall nooks, and even the finely crafted vases had all disappeared. Earlier, she had failed to notice the missing bits when she had rushed to his side, but now even she was dumbfounded.

Lord Sedley pulled out a map and, unsurprisingly, knew all the hidden entrances. He confidently threw aside the tapestry and walked into a barren land at the back of the house.

Even the ornamental hermit had vanished into thin air.

Eh? Dorothy's head spun in half delight, half astonishment. Overnight, the entire house and backyard had been cleared.

How was this possible?

Lord Sedley stared at the valet and frowned. After a moment, he turned to one of his men and asked, "Chopper, you were in the village. Did you hear anyone move through the night?"

Chopper shook his head. "Nay, even the roads were clear and silent with not a squeak."

The duke shook his head. "Lord Sedley, explain yourself. How dare you accuse an upright man of such things? A bosom friend of the regent, too. Ah, this is shocking."

"He had over a hundred artists, sculptures, paintings, caricatures." Lord Sedley reeled. "Search harder. Check the cellars!"

While Sedley's men raced about, the duke, Huxley, Dorothy and Penelope huddled in one corner, speaking in low voices.

"I am indebted, your grace," Huxley said humbly.

The duke waved his hand. "No matter, it is what I should do. But, what brought this on so suddenly?"

"Several things," Huxley replied. "George, the Regent, ignored the king's old advisors, and they were unhappy. Besides, the Regent has been spending lavishly on art, which the older generation sees as a waste. Since the Regent's biggest financer happens to be me, they decided to target me since they cannot hurt him."

"You knew this?" the duke frowned. "I never heard a word."

"Lord Adair had informed me that they planned to search my home a few months from now. The reason for the delay was that the Regent would not be in London at the time, and his guards would be unable to come to my aid. I would be sentenced before his return."

"But then Sedley lost his temper, and the plan to wait was changed," the duke said, enlightened. When Dorothy and Penelope continued to look confused, he explained, "Aron Selwyn is Lord Sedley's bastard child."

The women gasped in shock and quickly borrowed some peanuts to munch as they listened.

The duke continued, "Lord Sedley had been madly in love with a woman, a childhood sweetheart. They became engaged, but shortly after, his family's fortunes fell. In dire need of finances, he married an heiress to save his family. But, he had got the woman he loved with a child, and filled with guilt for ruining her life, he helped her as much as he could.

That woman died early, and all his guilt was now transferred to his son, Aron Selwyn, who should have been his heir but who, because of circumstances and his own weak will, he had abandoned. Thus, he spoiled young Aron Selwyn and grew attached to the child. So incredibly, blindly attached that when he heard about the beating Selwyn received at Huxley's hands, he decided to take his revenge a little earlier than expected."

Huxley nodded. "If not for Blinker's warning, I would have been caught in the trap. I had planned to move all the artists out of the house before the Regent departed, but this was sprung upon me so suddenly that I had little time."

"But it was enough," the duke smiled gleefully. "Look at his purple face; it makes me feel more joy than an exploding flower firework. An early New Year gift."

"The valet? When did you know?" Dorothy asked.

"I trusted the man, but not entirely. Then he started acting suspicious after we beat up Selwyn, so I started keeping an eye on him. Even so, if it hadn't been for Blinker... anyhow, I am used to being on guard since this is a delicate matter, and the servants are constantly changing. I kept the fact that I was aware of the brewing plot close to my heart. Only you knew about my vision to move them out."

"But where did the artists go?" Dorothy asked, still utterly confused.

The valet seemed to echo her astonishment, for he opened his mouth and spoke his mind for a change. "Where could they have disappeared? I swear I saw them all last night."

Lord Sedley glared at the valet. "Precisely. Where did they go? Vanished into the air? You cannot even cook that many people in a pot, or have time to burn all those things without leaving a trace of ash. Where did they go?"

"How can something that wasn't here vanish?" the duke called out. "Have you played enough? It is my breakfast time; therefore, I suggest you leave."

His relatives broke into thunderous applause at his words. Their expressions were proud, as if to say, "What else can you expect of our most powerful family member?"

"Wait," The valet suddenly cried. "They are in the Duke's backyard! It is the only answer."

Dorothy noticed Penelope bit her lower lip, and Huxley pressed his index fingernail into the pad of his thumb.

She was enlightened. The artists and the duke's guards had grabbed everything and scuttled over the border. They were currently hiding in the gardens of Blackthorne Mansion. Ah! This was brilliant. But would Lord Sedley dare to investigate a duke?

Attacking Huxley was one thing, but attacking the duke would be incredibly foolish.

Lord Sedley lived up to expectations by being very foolish. "I want to search your grounds, your grace."

The duke stared at him until he began sweating. "Pah! The nerve. You found nothing in this house; I have witnesses. There are three counts, one is an earl, and I am a duke! How dare you now suggest that I am involved in some unsightly plot without a whiff of evidence? Sedley, you are going too far."

The duke stood up with a cold face and, with a flick of his wrist, ordered his family and guards to follow him back home.

"Get out of my house. You have overstayed your welcome," Huxley said suddenly, appearing next to Sedley and almost frightening the old man's soul.

Lord Sedley wavered momentarily before grasping his courage and rushing after the duke. "If you have nothing to hide, let us search!" He climbed into his carriage and chased after them. His upper body swayed out of the carriage window as he hollered, "Let us in for a cup of tea. I want to apologise and admire your gardens, your grace."

∞∞∞

Back at Ansley Hall, Dorothy watched the last of Sedley's guards leave. "Now what?"

"Breakfast," Huxley replied, turning to the valet and ordering, "Inform the kitchens."

As soon as the valet rushed away, Huxley lowered his voice and explained to Dorothy, "Naturally, artists have already been informed, and now they are returning to our gardens. It will take them an hour to walk over, but the duke will stall Sedley before allowing him to search. This will give him a reason to attack Sedley in parliament."

Dorothy imagined the artists laden with statues and paintings scuttling from one backyard into another and then back again. She giggled. "This plan is so silly."

"Silly enough to work," he smiled back in relief.

They stared at one another, falling deeper and deeper into each other's gaze before recalling their last bitter conversation and then abruptly turning away.

Just as Huxley had predicted, the artists were back. What he had not predicted was that along with the artists, Lord Sedley was also back.

This time, he seemed even more dangerous and unhinged. He had just offended the Duke of Blackthorne and put his and his entire lineage at incredible risk. The duke could wipe out his whole family name if he wanted, and that thought entered his foggy brain too late.

Wide-eyed and manic, Lord Sedley stood at the entrance of Ansley Hall, his guards armed and ready to shoot arrows through the inhabitants who had once again gathered at the central doorway.

"Lor, how exciting," Blinker rubbed the sleep from his eyes and crowed. "You should have woken me earlier."

Dorothy pushed him back. "Go hide."

The valet paled when he spotted Blinker, and his eyes darted to Huxley. He suddenly realised why he had been kept busy by inane tasks for the last two hours instead of being allowed to venture back into the garden to investigate.

Huxley, in turn, gave him a faint smile that seemed to say, well tried, but alas, you lost. He lifted his hand and flicked the air, and the next moment, the valet was flung down the steps to Lord Sedley's side by a few burly guards. He would never be allowed to enter this house while he lived.

If he lived.

"Go inside and lock the door," Huxley told Dorothy.

She turned around, stuffed everyone inside, instructed the housekeeper not to let anyone in, and then stood beside Huxley.

"Dora, I need to reason with him so he does not try to barge in and hurt anyone," Huxley coaxed. "Go in with the rest of them. I will be with you in a moment."

Dorothy stared at the arrows glinting in the light of the blazing sun and pressed her lips together. She would not budge unless he did.

"The artists are scuttling back and forth," the valet called out. "Send someone to search Blackthorne at the same time."

"Childish nonsense," Huxley scoffed with a straight face.

"Let us in," Lord Sedley screeched back.

Huxley narrowed his eyes. "I already let you in, and you found nothing. I refuse to cower and allow you to trample all over my home as many times as you please. As for your threats... look around you, my lord. If you have surrounded me, then the Regent's men have surrounded you."

Sure enough, from trees and behind bushes, armed royal guards leapt out in unison.

Philbert Woodbead climbed off a horse and, dusty and crusty, bowed in Huxley's direction. "I repaid the debt of the sanctuary you gave me and saved your fine bottom. Here is the arrest warrant for Lord Sedley, signed by the Regent. He was not pleased that his friend had been accosted thus."

Lord Sedley roared angrily, lifted a pistol, and aimed at Huxley's heart. "I will kill you for the sake of this country. The wealth belongs to the people."

Dorothy leapt before Huxley, furious that her husband was risking his life to save a bunch of ungrateful, cowardly artists.

A moment later, Philbert Woodbead leapt in front of Dorothy, but it seemed he did not know why.

"I am scared," Woodbead muttered while trembling like an excited leaf before the rains. "I do not know why I am trying to save you, Miss Fairweather, but I suddenly feel as if my child is going to be killed. I have no children, so I do not know why my bosom is heaving with this maternal emotion. I am also not a woman. I am so confused."

Dorothy's eyes pricked with tears. The poet was really very sweet.

A random Regent's guard became impatient from hunger and suddenly shot Lord Sedley's hand; the gun went off, the bullet hit a tree, someone screamed, and someone swooned.

It became even more thrilling.

The next moment, the royal guards arrested Lord Sedley since his own underpaid guards were too frightened to go against the royal military.

One of the Royal guards approached Sedley and said sternly, "You have been stripped of your title and exiled to Africa without your family and will never be allowed to return. Meanwhile, Lord Huxley's valet is the only company you shall keep."

The men let out a wail of anguish, and Dorothy finally swooned and almost knocked into a pot before Huxley hurriedly caught her in time.

"If she had bled," Huxley said, his eyes dark and violet, "I would have demanded your death."

Then he scooped her up and took her indoors.

Chapter Thirty-Seven

Dorothy woke up early the following day, packed her bags, and moved back into the Blackthorne Mansion. A few weeks later, she was still firmly and morosely lodged in the duchess's guest room with no intention of returning home.

She poked her head out of the window and warbled a sad tune. A lovely little black and yellow bird squawked in protest and abandoned the branch it had been nodding off on.

She watched the bird flutter away, feeling even gloomier. She missed the music that used to sneak into her room every morning at Ansley Hall. She missed the sound of sculptors chipping away at marble and the smell of paint battling with the perfume of blooming roses. She missed the servants, the artificial lake she used to walk by every morning, the sound of tinkling fountains, and the—

"You have been moping for almost a month," Penelope said, gliding into the room.

Dorothy buried her face in the pillow.

"Come," Celine scolded. "You can't lie in bed any longer. We won't let you."

"Leave me alone," Dorothy wailed. "My heart has shattered, hope is lost, and I see only darkness."

"Have you been reading poetry again?" Penelope frowned. "You know it's not good for your countenance."

"We have to go to a ball," Celine said, drawing the curtains aside and tying them up with green silk sashes.

"Season is over," Dorothy muttered.

"It is, but this is a special ball," Penelope replied.

Dorothy peeked at Penelope curiously. "What do you mean by a special ball?"

"You will see," Celine replied mysteriously.

"Where is Blinker? I haven't seen him today," Dorothy said, sitting up in bed.

"He is playing with the children," Penelope responded.

"At least he seems happy," Dorothy muttered.

"I thought you loved Blackthorne," Penelope pouted.

"Not as much as I—no, you are right. I do love Blackthorne. I don't love that hideous creature I married. I am glad to be back," Dorothy said firmly.

"That's the spirit," Celine grinned. "Now come and have breakfast. After that, we have to find you a dress, curl your hair, and try a new hairstyle, which I saw Miss Drew wear a few nights ago. I think it will look lovely on you, so lovely that if Huxley saw you at the ball tonight, he would regret letting you go for the rest of his life."

"Huxley is in the country," Dorothy sighed.

"I heard the duke say he might arrive for the ball," Penelope confided. "He returned home last evening."

Dorothy sat up. "Do you think I can look that wonderful? I want him to suffer deeply."

Celine and Penelope bobbed their heads like two synchronised dolls. "We will make you look ethereal, enchanting, a veritable seductress," they promised.

A few hours later, Dorothy sat in the carriage, her heart fluttering in nervous anticipation. Would she see Huxley? And if he was at the ball, should she greet him?

She stared down at her fingers, tightly entwined on the gossamer skirt. Her sisters had done well. She was wearing a Paris green dress shot with gold and trimmed with amber leaves. Diamonds twinkled at her throat and ears, and her new hairstyle was less severe, full of loose curls and emerald pins that sparkled when she moved her head. It suited her far more than her usual scraped-back bun.

She didn't think she had ever looked more wonderful. Even the duke had gruffly complimented her, and he never noticed such things.

"We are here," Penelope said, her eyes sparkling.

Dorothy's head whipped up in surprise. That had been a short ride.

"Courage," Celine nudged her towards the door encouragingly.

Dorothy took a deep breath and stepped out.

A moment later, she leapt back into the carriage.

"Don't make me drag you out, Dora," Huxley warned.

"The ball is at Ansley Hall," she squeaked at Celine, ignoring Huxley blocking the door.

"The first ball in fifty years," Celine replied calmly.

"I don't want to attend."

"You have to," Huxley said.

"We had no choice, Dora. Oh, don't look as if we betrayed you," she nodded towards Huxley. "You see, Sophia has caught her prince. This ball is to announce their engagement. It will be scandalous if you don't attend."

"You, as my wife, have to be present," Huxley confirmed. "If not for me, then act as the hostess for Sophia."

Dorothy's shoulders slumped. For a moment, she had hoped he had wanted her here because he missed her … not for propriety's sake.

"You will do it, won't you, Dorothy?" Huxley asked anxiously.

Dorothy nodded resignedly. She exited the carriage without his help and pasted a smile.

This was going to be difficult.

Ansley Hall had never looked so beautiful, so inviting … so

homelike.

With every step, she felt as if her heart was turning into lead. She wondered how long she could hold back her tears.

She entered the house, and the glittering gas lamps almost undid her.

She recalled pestering Huxley to install them since she had loved them so much at Blackthorn.

The ballroom that had once been a cold, neglected room was teeming with people. The windows and doors were thrown open to coax the breeze in, and ice sculptures sparkled like jewels around the room. The work was so exquisite that she knew Huxley had enlisted the help of the artists. And the flowers ... she had never seen so many blooms in one room before. They dripped from the ceiling, were wrapped around pillars, and burst forth in a scented profusion from bowls and vases scattered throughout the room.

Sophia stood amid it all in a gold silk gown, glowing like a princess-to-be while her pudgy prince eyed her like a besotted fiancé.

Dorothy had barely any time to congratulate her sister-in-law before she was plunged into her duty as a hostess. She greeted the guests, smiled through tedious conversations, and coaxed the shy ones to dance.

It wasn't long before the engagement was quickly and formally announced. The prince, she learned, liked to sleep a lot. So, after a quick twirl around the ballroom with Sophia, he departed with his entourage.

The guests, robbed of the sight of the foreign prince and tired of the increasing warmth in the ballroom, began to trickle out.

Dorothy sighed in relief. She was ready to go to bed. Her feet ached, her smile felt stiff, and she barely had time to ogle Huxley through the dancing and the dinner.

It was well past midnight when she noticed something curious. A second wave of guests began arriving, and this new lot was decidedly odd.

First, Jimmy the Falcon entered with his wife. Next, Philbert Woodbead staggered in along with a few tipsy artists. Blinker raced in, bubbling with excitement. Perkins, the duke's old butler and Hopkins, his valet, Huxley's cook, the maids, Sir Henry with his famed white moustache, her sisters, Lady Bathsheba and her baby goats, and, oddly, even her mother and father and younger sisters crept into the room until Dorothy was surrounded by faces she had known and loved all her life.

Her heart sped up, and she turned to eye Huxley across the ballroom.

He was watching her.

Chapter Thirty-Eight

The crowd silently parted to let him through, and he slowly walked towards her in time with the music.

The music was familiar. He held his hand out to her once he was within dancing distance.

Dorothy couldn't help it. She took his hand and felt the reassuring warmth.

"You never sing in public," she whispered, knowing what was coming.

"And will hopefully never do so again. But this, one time, I must. It is to punish myself for treating you ill… and to prove my sincerity."

And so he did. His deep, warm baritone rang around the room, clear as a bell. The words were all too familiar, yet the tune was a touch different this time… happier, merrier … quicker.

> Let me kiss your lips, share your breath and your dew,
> Draw every torment away from your heart.
> Like the shade of a lamp, let my hands encircle your soul,
> Shielding you from the hurtful winds of the past.
> Good night, my sweet, sweet lassie
> Let the world fade away.
> Good night, my lassie, my sweet, sweet lassie
> Let the world fade away.
> My heart stops a moment,
> Time splits, and it lengthens

> A minute becomes a day.
> Your breath begins to flow,
> Easy and free, your lips tilt up in a smile.
> I weep, and I weep o' sweet lassie of mine.
> Don't sleep, my sweet lassie, my sweet, sweet lassie
> Don't sleep, my darling Dorothy May,
> For I will wither and curl, like a wild, wild grape
> If you leave me this fateful day.

He had sung the last verse ... the verse she had never heard before. Her sisters joined in, humming the song, and Dorothy realised this moment had been planned, possibly weeks in advance. Most of the guests knew the words, and even the evil ones joined in. Since the moment was so beautiful, they couldn't help it.

Spoons clinked on glasses, tables were thumped in time, the maids tapped the bannisters, shoes clicked on the marble floor, bracelets jingled, and Lady Bathsheba and her kids bleated.

It felt as if the whole world was dancing along with Dorothy and Huxley.

"You wrote that for me," she accused when he had finished.

"Woodbead helped," he replied with a faint blush.

"I thought you wanted nothing to do with me."

He gripped her gloved hand, his eyes dark and earnest. "The moment you walked out of Ansley Hall, my life disintegrated. I couldn't find my cigars; the ink pot was never filled, my quill never sharpened, the artists moped, the cook burnt everything—"

"You need a better housekeeper," she cut in sharply.

"I couldn't work," he went on. "I couldn't think. Everywhere I went, it felt as if every drop of happiness had been leached out from the air."

"You should have called a physician—"

"Every hour I ached, I brooded and moped—"

"A good dose of laudanum—"

"I read all of Woodbead's poetry. Every single one of them—"

"Oh!"

"I even memorised a few."

"Good lord!"

"And then I turned to romantic novels—"

"You didn't!"

"Things became even direr. I began to see your face everywhere. In pots and plants, in spoons and plates and pigeons."

"You have gone mad!"

"Loony, barmy and besotted. All because of you, Dora. Your absence has been torture. A living hell. If I am to function as a sane man, I need you to come back. To be my wife in every sense of the word."

"But the madness that drove your father to violence—"

His face darkened. "It's a risk."

"A risk worth taking?"

"I think so, but if you ever see any signs of it in me—"

"I will run as far as I can."

He smiled and pulled her closer. "Dorothy May, I love you with all my heart. Will you forgive me for behaving like a cad?"

She looked at the faces around her—some curious, some tearful, some jealous —and smiled. Yes, he had behaved abominably, but he had made up for it in the most touching way. He had surrounded her with people who meant most to her, opened his heart to possibilities and was willing to set aside his fears for the sake of love.

"I love you, too," she replied, feeling lighter than she had in months. "Everything is all right now."

His face lit up with pure joy, and he swept her off her feet.

"You are causing a scandal," she squeaked.

"I don't care a damn," he muttered, taking the steps two at a time. "I have waited too long, and I am not wasting a single more precious second in spending my life happily and completely with you. And Woodbead, if you dare ruin this moment, I will personally ship you off to the colonies!"

"I wouldn't dare," the poet grinned, raising a glass of

champagne in farewell.

Finally, after months of agonising, they headed up the stairs to consummate the marriage.

He swung her off her feet, carried her over the threshold into his chamber, kicked the door shut with his heel and lay her on the bed.

Nay, flung her on the bed.

He was too impatient, his eyes burning with need and passion.

She didn't mind since his bed was soft as a cloud with plenty of cushions.

It was well past midnight, and the fire burned low in the three grates in the chamber, almost down to glowing embers.

The soft crackle and their laboured breathing were the only sounds for a while as they gazed at one another.

Her upper body rested on her elbows as she watched him throw off his coat and walk to the edge of the bed.

She suddenly became nervous and uncertain, but before she could retreat, he grasped her ankles and took off her dancing shoes.

His fingers stroked her toes, heels and calves.

"Tickles!" She squeaked and tried to wriggle away.

He gripped her legs and pulled her closer until her mouth was close enough to kiss.

"Are you tired?" he asked, his warm, brandy-soaked breath brushing her cheek as he spoke. "I will let you go if you need sleep."

She wanted to lie and say yes because, although she had wanted this, now that they were so close to their union, it was too embarrassing.

He was going to strip her and do this, and that, and everyone downstairs knew what they were doing.

Oh, she wanted to bury her head in the blankets and hide forever.

"Mmm," he pecked her mouth. "You took too long to respond, and not responding means you are not tired. So, I will continue."

She wanted to argue this demented logic, but he had already begun kissing her, bringing her to a haze of erotic confusion with his firm, expert kiss.

"Open," he said, his voice low and gritty.

His tongue slipped between her lips, his fingers tugged her chin until her lips parted, and then he delved in deeper.

It had taken them a long time to reach this point. Huxley had needed to heal, escape from his past, and learn his character. This phase had been emotionally and intellectually difficult and resulted in him showing his worst side to his newly wedded wife.

Despite seeing his unpleasant self, Dorothy still chose to love him. He could see the adoration in her eyes, as well as the belief and trust she had in him. His cold heart would have never thawed if it had not been for her dedication and care.

She had cast her light on his shadows, illuminated every bit of his life and brought joy and laughter.

She had made him feel wanted, needed, and adored after years of loneliness and self-loathing. He had often questioned why no one could truly love him, but she had pulled out that deeply embedded hurt and replaced it with an understanding that he was not as terrible as he had assumed. He had simply not met the right person until she arrived in his life.

He kissed her, trying to show how much he wanted her, how he had longed to take her all these agonising months. How much he adored her.

"You will never part from me," he promised, biting her lower lip. "I shall not let you part from me."

The kiss turned fierce, but instead of becoming even more frightened, she suddenly relaxed. He had warned her of his cruelty in bed, but now that she was subject to his onslaught, she realised he had once again exaggerated and not understood himself.

This fierceness, this possessive kiss, was nice. He was kissing her breathless, leaving her weak and trembling, but she did not mind.

"Raise your leg, put your arm around my shoulder."

She followed his instructions obediently. It was better this way since she did not know what to do anyway. She could lie down and enjoy his skills, letting him twist her every way he pleased.

She no longer cared what he did to her. It was all pleasant, so wonderfully enjoyable.

"Turn over," he coaxed.

She happily did as he instructed and moaned when he began to pepper kisses on her nape while his fingers began unlacing her.

He flung the dress, petticoat, and chemise on the ground, leaving her naked.

She thought she would be cold, but her entire body was burning. Every inch of her was flushed and quivering.

He gripped her waist and flipped her back around, then began licking and sucking her nipple while his hands lifted her hips and put a pillow under it.

"Eh?" she squirmed.

"Shh," he soothed. "I do not want to hurt you. This will help."

And then his finger stroked between her legs, making her entire body clench and tense up. A soundless sigh escaped her lips when he repeated the movement.

Soon, his clever fingers had stimulated her to the point where she could barely stand it. She wanted to ask him to stop and go on at the same time. Her body twisted, but he held her firmly with one hand while the other continued its mischief.

"Mngh," she turned her head and bit the pillow while her fingers clenched the sheets.

He held her as she shuddered, stroking her stomach as she quietened. The next moment, he undressed, and his bare skin touched hers, making her gasp.

A finger entered her, slowly, gently, while she was still in a mindless haze.

It burned a little as if he had pushed a flame inside her, but after a moment of adjusting, the sensations changed.

It took a moment for his finger to enter fully, and her eyes suddenly cleared as a sudden stinging pain made her cry out.

"This will hurt," he warned her. "But, only this once, I promise."

"Mmm," she blushed, not willing to look at him. A tear formed at the corner of her eyes and dripped down, but she quickly turned her face and hid in the pillow.

He did not mind, understanding her shyness. His gaze was soft with passion as he stroked her arched hip, slim waist, dewy lips and silky mass of hair splayed all over the pillow.

Her hips were reacting to his touch, moving and shifting as if trying to reach for something. He knew what she wanted but refused to give in, cleverly avoiding touching the hood until she could barely take it.

He finally rubbed her clitoris, filling her with an intense glow of pleasure before pushing his entire length into her.

In one sharp, swift movement, he entered her and caught her cry with his lips.

"It is done," he whispered. "Bear with it a moment, and it will stop hurting."

He lay still, arms quivering with effort, while sweat beaded his forehead. He had never been so gentle in his entire life, and yet, now, he was fighting with himself with all his might.

After a moment, her delicate hands reached out to touch his back, and her hips moved. He understood she was ready and began rocking gently in and out.

She moaned, and he slipped his thumb between her lips. She absently bit, taking out her earlier grievance that the pain had caused her.

He let her bite him as his movements became rapid, and then he extracted his thumb from her mouth and rubbed the hood once again.

She spasmed along with him. Gasping, shuddering and moaning. Ah, this feeling was too intense; her entire body felt like it would burst into flames.

The pleasure turned her mind to soup, and she lay limp and defenceless while he panted next to her.

He turned his head and nibbled her breast. "A moment, and we can do it again."

Her eyes flew open. "Nay! That... was that not enough?"

"I warned you I am cruel in bed. You brought this upon yourself."

Oh, this was what he meant by being cruel. He was going to exhaust her with pleasure while she thought he would hurt her.

"No more," she pushed him. "I am tired."

"Once more," he insisted and then made her forget all her objections.

They ended up doing it three times that night, twice the following morning, and so on.

She didn't mind since, despite her token complaints, it was actually wonderful. But ah, to let him or anyone discover just how much she enjoyed . . . nay, it was so embarrassing, she could die of shame. Therefore, she protested every single time and then proceeded to enjoy herself thoroughly.

Epilogue

It was one of those perfect days. The sun emitted just the ideal amount of heat, the gentle breeze was not too cold, and the clouds were soft, white and sparse. And to top it all off, Huxley had grudgingly allowed Dorothy to call him nuggins and coo–coo bear that morning.

She smiled across the breakfast table at her husband. A year after the ball, he was still the same; his emotions clamped shut like an oyster, but he had begun to open slowly but surely when they were alone. He smiled, laughed at silly things, and teased her when they were alone, and it warmed her heart every single time.

He also sang more often—merry tunes, sweet ditties and her special song. His deep, caramel voice rang through Ansley Hall, warming the most frigid hearts.

It made anyone who heard him happy to be alive.

He looked up from his eggs, sensing her mushy gaze. He smiled, leaned over, and pressed her hand.

His touch was warm, comforting and ... careful.

She frowned.

"Who is this?" Lady Huxley asked, entering the room.

"Who?" Dorothy asked, momentarily distracted from brooding any further.

"Him," Lady Huxley squawked, staring at Blinker happily, slicing into a piece of bacon.

"My son," Huxley replied with a wink at Dorothy.

Lady Huxley gurgled.

"Don't you remember him?" Dorothy asked.

"I-I think so. When did you have him again?" She sank into a chair.

"Why years ago! Look at his size. You were present at his birth. Don't you remember all the blood and the screaming?" Dorothy shuddered.

"I see. I see. Yes, yes." Lady Huxley frowned and stared into the distance. After a moment, she asked, "Did Sophia, my daughter, marry him?"

"The butcher," Dorothy opened her mouth in mock astonishment. "Why, she married him years ago."

"The ... the butcher ... I thought the prince," Lady Huxley paled.

"Well, the prince was the first. I thought you meant her fourth husband ... the butcher—"

Lady Huxley shot up, hand on her heart. "I should lie down."

"It would do you good," Dorothy agreed with a grin. "You look awfully pale."

"You shouldn't tease her so," Huxley admonished once Lady Huxley had gone.

"I have to," Dorothy said, leaning forward to kiss him while Blinker made a face. "The best way to deal with bad people is to turn the whole situation into a jest."

"Wise words, wife," Huxley eyed her fondly. "Wise, wise words."

She popped a grape into her mouth and chewed thoughtfully. Her mind ricocheted back to where it had been interrupted by Lady Huxley's entrance.

Her life was happy. Blinker was coming along charmingly, the household was running smoothly, and she was managing her duties fairly well, and yet ... one thing bothered her. It hovered over her head like a noisy fly, refusing to leave her alone.

She pushed her plate away and grabbed Huxley's hand. "Come, I want you to do something for me."

He put the spoon down. "Now?"

"Now," she replied firmly, pulling him out of his chair.

He followed her, a tad grumpily, towards the Greek garden.

Dorothy took a deep breath and stood in the middle of the lawn.

He crossed his arms and eyed her expectantly.

"Pretend to hit me," she yelled at him.

Huxley stared at her in horror. "I shall not."

She bounced on the balls of her feet. "You have to. Just one punch," she thundered.

"Why?"

"I can see the fear lurking in your eyes. You still believe you are like your father, and one day, you will snap and hurt me. I am tired of being treated like a precious vase. I want you to treat me like a woman, not a thing."

"I am not going to hit you," Huxley said firmly. "I can deal with my fears."

"I want to show you that even if you did go mad, I am more than capable of taking care of myself."

"Dora, I am more than twice your size," he huffed.

"Just pretend, will you? I am not asking you to really hit me," she begged.

Huxley sighed, took a step forward, and prodded her shoulder lightly.

In a trice, she had him flat on his back.

He narrowed his eyes. This time, his attempt was slightly more earnest.

She got hold of his wrist before he could touch her and twisted until he was on his knees, wincing in pain.

The next bout was no better. Huxley lost spectacularly and landed on his back with a loud groan.

She stared down at him with not a strand of hair out of place.

He spat the dirt and let out a chuckle.

"How?" he asked in admiration.

"William Hartell Adair trained me for months," she told him proudly. "The famous spy who can finish off any man."

He grabbed her around the waist, none too gently, and pulled her into the tightest hug he had ever given her. "I never thought I would say this to a woman, but I am glad you can clobber me so well, my love." He grabbed her face and kissed her hard. "I didn't think I would ever say this either . . . next time, be gentle with me. I hurt in places I have never hurt before."

She chuckled into his warm, broad chest and snuggled closer.

He stared at the bright blue sky, holding her close, and thoughtfully observed, "George was right."

"About what?"

"The fact that the Fairweather sisters can take care of their own lovely selves."

"That we can, coo–coo bear. That we surely can."

The End

If you enjoyed reading this book and would like to receive a complimentary copy of Anya's next book upon release, you can email her at anyawylde@gmail.com *

You can also subscribe to Anya Wylde's newsletter to be the first to hear of any new release.

*Limited copies available, so hurry!

Sneak Peek: The Artist and the Earl

Mayhem and Petticoats Book 4

Chapter One

Jane Maryanne Fairweather pulled the sleeve of her morning dress down to conceal the vermilion and tin-yellow oil paint staining her arm. She hoped her gloves hid the worst of it.

She looked out of the window. It was a lovely summer's day. The sort that prompted some people to lose their minds and bound outdoors to engage in pointless physical activities.

Across the lawn, filled with nodding summer flowers, she spotted one such demented soul —the milkmaid's young son —running around an ancient oak tree. His legs were thin, like sticks, and his nose was round and spotted, like a baby spud.

She tutted, feeling sorry for mankind. All that running, bounding, and leaping was dislodging significant bits inside their heads. It was not the sort of thing to be encouraged. Why, even their king had gone mad! No doubt, his nurse had encouraged him to play rather than read.

As for the regent, she shuddered; he was afflicted with something far worse. Idiocy.

"Jane," her mother screeched. "Hurry, Lord Hickenbottom is waiting."

Her shoulders drooped. Lord Hickenbottom. What had possessed the deuced man to call on her? Another shout from her mother had her racing to the mirror to pinch her cheeks and tuck a long, dark copper tress behind her ear.

"Jane!"

She ran a finger around her collar, irritated by the lace. "I am *hurrying!"*

Another quick glance in the mirror confirmed that she looked as she always did, like a skinny white owl: eyes too big for her small pale face, a thick mass of coppery waves piled on top of her head like a heavy crown, and a slim figure clad in soft buttery muslin.

She darted out of the sunroom and flew towards the kitchen. Her eyes were a bit feral when she burst into the room.

An old, wrinkled head that looked uncannily like a cabbage with kind eyes smiled at her. "Miss?"

"I have a caller!"

The cook grinned. "You did look lovely last evening in the pink ball gown. I knew someone would take a fancy to you."

Jane looked around the room. The maids were busy bottling dried herbs and pickles, and the valet was asleep with his mouth open by the fire, yet she lowered her voice and sidled closer to the cook.

"Did you get it?"

"I did." The cook surreptitiously handed it to her.

Jane pocketed the juicy tomato and made her way towards the morning room. Her steps were now eager, and her smile sparkled with mischief.

She found Lord Hickenbottom standing by the pianoforte.

She observed him for a moment. He was wearing yellow breeches, a cream shirt, and a fawn waistcoat and held a gold-rimmed black hat.

He looked like a plucked daffodil, which was turning brown on the edges.

She suppressed a shudder. "Do you play, my lord?"

"Pardon?"

She hated this. Hated conversing with strangers. "Do you play?" she asked a touch more loudly.

"A little." He bowed and approached her.

She smiled nervously and took his arm. They sat on the chaise longue.

He stuck his hand in his pocket and pulled out a dark red

rosebud.

"When I saw this," he stroked her cheek with the petals, "I thought of you—young, fresh, and delicate."

She smiled, turned her head and bit the rosebud clean off the stem.

His Adam's apple bobbed up and down as he stared at the bare stem with only the thorn and two leaves remaining.

She swallowed and let out a delicate burp. "Thank you. I was hungry."

"You ate the rose."

"I ate the rose."

"You ate it."

"I did."

"Why?"

"What else was I meant to do with it?"

"Put it in a vase?"

"But I was hungry."

"Eat a biscuit?"

"I will when the maid brings it."

"But the rose?"

"It was delicious."

His right eye began twitching alarmingly.

She wiped her lips with a lace handkerchief and let out another burp.

He shook himself as if brushing off the incident and forged ahead. "Those watercolours," he pointed to the framed pictures on the wall, "did you do them?"

"I did not," she lied.

"Ladies are so accomplished," he inched closer to her and took her hand. "Do you sew?"

She smiled widely. "I enjoy hunting."

He frowned. "Hunting? You shoot?"

She batted her lashes. "I hunt rabbits. I catch them by their throats and toss them in the fire. Such fun."

"Oh."

"And I like watching the butcher."

He blinked. "Eh?"

"Chop, chop, chop. The way he cuts the meat, the smaller, the better. Blood trickling down his sharp knife."

He dropped her hand. "He allows you to watch him?"

She licked her lips and squished the tomato in her pocket. "He is an old friend."

"Does your mother not object to such a friendship?"

She shook her head and surreptitiously eyed the wet red patch forming on her dress as the juices of the tomato began seeping through. "Even the cook allows me in the kitchen every time they have a piece of meat to skin."

"Goodness, is that blood?" He leapt off the couch.

"Oh dear," She pulled her hand out of the pocket and let her sleeve fall back. The tomato bits had mixed with the crimson oil paint and coated her hand. It looked as if she had probed the insides of a living creature. "That was Lord Thomas."

He wiped his forehead with a green silk handkerchief. "I beg your pardon."

"A lonely squirrel whose wife died. I kept him in my pocket to comfort him, but your presence distracted me, and I squished him."

He eyed her uneasily. "How did his wife die, Miss Fairweather?"

"I ate her. They are delicious straight off the tree."

"Uncooked?"

"Naturally."

"Egad!"

She ran a toe over the lush Persian carpet. "Tea, my lord?"

"I have to go. An urgent matter I just recalled. Perhaps another time. This has been delightful."

"Please stay," she said, grabbing his arm and pulling him back onto the seat. "The cook has made the most wonderful cakes. Light as air."

On cue, Rose walked in with a tray laden with tea and cakes.

Jane poured some tea into a cup and then upended the entire contents of the sugar bowl into it.

"Drink," she ordered and handed him the cup.

"I would prefer something stronger. Brandy. Your father may have some in his study. I will ask him—"

She began to howl like a wolf.

He drank.

He downed the contents in one gulp, then leapt up and sped out of the room.

Jane watched him scurry, and the moment he was out of sight began to laugh in triumph. She twirled and hugged herself. Another suitor thwarted. This one had been easy—she paused mid-spin, and her smile faltered.

Outside the window, a bush was rising. A spotted laurel, or was it a dogwood? It had leaves of both plants. How curious. She had never seen this bush before, but had seen those round, shiny eyes spitting fire at her through the leaves.

It moved again, rising like a whale in an ocean.

She gulped.

Her mother, dressed up like a bush, had heard every word and was now glaring at her.

"It seems," her mother said, flicking away a slug. "I will have to take matters into my own hands.

Chapter Two

The deep, comforting scent of linseed oil blended with the intoxicating fumes of turpentine and oil paints permeated the sunroom. The faint breeze trickling in through the tall, open windows did nothing to alleviate its headiness.

Jane adjusted the wooden easel so the sunlight fell directly on the canvas, and with eager fingertips, she stroked it. The gesso was dry and the sketch ready.

She dipped her brush in malachite and swirled the pigment around. A shout erupted from somewhere in the house, startling her, and she dropped the brush, splattering paint on the floor.

As she mopped the green pigment, a sudden, intense longing for her peaceful home in Finnshire gripped her.

Her wealthy brothers-in-law had held her father's hand and helped him toddle towards the right sort of investments. Now, their situation was greatly improved, and Mother had decided to buy this townhouse.

She scowled. A manicured garden had replaced the pastoral field full of daisies and buttercups. The chirping of birds was drowned by the yapping of maids and thundering carriages.

Why, even the simple, delicious fare they had eaten in the country was replaced with white soup, odd dishes, and watery wine at frightfully late hours. So late, in fact, that she had fallen asleep at the dining table six times in the past month.

Even the sun seemed different here. It was as if he were

trying to hide behind the clouds all day, unable to see the filth on the streets or the dark, suffocating smog suspended in the air.

And yet, London, like an insistent, dirty, smelly stray pup, was slowly charming her.

She had seen so much in the past year, and the more she saw, the more she improved as an artist.

She had been tired of painting sensible trees and mountains.

Here, she could capture the chaos of Gin Lane, the vibrancy of ball dances and the tragedy of broken hearts.

A part of her was breaking away from Finnshire, childhood innocence, and slowly disintegrating.

Was that why she suddenly wanted to go back to the village? An attempt to hold on to her peaceful past and avoid the eddy rising ahead, full of unknowns?

She dipped an expensive red sable brush in walnut oil and added it to the bone black on her palette. With steady fingers, she added the paint to the canvas.

"A new painting, Jane?" Miss Georgiana Berry, her bosom friend, called from the doorway.

Jane added a touch of Prussian blue and white to the black, marvelling, once more, at the recently created synthetic pigment. She wondered if it would last the test of time or fade away as the years passed.

"It's a lamplighter." Her mother walked in just then and gestured at the painting. "And you, Jane, are just as unsightly as he."

Jane tilted her head and smiled at the canvas, pleased with the blue-grey wash. She thought the man looked lovely.

"Rosey!" her mother screeched at her lady's maid. "Get a bath ready."

Jane stuck her tongue out in concentration and picked up the brush again. She carefully added a touch of grey to the lamplighter's skin. Her fingers paused uncharacteristically and hovered over the lamplighter's eyes.

An odd feeling shot through her as she looked at him. His

eyes were hypnotic.

Her paintings had affected her before, but this was an undefined emotion.

"Looks like years of soot have collected in his wrinkles and cracks," Georgie marvelled. "I wish I could paint so well."

"You do paint well," Jane said, setting the brush down and wiping her hands on a rag.

"A lamplighter." Her mother peered at the painting. "It is ghastly. All smoke and dirt. Women should paint trees and flowers. Not soot-laden, dirty commoners. No wonder you are not getting married. Four seasons and not a single suitor. With your dowry and connections, one would have expected you to be snatched up in the first year itself—"

"Mother," Jane whirled around. "Let me work."

"That's not work. That is a waste of time. You have a ball to go to—"

"It is in the evening."

"You need to get ready."

"It's hours away! Besides, after attending five hundred balls, I think I can get ready in under an hour."

"You need four hours to look presentable," her mother responded curtly. "The paint alone takes an hour to scrub off."

"I don't want to get married, Mamma," Jane snapped.

"We had barely any money, yet your sisters married well. Now that our fortunes have turned, I expected you to get married more quickly than your sisters, but here you sit, gathering dust, inching closer and closer to spinsterhood. The callers have started dwindling. Soon, no one will want you."

"It was Penelope who had nothing."

Mrs Fairweather narrowed her eyes. "I sent her to Blackthorne."

"You did not think she would marry the Duke. You had no faith in her."

"Nevertheless, it was my doing. That girl owes it to her sisters to help them after all I did for her."

"You did nothing. You still treat her cruelly."

"Enough. Do not try to divert me from the subject."

"Is it because she looks like her mother?"

Mrs Fairweather scowled. "What has got into you?"

"What if you fall in love?" Georgie interrupted quickly. "It's the most wonderful feeling."

Jane's eyes blazed. "I shall not fall in love. I cannot afford to fall in love. Hundreds of women with extraordinary talents have faded away simply because they got married. A vast majority died in childbirth."

Mrs Fairweather placed her hands on her hips. "You have been reading naughty books again."

Jane spoke through gritted teeth, "Men and the proof of their talent live on in the pages of books, sculptures, and thousands of paintings. While women . . . What of our talent? What of our history? What of our contribution to the world of art and culture?"

"Jane." Her mother's voice turned cold. "We have all had childish aspirations. I wanted to sing and dance on stage. Naturally, now that I am older, I see the foolishness in it. You will see the foolishness in your pursuit once you are wiser. It is the young blood in your veins creating windmills in your head. Women cannot be painters. They are born to be wives and mothers."

"I shall be an artist and nothing else."

"I do not have time to waste on this foolish debate. Get into the bath."

Rosey and two other maids appeared carrying buckets of water. They threw a sheet inside the bath, placed a chair in the middle, and began pouring hot water into the tub behind a changing screen.

Mrs Fairweather turned to Georgie. "It is your responsibility to see that she bathes. Do whatever it takes to get that paint off her. If you like, toss her in."

The girls watched Mrs Fairweather march away and, in unison, let out a relieved breath.

"Your mother," Georgie paused, searching for words, "means

well."

"I know." Jane put the paint and the brushes away. She could not do more today since she had to wait for the grey wash to dry.

She turned away in frustration. She hated waiting for the paint to dry. Her fingers itched to move on to the next layer, and the image of how she wanted the result was vivid in her head.

"You are an odd one." Georgie poured water into a bowl full of beaten soap and placed it near the head of the claw-footed bathtub. "You have converted the sunroom into a bedchamber and a bath."

"I spend most of my time here. I thought it best."

"But to sleep in the sunroom?"

Jane shrugged. "It's no different." She stepped behind the Coromandel screen and, with the help of Rose, the lady's maid, began undressing.

"It's away from the main house! How does your mother allow it?"

"She does not. Father does."

"He has spoiled you rotten."

"He is simply more sensible."

Georgie sighed. "I hope you get a husband half as loving."

Jane's red face popped out from behind the screen. "How many times—"

"His eyes," Georgie cut in quickly. "His eyes are sinful."

"Whose?" Jane frowned.

"The lamplighters."

"I knew I had made them too handsome," Jane said, running over to the painting.

Georgie shrieked. "Goodness, you are stark naked and dripping water everywhere. For shame, Jane. What if someone walks in? Go back and finish your bath."

Jane frowned. "I don't think I have met anyone with eyes like that."

"We are no longer children, Jane. If your mother sees you

like this, she will—"

"I will?"

"Mamma!" Jane's eyes widened, and she dove behind the screen.

Mrs Fairweather's lips tightened. "Anyone could have been out for a walk and seen you running around stark naked like a crazed loon. You have ignored my advice, and despite the excellent school we sent you to, you behave like an uncouth woman with no morals and values. Now, it seems you have also let go of your senses. Your father insisted on giving you this sunroom. I have complied with his wishes up to this point. No more. I have had enough."

Chapter Three

Once again, the little London townhouse was creaking and groaning as the Fairweather household rushed about like enthusiastic locusts sweeping through a field of rice.

The sun began to dip, and the maids began pulling the curtain ties around the house. The heavy silk draperies closed with a swish, plunging them all into darkness. Oil lamps blazed to life, and the sound of flint striking steel filled the air. The maids scampered again and began carrying steaming buckets, dried flowers, burning incense, and lotions and potions from the kitchens to the sunroom.

In the sunroom, Jane and Georgie were getting ready for the ball. The place was strewn with gloves, stockings and headdresses. Pearls, brooches, and necklaces lay on the bed while dancing shoes and satin slippers sat on chairs.

Jane flung the chemises on the ground and sat on top of them while Georgie tripped and upended a box full of ribbons, sending them flying into the air.

Jane watched the coloured strips of fabric rain down and moaned. "It's one of those days. I have a feeling that something terrible is going to happen."

Georgie threw herself on the chaise longue, her red curls shining in the golden light. "I cannot get dressed in this chaos."

"You have an hour." Mrs Fairweather's head, full of curling paper, popped into the room. "Wear the rubies, Jane, and get off the floor." She disappeared without waiting for a response.

Jane sighed and heaved herself up. She went and stood in front of her painting and cocked her head. "I should add some wrinkles around the eyes."

Georgie tutted. "You have a maggot in your brain. For once, forget your painting and enjoy yourself. Dance and live in the moment." She took a deep breath and yelled. "The pink, Rosey."

"At once, Miss."

Jane lifted her arm as Mary, her maid, pulled the morning dress off her. Her eyes remained glued to the painting. She shivered in her chemise, her hands coming up to caress her pale arms.

"Your mother asked you to drink this." Mary handed her a cup of tea.

Jane drank it absently, grimacing at the sharp taste. "Rubies," she snapped irritably. "Mother wants me to wear rubies with the white crepe. It will look ghastly. I will wear pearls in my hair and nothing else."

"Your mother means well, even if her taste is questionable," Georgie comforted.

"She wanted me to wear a yellow brocade dress with gold flower ornaments for Lady Dunne's dinner party," Jane grumbled.

Georgie shook her head, making her stunning auburn curls bounce and catch the light.

"Soup," Rosey flew in and deposited a tray. She hung the pink dress with flounces on the bedpost and retreated.

Jane sat down at the dressing table and touched her stomach to still the flutters. "I feel a hint of collywobbles coming on. I feel green. Am I green?"

Georgie cocked her head. "You look lovely. Pity you can't go to the ball in your chemise with your hair down. Somehow, you transform into a beauty in a state of dishabille while I need all the help I can get."

Jane looked at her reflection and frowned. Her eyes were brown and bright without the need for Olympian dew. A touch of crushed strawberries had reddened her lips while her cheeks were naturally flushed from summer's heat. The chemise had slipped down one arm, exposing a delicate white shoulder where a strand of dark, copper hair lay in sharp contrast.

She looked fey.

"I look demented," Jane objected. "While you look beautiful as usual. That's why Lord Plaskett proposed to you within a week of seeing you."

Georgie, round and soft, clutched the bedpost while her lady's maid tied her corset. She changed the subject. "Did you hear about Lady Green?"

"No, what happened?"

Georgie lowered her voice, "She eloped with her butler."

"Goodness," Jane exclaimed while Mary took a strand of her hair and allowed the smoke of myrrh and sandalwood incense to flow over it.

Georgie pinched her cheeks and rubbed her lips to add some colour. "As for Miss Darlington—"

"The one who was to marry Lord Drake?"

"Aye, she was caught kissing Lord Drake."

"So? They are engaged, are they not?"

"She was kissing the older Lord Drake."

"You mean his father?"

"I mean the grandfather."

Jane coughed and spluttered while Mary dropped the incense holder and swooned.

"And I thought they were madly in love," Jane rolled her eyes. "Look around you, Georgie. This chaos is all for me. This madness is that I find a man I don't want and get married. The entire household is racing about trying to get us ready for a silly dance. I don't understand it."

"Give love a chance," Georgie replied. "It's wonderful. I cannot wait to be Lady Plaskett."

"And if Lord Plaskett dies? What then? Will you live a spinster's life, miserable, haunted, alone and shunned? You may not even own your house and will have to depend on the largesse of your relatives. Wouldn't it be better to earn your own fortune? To live your dreams, to make your name and fame?"

Georgiana stared at her friend in shock.

Jane sighed. "Georgie, I am sorry. I don't know what's got into me. I have the devil's blues. I feel like something awful will happen, and I cannot shake the feeling."

"It is a thought that plagues most women. Jane, I have learned to accept the fear and take what happiness and days I can get with him. That is love, where living without him is impossible."

"You are too soft-hearted for your good. You shouldn't forgive me. You should storm out of here and never see my face again."

"Mother says we used to babble at each other as babies, and I am not going to stop babbling at you just because you had a little tantrum and said unkind things. I have done my share of it."

"Wise and sweet." Jane smiled. "I would have hugged you, except the incense Mary dropped earlier has set my chemise on fire."

Georgie swiftly pulled out the roses from a flowerpot and upended the water over Jane, carefully avoiding her hair.

"You saved my life," Jane exclaimed dramatically. "I will save yours one day."

"What happened? I heard a scream." Mrs Fairweather hurried in.

Georgie indicated the maids lying on the floor. "Embers from the incense set Jane's chemise on fire. And then the maids swooned."

"Honestly, Jane, stop wasting time! Stick a shoe under her nose and get on with the dressing. Here, I have mended your dress. It had a tear in it. We have only an hour left."

"Yes, Mother, I will try not to go up in flames again and inconvenience you."

"I expect nothing less."

Chapter Four

Jane floated into Lord Moore's mansion, gave her coat to the attendant, and changed into dancing shoes. She was wearing a soft, white, gilt muslin dress scattered with tiny blue flowers and, for a change, felt pretty.

They were soon announced, and while her parents greeted the host, she and Georgie slipped away.

"Lady Moore has outdone herself," Georgie breathed.

Jane had to agree. Ornate mirrors hung on the walls, reflecting the light of three hundred candles, which made the ballroom gloriously bright. Everything seemed to twinkle, from women wearing glittering fabrics and precious gems to polished silverware. Amongst the candles sat fat blooms that alleviated the stink of sweat and partridge pie.

They danced for a bit before heading to a secluded corner by the large French windows. A footman appeared before them, holding a silver tray with little bowls of Roman punch.

"Do you want one?" Georgie asked Jane as she dipped a spoon into the frozen drink.

Jane shook her head and grimaced. "I wish they would hurry and serve supper. I want to go home."

"If I see another bowl of white soup, I will scream," Georgiana muttered. "Oh, look, Lord Plaskett has arrived."

"I can't look since I don't have a spyglass."

"Do you want mine?"

"I want a drink that is not champagne or punch."

"My parents have also arrived. Mother should have worn a

shawl, and father should have worn the grey coat, not the peacock blue." Georgie put away the spyglass. "Lawks! Jane, you have turned green. You are not going to swoon, are you?"

"I don't swoon," Jane snapped.

Georgiana frowned worriedly. "I am going to get some wine. Sit." She pushed her into a chair hidden behind a thick drapery.

Jane shook her head. "But Lord Plaskett is here. You must greet him first."

"Pah, he won't mind. I will be back with the wine, and Jane, whatever happens, do not swoon."

Jane was glad of the rest. It was hot, uncomfortable, and crowded. Her chemise was soaked with sweat, and her stomach ached. Perhaps skipping the soup had been a mistake. As for breakfast, she had forgotten to have any in the excitement of getting started on the painting.

She watched the people for a while, wishing Georgie would return. The fans were out and fluttering madly. Skirts swirled, plumes bobbed, and flushed faces danced past her blurred vision. The orchestra was loud where she sat, the music sharp and unpleasant to her ears.

Her chest began to feel tight, and her body felt odd, as if someone had wrapped her up like an Egyptian mummy and tossed her into a coffin. She closed her eyes, trying to breathe through it all and regain control.

"Jane," her mother hurried up to her. "Georgie said you were feeling unwell."

"I just need a moment."

Her mother crouched next to her. "Why don't you get some air? The balcony is a few steps away. Go on, child."

Jane was too weak to argue and did as she was told, stumbling towards the arched doors and heading outside.

The shock of cool air on her face was bliss. She grabbed the railing, leaned over, and breathed in the rose-scented air in relief.

Her mother had been right. She did feel better.

Slowly, her limbs loosened, and her breathing began to

improve. She slipped her hand into the hidden pocket sewn into her skirt and gripped the charcoal pencil in relief.

After a moment, she realised someone else was on the balcony. From the corner of her eye, she spied the glow of a cigar.

The scent of damask roses and expensive tobacco flirted with the dancing breeze, teasing her nose until she turned to face the stranger.

The full fat moon peeked out from behind the clouds just then and illuminated the man's face.

Her heart stopped.

Those eyes! The same perfectly arched brows, the almond-shaped, dark eyes framed by thick lashes. The lamplighter from her painting stood before her.

It couldn't be!

She ran her eyes over him. He was far younger than the man she had drawn, more handsome and powerfully built. Not a speck of dirt on his fine clothes. And yet, the eyes were the same.

She felt her head spin, and his hand shot out to grip her arm and prevent her from falling.

A moment later, she wrenched herself out of his grip. "Pardon, I stumbled."

"You were about to swoon." His voice washed over her like expensive brandy.

Her fingers flew to her stomach, and she backed another step. "I am not the sort that swoons."

His tone gentled. "Pardon, I must have been mistaken."

Her back straightened, and she dipped in a curtsy. "I will leave you to your solitude."

She turned on her heels and found her mother staring at her in shock.

"What's the matter?" Jane frowned.

Her mother stumbled forward and clutched her shoulder, "You have ruined her, you brute."

Jane blinked. "Who is ruined?"

"You are," her mother cried.

Georgie came running onto the balcony and skidded to a halt. "Gack!"

"Mother says I am ruined. But wouldn't I know if I were?" Jane stared at her friend in confusion.

Georgie's voice shook as she spoke. "Your dress."

Jane glanced down and found her sleeve had come away. Her mouth dropped open in horror. When had it happened? How had it happened?

"I did nothing of the sort," the man said. "I don't know how her dress is in the state it is . . . ask her . . . Speak, deuced woman."

"I don't even know him," Jane agreed. "I wanted some air. Mother, you saw me but a moment ago."

"You took advantage of her when she swooned."

"I did not swoon."

"She did not swoon."

"My precious, delicate daughter ruined!"

Jane realised that several people had arrived on the balcony. "Mother, hush, it's a private matter. Nothing happened, believe me."

People began talking, and Jane shook in distress.

"Who is ruined?" a powerful voice cut short the chatter.

Jane closed her eyes and sank to the floor. It was the Duke of Blackthorne.

"Miss Jane Fairweather," someone replied.

"My sister?" Penelope, the Duchess of Blackthorne, cried out. "Impossible."

"Jane?" Dorothy and Celine, her other sisters, dropped down next to her. "Is this true?"

"No!"

"But the sleeve…" Dorothy bit her lip.

"Yes, the sleeve," wailed Mrs Fairweather.

"The sleeve does not look good," agreed Penelope.

"Then dose it with laudanum and let me go home," Jane cried.

"What happened?" the duke demanded.

Jane took a shaky breath. "I was unwell. I came here for air. I stumbled, and this man helped steady me. Perhaps my sleeve came off then."

"Speak up, girl," someone called out.

Jane ducked her head and repeated herself a little more loudly.

Mrs Fairweather frowned. "Sleeves don't have a habit of coming off like that."

Jane scowled. "Well, this one did. Perhaps it dislikes being attached to a dress. Mayhap it wanted to dance and tried to flee indoors."

Penelope's hand on her arm stopped her. "Hush, you are making things worse. You sound foxed."

Jane hid her face in her hands. "Oh, Penny, I swear to you, nothing happened."

Her sisters looked grave, and the silence that followed did not bode well.

The Duke of Blackthorne stepped forward. "Savill, a duel at sunrise, name your second."

Savill? Jane frowned. She had heard the name before. Her confusion must have shown, for Georgie whispered in her ear, "Richard Henry Bellmore, the Earl of Savill and the wealthiest man in England."

Jane's mouth went dry, and her eyes flew to her mother, whose ostrich feathers were quivering in delight. Lord Savill was the most eligible bachelor in England and wealthier than all her brothers-in-law, including the Duke of Blackthorne.

Her mind flew back to the tea she had drunk, the dress her mother had taken to 'mend', the sudden urgency in her voice as she had pushed her to the balcony for fresh air, the way she had bounded up to her and grasped the very shoulder whose sleeve had come off, and then announced that her daughter was ruined in a thunderous voice.

"This is clearly a plan concocted by mother and daughter." Savill appeared to be thinking the same thing. "The idea is hardly original. But your plans will fail."

Celine stepped forward; her hands curled into fists. "She is a Fairweather, with a substantial dowry, excellent connections and beautiful. She does not need to stoop to underhanded tactics to trap a man."

"Beautiful?" Lord Savill looked at Jane, and his lips twisted. "You are blinded by familial love."

The duke was at his throat. "Take back your words."

"It's the truth."

Penelope pulled her husband off. "Don't be foolish. Let the man go."

Lord Savill's voice rang out, clear and confident. "I will not marry her, come what may. I will see you in the morning, Blackthorne."

A sudden gust of cold air chilled the occupants standing on the balcony, and they gasped. It boded ill. The north wind had turned just as the duel was announced.

Her sisters gripped each other's hands, looking uneasy.

"Pah! This is utterly foolish," Jane cried. "Nothing happened!"

"The sleeve, according to the *ton*, my dear," Penelope said resignedly, "holds more import than your words."

"Then the *ton* is comprised of mutton-headed fools," Jane snapped.

"Very powerful mutton-headed fools," Penelope agreed. "Now, slip out the back and head straight to your carriage with Miss Berry. When you get home, go straight to bed. We will find a way out. I will not let two men endanger their lives over this foolishness."

"I—" Jane hesitated.

"Please," Penelope said. "You are deathly pale, love. Go home. I promise to send word the moment we have come up with a solution."

Georgie pulled her hand. "You are making matters worse by staying, Jane. Another word from Lord Savill about you and his Grace will shoot him on the spot."

"All will be well," Dorothy said with a smile while Celine kissed her goodbye.

"Mother did this," Jane told her sisters quietly, then, with trembling legs, left the scene.

About the author

Anya Wylde lives in Ireland along with her husband, children and a fat French poodle (now on a diet). She can cook a mean curry, and her idea of exercise is occasionally stretching her toes. She holds a degree in English literature and adores reading and writing. Connect with Anya Wylde on Facebook, or Instagram to be notified about her upcoming releases, or follow her on her Amazon Author Page.

Subscribe to her newsletter **here**.

Website: **www.anyawylde.com**

Other Books By The Author

Regency Romantic comedy

Penelope
Seeking Philbert Woodbead
Dorothy
Elizabeth

Regency Romance

A Duke Confounded
When the Rogue Came Calling
The Artist and the Earl
Unmasking Miss Fairweather

Regency Mystery

Wicked Wager
Murder At Rudhall Manor
Death of an Aristocrat

Contemporary Romantic Comedy

Love Muffin And Chai Latte
Goodness Gracious Gracie

Fantasy

Meara
Destined

Printed in Dunstable, United Kingdom